INDIAN POLICE AND *NEXUS* CRIMES

INDIAN POLICE AND *NEXUS* CRIMES

James Vadackumchery

PUBLICATIONS

KALPAZ PUBLICATIONS

Delhi - 110052

INDIAN POLICE AND *NEXUS* CRIMES

ISBN : 81-7835-037-8

Published in 2002 in India by
Kalpaz Publications
C-30, Satyawati Nagar Phase III, Ashok Vihar,
Delhi 110 052

Laser Typesetting: Grow Computers, Delhi
Printed at: Mehra Offset Press, New Delhi

To

My dear wife Mary

and

loving daughters

Neethu and Neethie

CONTENTS

PREFACE

I was invited once to deliver a lecture on computer crimes. I said that I was a computer illiterate, but I said further that I could give a lecture on *nexus* crimes. Internet and intranet crimes may be there as a lot of crimes is committed in that area, but I have little information about them. At the same time, I know a lot about *nexus* crimes. In a meeting of the members of the syllabus committee for police, I prepared the syllabus for criminology and included *nexus* crimes as a new subject. The additional director general of police (Training) who was the chairman of the committee asked me: "What do you mean by *nexus* crimes?" I expected such a query, for, I was probably the one who might have used the words *nexus* crimes in criminology for the first time, as I have not come across such a crime in eastern or western literature in criminology.

The aim of this book is to make the people aware of the *nexus* crimes which exist in society and to give a distinct identity to the epidemic. Police being the most powerful enforcement agency in the country, the problem has been exposed by taking police department as the point to start with. Other departments may have established worse *nexuses* with criminal politicians, criminal bureaucrats, criminal businessmen, underworld criminals and so on and the problem ought to be studied. The crimes defined in the Indian Penal Code - 1860 are not the crimes which take the nation to destruction. It is well established that the *nexus crimes,* syndicate crimes, white collar crimes, enforcement crimes, political crimes, ideological crimes, terrorism, etc., are serious and heinous crimes which will blast the country into ashes and that is the precise reason why the book becomes important.

There exists little or no literature on the subject. The contents of this book are therefore derived from my observations and researches conducted on the subject. Hence, the views and opinions expressed in the book are personal. They do not reflect the views and opinions of the Government of India, State Governments, Police Departments or Home Offices.

I have to thank my wife, Mary and my daughters, Neethu and Neethie for their support and encouragement to write this book. They always tell me: "Write - write more and let the generations benefit by the writings". What an encouragement! Thus this book has come out. I hope that it gives light on the subject and brings out the nature of *nexus* crimes in today's world.

James Vadackumchery

INTRODUCTION

Nexus in dictionary means 'a means of connection or link'. A sort of binding, fastening or joining. Nexus crimes mean crimes which people commit as a result of a link among them—a sort of binding, fastening or joining. Who are the people who are bound together for the commission of crimes? In a democracy, there are three wings—the Legislature, the Executive and Judiciary. Political parties rule the country and the politicians become the ministers in the Government. Under the politicians comes the executive. Necessarily and naturally, there comes a link between the politicians and the executives. Politicians have their vested interests and they need authority, power and finance to promote their political interests, and they require support from the executives—the civil servants—for the purpose. This is precisely why they consciously make attempts to establish a link between themselves and the civil servants; why the civil servants are transferred as soon as a new government assumes power in a democracy. The nexus which the politicians establish with the civil servants can be used, misused and abused for political advantages or for mutual benefits. A nexus comes into being and sometimes, the nexus so established becomes a source to commit crimes in various forms. Crimes here do not mean the traditional crimes defined in the Indian Penal Code—1860 drafted at a time when democracy was not in existence.

Crimes which have been Excluded in Indian Penal Code-1860

The Indian Penal Code (IPC) does not include within its precincts many crimes. Nevertheless they are crimes. Some of the crimes are: (1) White collar crimes, as defined by Prof. Edwin H. Sutherland, are not mentioned in the Indian Penal Code, therefore some criminologists and lawyers say that they are not crimes within the strict meaning of the term. Nevertheless, Sutherland and many others claim that they are in every sense crimes. (2) Likewise, organized crimes and crime syndicates as defined by the experts at Oyster Bay have not been mentioned in the Penal Code—1860. Yet, the criminologists argue that they are crimes of the first order. (3) Mafia criminals engage in criminal activities and their crimes cannot be treated as simple crimes. (4) Political crimes are not defined in the Penal Code—1860. When an offence affects primarily individual life and property, but is closely connected with acts like treason, sedition, espionage, insecurity of the State, rebellion, incitement to civil war, etc., then such an act may be considered as a political crime. (5) Enforcement criminality is in vogue and the offence as such is not defined in the Penal Code, yet it exists. Enforcement criminality by definition, may be an act committed by an enforcement officer during the course of his work with the aim of making profit for himself or for others in whom he is interested with the knowledge or approval of the person for whom the act is committed. (6) In nexus crimes, elements of white collar crimes, organized criminality, political crimes and enforcement criminality may be seen. These will be discussed in detail in the chapters that follow.

In the address to the Nation on the eve of the independence day, August 15, 2000, the President of India spoke about the unholy relationship that exists among the politicians, bureaucrats and businessmen for the commission of offences and he pleaded for breaking the link among them. The crimes they commit jointly may be called *Nexus* crimes. They are organized crimes. All criminal activity which is not spontaneous and impulsive is organized and in nexus crime, the purpose for which the politicians, bureaucrats and businessmen join together must be analysed. Vohra Commission spoke about the unholy nexus among the senior level politicians, bureaucrats and businessmen and their combine or organization is called criminal nexus. All of them may be classified as criminals although they occupy high positions in life and service or otherwise. The organization varies considerably depending upon the purpose for which they form an alliance. A simple activity needs only minimal organization and correspondingly the number of persons needed to execute it also will be small. Think of a situation in which an owner of a bar wants to sell liquor during prohibited hours. A police officer or an excise officer can just shut the eyes. His bar will sell the liquor and the police/excise authority will get the share. This is a simple form of a nexus crime. The nexus may become very complex as the nature of the activity demands- thus needing a highly complex kind of organization.

Nexus can be a simple understanding between a police official and an individual criminal. Once, a commissioner of police in a city suspended a police constable. The reason was that he did not take a pickpocket entrusted to him by the passengers in an omnibus for pickpocketing. Further investigations revealed a 'policeman-pickpocket nexus' where it was agreed that the pickpocket would operate in the public transport buses. If and when he was caught by the victims of pickpocketing or any other fellow passengers, then the policeman would intervene and take charge of him claiming to put him behind bars. Being reassured by the policeman the commuters thus entrusted the pickpocket to the policeman in uniform. What was actually happening was the reverse. The policeman who took the pickpocket in custody got out of the omnibus and resumed their operations in another bus. If not detected while pocket picking, the earnings were shared. Finally they were apprehended as some passengers sensed the unholy liaison between the policeman and the pickpocket and that brought out the nexus crime and subsequent suspension.

During 1971-73, when the author was a student in Karnatak Arts College, Dharwar doing B.A. (Criminology) course he had a cousin who was then studying in a medical college in Hubli. One day, his pocket was picked and he lost Rs. 50. At that time this amount was as good as Rs. 500 of today and therefore, he preferred to make a complaint to the sub-inspector of police who happened to be a friend of his. Immediately, the sub-inspector called the police constables who had an escort duty—escorting prisoners from jails to the court. The sub-inspector asked the constables: "How many pickpockets were there today for production before the court?"

The constables said: "Three". To them, the sub-inspector then told calmly: "This doctor lost his Rs. 50 today in the bus. You and the pickpockets were in the same bus and therefore please give Rs. 50 to this doctor". The constables smiled meaningfully and gave Rs. 50 to the doctor. The sub-inspector then consoled the doctor: "See, there is a secret understanding between the pickpockets and these policemen, i.e., they must pickpocket someone on their way to the court so that they can have a good breakfast before they enter the court room". No doubt, nexus crimes have been in existence in the past. But, their presence was not discussed openly by people as they were afraid of.

Apart from a nexus between police officials and criminals, there is also a nexus among the police functionaries themselves. Simon was a student of engineering during 1970s. One day, his wrist watch was stolen from his room. He filed a complaint before the police. They started investigation. At 4 o'clock, an assistant sub-inspector along with two or three constables would come to his room and together they went to the nearby hotel from where they used to have tea and *paratha* with chicken. The watch was Henry Sandoz which then cost Rs. 110. The visits everyday cost him as good as Rs. 35 for the evening tea. After four days, he humbly and politely requested the investigating team to stop further probing into the theft as the overhead expenses went far above the loss incurred. People are intelligent enough to read the police mind when they see how the police perform their functions. In a police station, petitioners used to come in the morning at about 7.30 a.m. and the constable who made inquiries in to a particular petition made it a point to take the petitioner to the nearby tea shop to elicit more information from the petitioner. While they enjoyed the breakfast, other constables visited the tea shop and they too could join the breakfast. The nexus among the constables became a talk in the locality and some laughed at the breakfast stories. Of course, the petitioners had different state of mind. Eventhough they were petty nexuses, certainly, the behaviour damaged the image of the police functionaries. Such types of petty nexuses do not take place now as much as they used to in the past. Nevertheless, allegations are heard even today about such petty nexuses.

Just as little children commit little crimes, the lower level functionaries in police may involve in petty nexuses. A film once showed a burglar being told to commit thefts during night hours by the jail wardens.

After the commission of the offence, he used to return to the jail and the earnings were shared among them. This was a story of a film and can be taken as unrealistic. Being an entertainment programme—or at least, we wish it to be so. But in reality it is a known fact that the subordinate staff direct the offenders/petitioners/complainants to go and see the higher ups to get favoured treatment when they file complaints before them so as to please everybody in order to create facilities for each one in the chain of superiors. The constable may tell one who needs the service to 'see properly' the head constable who advises, in turn, the complainant to see the sub-inspector 'properly'. The sub-inspector then advises him to see his higher up 'properly' and thus the vertical mobility in nexus is ensured. Prof. Edwin H. Sutherland speaks of fee-splitting among medical officers and he calls it to be a 'white collar crime'. More about the relationship between white collar criminality and nexus crimes is discussed elsewhere in the book. Everyone knows what is going on and all of them prefer to play deaf and dumb games!

Nexus/Consensus Crimes

Though no one has defined nexus crime, many speak about nexuses which are criminal in nature. Can we assume nexus crimes to be consensus crimes? In other words, crimes committed after reaching a consensus about the sharing of the profits? Yes. In Excise Department, it is told by Abkari contractors that they pay regularly a fixed amount to many. They have fixed terms and conditions after making a mutually accepted agreement in which they fix different rates for different duties like—patrolling the jurisdiction, conducting raids, for harassing people, etc., and according to them, there exists a sort of consensus for a regular pay off on a monthly basis. Certainly, it is a nexus crime and both the Abkari contractors and the officials are benefitted.

In police, one can not see such interested contractors to make regular payments, but people say that police is an enforcement agency in whom many business-men are interested. Sometimes, news comes in the press that some Abkari contractors' account books and diaries have entries (purposeful or not?) showing regular pay off to police officers. Automobile owners, restaurant keepers, mill owners and so on too make similar complaints. Well founded or not, such complaints and allegations are of bad taste to the reputation of any department.

Again, in one film a head constable tells his sub-inspector: "Sir, we wear this uniform for the Government. But, remember that it is these Abkari contractors who stitch and give the uniform to us". The sub-inspector who was just out from the police academy could not understand the full meaning of what the head constable told him—or better advised him. Nevertheless, as days went on, he was made to realize the necessity of establishing an unholy nexus with people, businessmen, underworld criminals who mattered in his jurisdiction. This may just be another dialogue in a film. Yet, these films show us what is going on in society or what impressions the society entertains about the law enforcement machinery. Once a deputy superintendent said: "I felt so small in front of my boss, the superintendent of police, when I saw a criminal businessman in my jurisdiction smoking a cigarette in front him in his very office signifying his closeness with him. The criminal businessman was seated before him while I was not even offered a seat while talking to him". Why so? The superintendent of police had to treat him so because he had received some advantages. That is the reason why a better treatment was offered to that criminal businessman by his superior officer. Leave alone the superior officer, even the Minister of Home Affairs himself offered VIP treatment to some criminal businessmen!

Nexus thus becomes omnipresent and inevitable in the present day society. The businessmen have money and political connections. The law enforcement officers have power and authority. Their combine leads to the commission of crimes without fear and with immunity in law. If the versions of the law enforcement officers are believed in toto, then one may have to take note of the fact that nexus crimes will be a consequence of the helplessness of the enforcement functionaries. A nexus crime is therefore a crime committed by officials in government as a result of the dirty links they establish with criminals of all descriptions. A sub-inspector once was candid enough to say that he could not but become a part or member in the nexus which existed among criminal politicians, criminal businessmen and criminal superior functionaries in his own department. All of them have their interests and expectations which may be criminal in nature, form and magnitude. All of them are tied together with mutual benefits and nexus crimes come as a logical consequence of this unholy binding together.

There is a relationship between organized crimes and nexus criminality. In organized crimes, fear and corruption play an important role. The crime syndicates threaten the law enforcement officials too and give an impression that their lives are in danger if they do not yield to their activities. Instances are plenty to show that law enforcement officials are attacked by the goondas of the syndicate and sometimes, they do so with the full connivance of politicians and senior police officials in the hierarchy. The lower level functionaries in law enforcement who usually come from the poor or average economic strata of the society find it extremely difficult to withstand the pressures of the situation. They, therefore, have no option but to yield. If the officials do not yield to the wishes and desires of the syndicate as said earlier, then their very existence and survival becomes difficult, if not impossible. They have such a powerful influence at the top level of the enforcement hierarchy and political administration that police officers at the middle level or still lower level become fragile and defenceless to fight against such mammoth monsters.

Who is after all a constable—a head constable—an assistant sub-inspector— a sub-inspector of police? Or, who is after all an inspector, deputy superintendent or superintendent of police? All of them, at least most of them, come from families whose survival depends to a great extent on the income they get from the salary they receive every month. These officers have statutorily conferred powers and authority, but they can exercise them only if and if only there exist conducive atmosphere for the same. Often, such an atmosphere may be lacking, so much so, that they can not, as a rule, play with their salary and job.

As assistant superintendent of police in the Indian police service had his poor parents, three sisters and two younger brothers. They depended upon his income. He was caught between the devil and the deep sea. The conflict within him was: "Should I fight with the Mafia criminals and criminal politicians and suffer the evil consequences or should I yield to them and save my family and myself?" Most obviously he is influenced by his survival instincts more than his sense of justice and in such situations, he takes a decision and often, it may be in favour of becoming a part or a member or a silent sufferer or a mere spectator of the nexus operations.

Hedonism and Nexus Crimes

People desperately want to be happy. They want to enjoy life. They have needs and greeds. Policemen are not exceptions to this. They want to be happy and secure in life and if their participation in nexus crimes can ensure happiness and security in life, why not become a nexus criminal? This seems to be the attitude of some police functionaries as well. Those who seek worldly pleasures and luxuries can easily get them if they establish unholy nexus with corrupt politicians and criminal businessmen. Even Aristippus, a wandering Sophist of Cyrene (c 430 - 350 BC) said that all men, consciously or unconsciously, seek pleasure and people do obey this imperative of nature. Pleasure is man's natural goal in life. A nexus criminal can and does make a lot of fortunes in life and others see them. Pleasures of the senses—that is what people want more than the pleasures of intellect–or–moral pleasures. Nexus crimes can guarantee the pleasures of the senses. I think that policemen/officers who desire the pleasures of the senses have conscious or unconscious inclination to become nexus criminals.

William Adrian Bonger (1876-1940) spoke about 1) criminal motivations and (2) stimulating situations through which the criminal motivations are executed. A police officer who becomes a nexus criminal is understood to have criminal motivations. He wants to make pleasures and luxuries in life through easy cuts which can be obtained through politician-police nexus. Police officers who fail to control or refuse to control their desires for pleasures–their criminal motivations search for situations through which their criminal motivations find actualization. Some offer huge amount to politicians to get a favoured posting and if that is true, certainly such people may go after nexus criminals to make money. Poison is treated by poison–that is an old saying and if that is a truth, corrupt money given to nexus criminals is obtained back only through corruption. For this, nexus crimes become a must. Again Aristippus said: "It is not abstinence from pleasures that is best, but mastery over them without ever being worsted". Some people have been noted to be seeking pleasures after pleasures and ultimately landing in the nexus camps.

It is Gabriel Tarde (1843-1904) who said: "Man learns crime just as others learn a trade through training and association with others". When nexus crimes bring money, position, status and fortunes, a crime-prone police officer wants to learn means and methods to establish stronger ties with the people in the nexus. In order to do so, they faithfully and submissively do many things for them by misusing or abusing their power, authority and official position. Many joining the service see many things which are going on inside and outside the department and those who have a nexus inclination learn the means and methods just like they learn a trade. Sutherland goes on to add: "Criminal behaviour is learned. It is learned in interaction with other persons in a process of communication. This communication can be often verbal and at times through gestures". He continues: "The principal part of learning of criminal behaviour occurs within intimate personal groups. And when criminal behaviour is learned, the learning includes (a) techniques of committing crimes; (b) the specific directions of motives, drives, rationalization and attitudes."

What is the *modus operandi* of a particular police officer to maintain his nexus relations? This becomes a talk in the village so much so that the people openly start saying that 'such and such police officer is so and so's man'. What does it show? It shows that the people are well aware of the nexus between a police officer and a businessman; between a police officer and a politician. Not necessarily true always but some films of the recent past show such unholy relationship between politicians and the police. In one such film, as instigated by a politician, a police officer arrests an innocent man and locks him up–manhandles him–registers false case against him and thus the crimes of atrocities committed against him are many. Somehow or other an idea has gone into many police functionaries that political support and patronage are necessary for stability in a lucrative position. It is a "give and take" policy and precisely therefore the politicians expect many things from their police officers just like police officers expect many things from their politicians.

Nexus and the advantages of having a nexus instigate many to violate laws. Pleasures of the senses and pleasures of the moment–desire for authority and desire for power lead many police functionaries to establish nexus with the nexus criminals. Nexus crimes are committed not only by police, but also by anybody who has an inclination to it.

Nexus crimes have come to public visibility in the recent past in India. During the British rule, there were no crimes like nexus crimes. Politicians were not rulers then. It is only in democracy, the politicians become rulers and if they are unprincipled men, then they establish unholy relations with law enforcement officers, businessmen and people of the underworld. Even the Indian Penal Code which was enacted in 1860 does not speak about nexus crimes. The crime is not defined and punishment is not prescribed. Traditional theories explaining criminal behaviour have no applicability to nexus crimes. Several cases are reported in the newspapers of raids in the houses of bureaucrats unearthing several millions of rupees. Bureaucrats become richer and richer everyday and the nexus among the politicians-police-businessmen-underworld criminals becomes more visible with the passage of time. Opposition political parties hold press conferences, deliberate in the Legislatures/Parliament/speak in street corner meetings, etc. pressing about the issue of rampant nexus crimes. Of course, there might be exaggeration in their versions, but one can not simply ignore them as there is a lot of truth in what they say.

Emile Durkheim (1858-1917) said that crimes were the inevitable consequences of the social complexity and individual freedom. Can we say that the nexus crimes are the inevitable consequences of the social complexity and individual freedom? Democracy has its complexities but, can we say that the nexus crimes are the inevitable outcome of the democracy's complexities? Individuals have freedom as guaranteed by the Constitution of India. But should there be necessarily *nexus* crimes? Politicians present in democracy are of varied descriptions. At the village level, there are political workers who claim themselves to be politicians and they rush to police stations with their needs and greeds. They have linkages with higher level politicians in the political hierarchy and it is this linkage which is their strength. The political workers of the ruling political party/parties–particularly those who are the members of the political party to which the Minister of Home belongs–make attempts to establish nexus with police functionaries at the operational level–with police stations, with circle offices, with subdivisional offices, etc. The result has been that there comes into being a police-politician nexus.

Political Parties Sponsored Postings

Studies conducted in the area attest to the view that the politicians interfere with police work from petition inquiry to investigation of serious offences. Some of them make a living through their uncalled for interferences in police work. Durkheim further speaks about individual freedom and many a time, the police functionaries are not able to exercise their freedom and discretion. These politicians, sometimes, make attempts to humour the police personnel and in any case, they patronize their policemen/officers. Instances have been reported that some politicians name the policemen/officers to work in certain areas where they have special interests. They know it for certain that the nexus which they have with their policemen/officers can help them to manage and manipulate matters to their advantage. The political hierarchy favours it and effects necessary transfers in such a way that their political interests at the grass root level are not jeopardised by the posting of ethical police officers. The policemen/officers who come thus to a particular jurisdiction often see to it that the political interests of the party which posts them to a particular locality are not destroyed by their presence. They manage and manipulate police affairs in such a way that political mileage is guaranteed to the political party which sponsors them. Not only that, some policemen/officers identify themselves with political interests so much so that some of them go even to the extent of collecting party fund for their political godfathers. The opposition political party men call such policemen/officers 'party men in uniform'.

According to Emile Durkheim, crime is the price paid for freedom. Moreover, crime is a way through which the individuality expresses itself. In nexus crimes, one may notice that the freedom which the policemen/officers have is exercised to their advantage and the advantage of the politicians. Naturally, the individuality expresses itself. For example, a raid organized in a conspicuous manner in the house of a person may put him down and a paper report appearing in the press may further put him down. If politicians and police officers join together, they can do it. There is misuse of authority and abuse of power in such nexus crimes.

Freedom, Misuse of Authority and Abuse of Power

In nexus crimes, one notices the exercise of freedom and consequent misuse of authority/abuse of power by police. The politicians make use of the police power and authority for their mutual advantage. What is meant by the expression 'freedom in police'? Are the police free to act as per law and procedure established by law? They are free, but nexus criminals in police do not feel free to act according to law and they can not. For, then they lose their mutual advantages. Soren Kierkegaard is very true when he says that one 'chooses himself and not another'. If a police officer chooses to do things as per the nexus, then he does not exercise his freedom for administration of justice. He cheats himself and he does not choose himself. His choice results in misuse of his authority and abuse of power. He becomes successful in using his creative genius to break the laws in society and to cause distrust among the people. People show their distrust in many ways and they insist, sometimes, that their cases must be investigated by the CBI of the Government of India and they do so because they think that there will not be any political interference in such cases. In other words, the nexus does not work–they think so.

Nexus crime in police means that a policeman/officer misuses his authority or abuses his power for the benefit of those who are in the nexus. They can be politicians, social higher-ups, financially well-to-do, administratively very powerful or those who are notorious in committing crimes and underworld activities. If a police officer arrests a man in an informal or unlawful way and takes him to his custody with an intention that his arrest is likely to benefit his people in the nexus, then it is a nexus crime.

In nexus crimes, the policeman/officer knows pretty well that he is violating the law, but he does so to satisfy the nexus criminals. There is no 'ignorance of law' here. He treats his violations as necessary, though not acceptable to his conscience. Violations for him become necessary if he wants to survive in a position or post which has been given to him out of the benevolent attitude of politicians, the affluent or social higher-ups. Some police officers may desire to do things as per law and procedure established by law, but they do not as they find that the nexus they have with the nexus criminals is so demanding that they have, as pointed out earlier, no option but to yield. Once somebody is in, then he can not get out of it. He has to abuse his power/misuse his authority.

Anomie Approach to Nexus Crime

Emile Durkheim and later Robert K. Merton speak of anomie to explain criminal behaviour. Can the anomie explain nexus crimes seen in Indian democracy? There are a number of laws to regulate police behaviour. Nexus crime means that there takes place a breakdown of the regulatory norms and it takes place for the benefit and advantage of the nexus criminals. Indian police had a culture which existed during the British rule when nexus crimes did not take place. When India became independent, the colonial culture of police underwent a change to a new culture of democratic police and ultimately to a change in which nexus crimes became very conspicuous. The politician-police nexus may be the worst among many nexus crimes.

Nexus crimes are not the effect of impulses or instincts of human beings. They are the after-effect of an understanding among the nexus criminals. Democracy has certain goals and the well meaning politicians and the bureaucrats are expected to achieve the goals of democracy. Nevertheless, some unscrupulous politicians and bureaucrats join together for mutual advantages. The anomie approach therefore does not explain nexus crimes.

Democratic Disorganization and Nexus Crimes

Democratic disorganization consists in a breakdown or disruption of values in a democracy - the morale among political leaders get deteriorated. Edwin H. Lemert speaks of systematic deviation of which nexus crimes are the best examples. The nexus criminals develop a rapport among each other. Once the rapport is developed, then they together manage and manipulate everything in such a way that their crimes become organized or systematic deviations. An inspector of police once said that he arrested some innocent people as he was pressured by his superintendent of police who was having connection with some politicians. The nexus between the superintendent of police and the politicians of the ruling government forced a subordinate to submit himself into committing a crime for them. Nexus crimes are thus committed by a higher rank either by himself or by his submissive subordinates. Lower levels too indulge in nexus crimes. Why do they do so? They say that they see nexuses among the higher ups and they want nexuses at their levels too. The nexus crimes are generally non-violent and nexus criminals are said to be professionals. There is a view among the policemen/officers that all policemen/officers can not become corrupt. An efficient, intelligent and professionally competent policeman/ officer can only become corrupt; otherwise, he will be caught.

Commonality of Abilities and Attitudes

Nexus criminals too are generally efficient, intelligent and professionally competent. They have public relations skill and they please the politicians, businessmen and all others in their gang. In many cases, 'wits' or the ability to manipulate the political, affluent, influential members of the nexus counts heavily for the success. A nexus police officer could make a lot of money from private bus operators. The understanding was that each bus would give him Rs. 100 every month so that they could operate their vehicles without being caught by the policemen. Some have nexus with bar owners, hotels, toddy shops, theatres, etc. and everyone carries on his business with some immunity from legal actions. They thus exclude themselves from being considered illegal operators, knowing fully well that they can be caught for criminal activities if they do not have the nexus with police and other law enforcement agencies. In this direction they try to please their bureaucratic brethren. The nexus criminals (not the bureaucrats in the nexus) exhibit relatively positive attitudes towards all individuals who have similar nexus with the police.

For instance, an *abkari* nexus criminal has a positive attitude towards a politician nexus criminal. The forest (Mafia) nexus criminals have a positive attitude to the *abkari* nexus criminals. They know that all nexus criminals belong to the same family and all of them want to obtain bureaucratic support for their free involvement in committing crimes.

The Nexus World and the Criminals

Nexus criminals—both bureaucratic and otherwise—tend to view the nexus world as made up of people like them. Hence, they speak it out. They involve in learning experiences by their association with nexus criminals and they consider their activities as a necessary way of life. A nexus criminal violates the laws designed to regulate his occupational activities. Because of the nexus those who are involved in violating the laws do not reach criminal courts.

A journalist once questioned a police officer if there was any relationship between the police and goondas as he thought that a gang could operate only if it had the support from the police. True or false his view on police, there are people who think that the police subculture is nexus-prone to gangs or *goondas*. A subculture is a way of life and it has become very traditional among a particular group of people. Police is a group and therefore a subculture may be seen among them.

Subculture in Police

Consensus crimes- i.e., crimes committed by the members of a subculture after having a consensus—may be a nexus crime. The members of the group have a nexus here. The use of third degree methods, employment of torture, using of filthy expressions and epithets may be rightly called consensus crimes—nexus crimes - in police subculture. Police Commissions, research scholars, people and media take note of such subcultural behaviour. Why do the policemen/officers commit consensus/nexus crimes? They have some special advantages in kind, in cash or otherwise in committing such crimes. As said earlier, a subculture might be a way of life and a nexus subculture is certainly a way of life. A nexus subculture in police revolves around utility, advantage and benefit of the policemen/officers and certainly it is malicious and negativistic. Many of the subcultural behaviour in police is found to be motivated by interests other than administration of fair justice!

Albert K. Kohen has carried out extensive research on delinquent subcultures and he observed malicious and negativistic character of delinquent subcultural behaviour. His studies were on delinquent boys. He characterized their subcultural behaviours in terms of short run *hedonism* which is also a part of nexus crimes. No one who has a long-term vision or goal may indulge/involve in nexus crimes. How did consensus crimes–nexus crimes— a subculture develop in police? No serious studies have been conducted to know the causative factors although police commissions and research scholars speak something about it in their reports. If the use of torture or epithets is considered as a consensus or nexus crime, then the etiology of such a subcultural behaviour can be anything from ignorance to egoism, authoritarianism, lack of socialization, wrong concepts of policing and what not?

Anticipation Vs Aspirations in Job

'Success in life - in the career' - this may be the cause of nexus crimes. 'Success in life' is measured in terms of acquiring money and valuables and 'success in the career' is counted in terms of lucrative postings, promotions, name, fame, etc. Nexus criminals want both. They can not achieve them by being or becoming legal and moral in life. What do the *nexus* criminals want out of their police career? An answer to this question will be an answer to their nexus involvement. Policemen/ officers who are posted in certain units anticipate what they can make from such units and they compare their aspirations and expectations. Their expectations are what they want out of the job and aspirations are what they anticipate that they will receive. Relative deprivation in job may be seen in some to be the cause of being nexus prone in their career. While examining in life as to "what one wants and what is actually available to him?", it is seen that those who face serious difficulties or limitations to achieve their wants or greed through legitimate avenues become nexus criminals. They do not revise their aspirations downward and one of the main causes of nexus crimes is the greed which people have. Cloward and Ohlin speak about the development of delinquent culture and opportunity structures. According to them, those who find difficulties to achieve material success through legitimate and conventional means–or those who perceive their chances of success as circumscribed make attempts to achieve their goals through illegitimate means. They were not talking about nexus crimes, yet their views can be accepted as a good etiological explanation to nexus crimes seen in today's society. More about the etiology of nexus crimes are discussed in the chapters that follow.

Problem Vs Solution

After a television interview on nexus crimes, the author got a number of telephone calls asking him to devise some solutions to the widening and spreading epidemic in India. The problems are identified, but solutions are limited. The area calls for indepth research and study as the problem is seen in all departments–perhaps more in other departments than in police. Sales tax, Income tax, Central Excise and Customs, Railways, Banks, Industries, Commerce and all departments may have their nexuses and necessarily the issue must be studied by research committees appointed by the Government at the national level.

1

POLICE : NEXUS CRIMES AND ORGANISED CRIMINALITY

In an interview by *Surya* Television, a question was raised to the author: "What sort of crime is most prevalent today?"-to which he replied "Nexus Crimes" wherein the *Neta* (Leader), *Babu* (Bureaucrat), *Dalal* (Agent) and *Dada (Goonda)* have connections in the commission of such crimes. The nexus among them brings out wonders of the kinds witnessed nowadays. Who is the *Neta*? *Neta* is a leader and he leads, guides and directs others and such leaders are seen in politics, in trade unions, in religion, in underworld activities. A leader has his followers and leaders who are interested in the commission of crimes have their favourite *dadas* who are called *goondas* (gang-men). Their authority is absolute and unquestioned within their jurisdiction and group, i.e., among the gang-men. In this sense, theirs is an organization which has the characteristics of a crime-syndicate.

Organised Crime

The term organized crime was so confusing that forty experts had to spend an entire day at Oyster Bay to agree upon a proper definition. According to them, an organized crime is described as

"..................the product of a self perpetuating criminal conspiracy to wring exorbitant profits from our society by means—fair and foul, legal and illegal. Despite personal changes, the conspirational entity continues. It is a malignant parasite which fattens on human weakness. It survives on fear and corruption. By one or other means, it obtains a high degree of immunity from the law. It is a totalitarian organization, a way of life that imposes rigid discipline on underlings who do the dirty work while the top men of the organization are insulated from the criminal act and the consequent danger of persecution".

The description above is of some value and importance to understand nexus crimes. Nexus crimes are not self-perpetuating. Self-perpetuating means that the organization or syndicate continues to function if at all any of its leaders die or is sent to jail. In nexus crimes, there comes a link between the bureaucrats and organized criminals. What is the need for establishing the link? It is to get the goodwill of the bureaucrats. In organized crimes, fear and corruption do play a decisive role in its operation. The organized criminals are afraid of the law enforcement officers. In order to gain their support and cooperation, they corrupt the law enforcement officers. A nexus between the organized criminals and the corrupt law enforcement officers can ensure mutual benefits.

Prostitution Syndicate

One of the oldest and widely practised forms of syndicate crimes is prostitution and recruitment/ enlistment of young girls and women for prostitution. There are five-star hotels where prostitution is going on and the police may be well aware of such illicit activities. Nevertheless, they do not initiate any action against the hotel management. Why? It is because of the nexus that is established between the criminals and the police. Prostitution in any hotel will be known to many although not highly visible. Besides hotels, there are houses of prostitution peopled by a 'madam' and a collection of young prostitutes. Prostitution in such houses becomes an open secret. About the interaction between the police and prostitutes in United States, Don C.Gibbons writes:

"The metropolitan police were involved in the regulation of this business, rather than its suppression. In return for tolerating the vice operations, and the payment of their actions in controlling unruly clients and other contingencies of this sort, the police extracted a sizeable share of the proceeds from the persons operating the prostitution outlets. This 'payoff' was then distributed among various policemen, politicians, city officials and other citizens".

This is exactly what is seen in India too and in the nexus, one takes note of the link among the prostitution syndicate criminals, the police officials and politicians. The nexus is:—

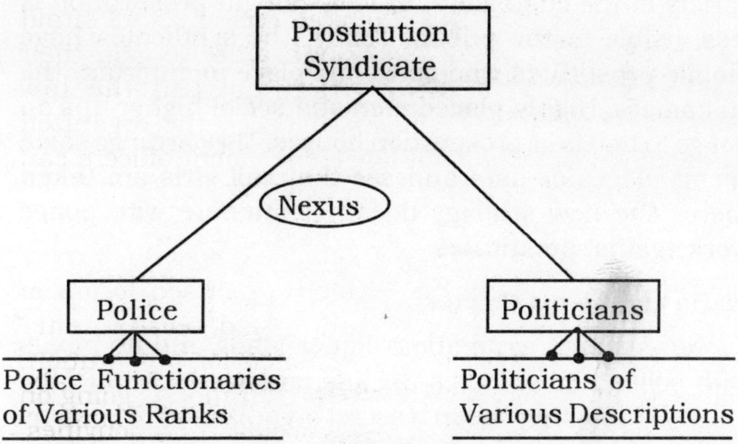

How do the police maintain the nexus? The police would inform the syndicate criminals before they conduct a raid or stage token raids in houses of prostitution. A press release would be given without mentioning the names of hotels/houses of prostitution. After the press release, the police would permit the business to go and the tender flesh trade would be back to normalcy with prostitution running at a much higher speed. The policemen and politicians get their regular pay-off and the syndicates make exorbitant profits.

The common people are not very much concerned about hotel prostitution or prostitution in the houses of prostitution unless it affects their peaceful living. Hence the people are maintaining a tolerant attitude towards this branch. The owners of hotels entertain prostitutes as they are stimulants to their business and sometimes they arrange call girls to attract customers. If the police are not informed of prostitution, they keep silence and make an income through their purposeful silence. Call girls willingly come to the hotels as they find the career more lucrative and handsome earning than alternative options available to them. The same girls go to different hotels and the syndicates encourage them as they ensure variety to the customers. In fact, call girl prostitution is less visible to the public. Today, the syndicates have mobile prostitutes who go to any place to entertain the customers. Highly placed men and social higher ups do not go to hotels or prostitution houses. They arrange some secret places or flats and see that call girls are taken there. The new strategy does not interfere with police work against prostitutes.

Mafia and Nexus Crimes

Newspapers write about liquor Mafia and its nexus with police, excise, sales-tax and motor vehicle officials, etc. By Mafia, they mean a secret organization of persons engaged in criminal activities to make money. No doubt, there is criminal conspiracy among the Abkari lobby, self-serving criminal politicians and corrupt police/excise functionaries. A raid in a south Indian State recently could unearth this criminal nexus between the police officials and liquor lobby.

The liquor Mafias in many States in India are only local *mobs* (organized criminals) and often they exist as they lavishly finance the political parties in power. They can not survive without political support. Though there is no national network in India for the liquor Mafia to operate, there exist a number of loosely coordinated regional syndicates in the entire country and they do their business after establishing a nexus with law enforcement officers. The liquor shops are auctioned and every year the auctioned money goes up. In a particular State in south India, alcohol is prohibited. Hence the liquor shops sell only toddy and Indian made foreign liquor. It has been found out that the entire natural toddy collected from the State could only satisfy the need for a few liquor shops. But every liquor shop has more than sufficient toddy! How? They manufacture it and it goes on with the blessings of the enforcement officers and after establishing a nexus with them and political leaders. They run their business with the help of *goondas* and are undergoing an upward mobility as far as their wealth accumulation is concerned.

Bootlegging, i.e., alcoholic liquor unlawfully made, sold, transported without registration or payment of taxes—nexus may be as under

A Bootlegging Nexus

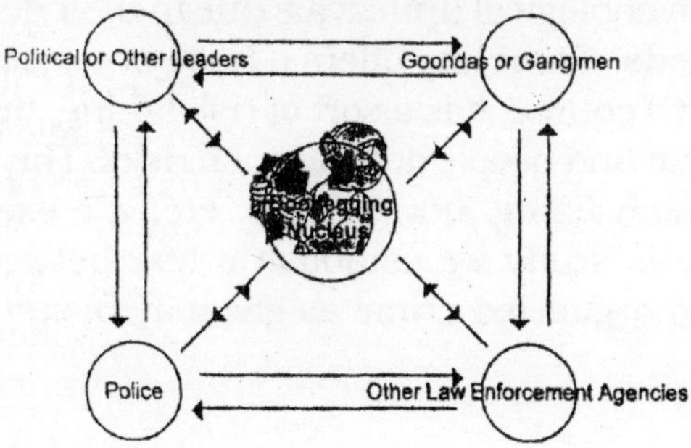

The nexus is found to be profitable and income generating for all its members. The gangsters and mobsters are viewed with respect and admiration as they are found to be very successful in their careers. Officers who establish nexus with such gangsters and mobsters too are counted to be successful in their career with the result that there exists a rush to get postings to such places where they can establish nexus with Abkari gangsters and mobsters. The interlocking structure of politicians and criminals becomes very essential for the success of nexus crimes. Thus, the nexus crime is a way of life managed by the local or regional mobsters bound together into a whole by the link established with the local or regional politicians, bureaucrats and *goondas* and where they establish a sort of association for making money and success in their careers.

Gambling and Nexus Crimes

It is an open secret that gambling in various forms and magnitude goes on in Indian society. Gambling, no doubt, is an organized crime in many situations and it can never be conducted unless some nexus is established by the gambling dens with the police/law enforcement agencies. Gambling is a 'big business' in many cities in India although an exact measure of their existence is not known. There are the government sponsored lotteries and their success is inevitable. People gamble in these in large members sometimes going through psychological upheavals due to their deep seated human needs. Gambling offers a hope of success for the gamblers. Of course, it is a sort of risk taking, but there is pleasure in it and people do take such risks. The notorious cricket match-fixing, horse races, etc. are examples in point. In this study we establish a link between nexus crimes and organized crime as given at Oyster Bay.

Nexus crimes, like organized crimes, have a high degree of immunity from law as the law enforcement officers themselves become a part of the nexus or better, they are made a part of the nexus. Their support and willing co-operation thus become essential for the success of nexus crimes.

Pattern of Nexus Crimes

The police and other enforcement officials are not normally members of the criminal gang— rather are parts of the criminal nexus. In order to get the support from the law enforcement machinery, the criminal gang with politicians rush after officials who are succeptible to them. This is necessary to ensure immunity from law. The law enforcement officers thus become members of the nexus subculture. They know that they are a part of the nexus subculture simultaneously making all efforts to show that they are not its members. Hence, they stage some raids or searches and give press releases to impress the people and the media that they are active against organized crimes. Some observations convince the researchers that the police/law enforcement officials in the nexus gangs make mock raids/searches etc., with the connivance and blessings of the nexus criminals so as to save their face.

Nexus crimes are committed in a clandestine manner and they fear the leaking of the nexus relations. As the law enforcement officers accept corruption pay-off, they are always anxious of the possibility of leaking of the sweet-heart dealings. In organized crimes, fear and sometimes violence play an important role. Violence is employed to ensure success in the operation of syndicate criminals. The question does not arise here as the law enforcement officials have no one to be afraid of. If at all they are caught by the vigilance and anti-corruption officials, usually an inquiry is ordered and more often than not, such inquiries may not become successful or yield any good results.

Unlike the syndicate criminality, nexus organization is not a totalitarian one. Nexus criminals want to maintain the secrecy of everything they do.

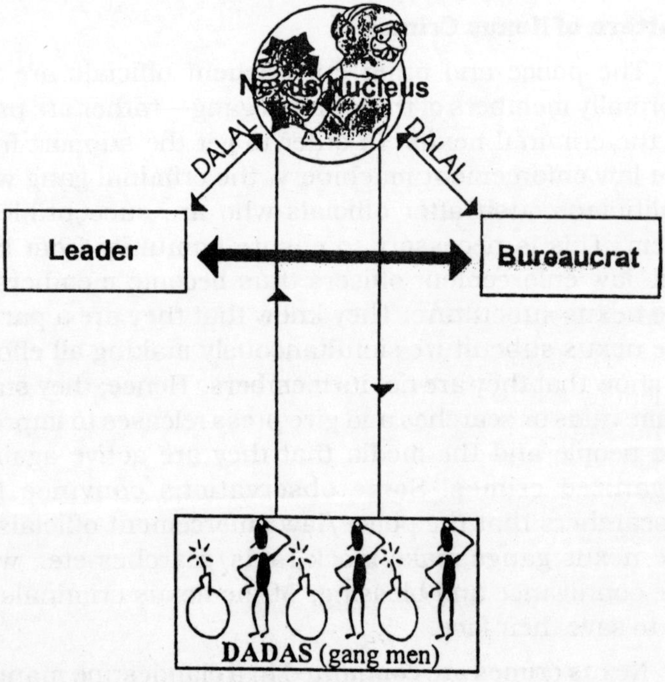

Organization of Nexus Criminality

The pattern of nexus crimes is of great importance. The nexus criminal (the criminal businessman) manages and manipulates everybody in the nexus and he has, in many instances direct contact with the bureaucrat, to the *dalal* (go-between) and to the *dadas* (gang members). The *dalal* is a go-between and he is used for many transactions such as passing information, money and privileges whenever necessary. At police station levels, some small scale politicians may play the role of both leader and *dalal*. They collect money from people and hand over the same to policemen/officers and pocket some for their use. The *dadas* and *goondas* may be utilized only when necessary.

In organized crimes, the pattern is different. The pattern is feudal in character. At the top, there is the boss whose authority is absolute and unquestioned in the group. But in nexus crime, the question of authority does not arise as the law enforcement officers have the authority with them; the politicians have their political power. The nexus gang in fact want to get the support and goodwill of the police (bureaucracy) and of the politicians. They want their full support to carry on their criminal activities without fear.

Mini Nexus or Simple Nexus

The complicated pattern of nexus crimes, i.e., the leader, the *babu*, the *dalal* and *dada* (LBDD) pattern--is not applicable in mini nexuses or simple nexuses. People have fear of police and some apprehend that the police may employ torture on them. This was more so in the past than at present. Those who have friendship with policemen/officers approach the police with a request to use, misuse or abuse their power and authority to see that everything is done in their favour. The police may yield to their request and as a result of the relationship, the police may do many things which they are not supposed to do in ordinary course. This may be called "Friendship Nexus" which dissolves and forms according to the needs. As soon as their need is over, the 'Friendship Nexus' is broken and the pure friendship is once again strengthened and they continue as friends. If the Friendship Nexus results in miscarriage of justice or administration of injustice, then it results in being called a nexus crime. There are times when the police officers direct their subordinates as follows: "He is a man of social standing and therefore just bring him to the police station and threaten him"– and the police do so as a result of the friendship which an individual policeman/officer has with the one who says so. This is a *mini nexus/simple nexus* crime. Police need introductions and recommendations to initiate action–not to initiate action-to do something in a particular way and people say so or think so because they are afraid of the mini nexuses (simple nexuses) that are at work in police subculture. This sort of simple nexus is also called Direct Nexus as the transaction is direct whereas if the transaction is through a third person, then it is called 'Indirect Nexus'.

SIMPLE/MINI NEXUS

FRIENDSHIP NEXUS

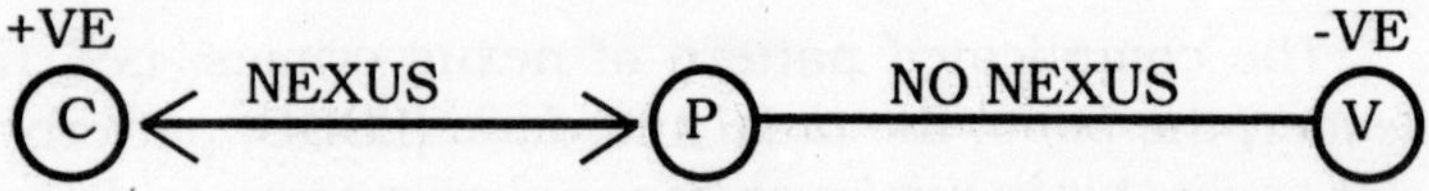

Where C - Criminal

P - Police

V - Victim

In Friendship Nexus, the criminal out of his friendship with the police establishes a nexus and thereby they together administer wounded justice to the victim. The nexus is not enduring or lasting and does not have any sort of relationship with organized crime patterns. Here NBDD nexus is not seen. The policeman/officer may strengthen his friendship and there ends the matter, although miscarriage of justice may have taken place.

Triangular Nexus

In Triangular Nexus, the criminal does not have any direct relationship with the police. Hence, he approaches a common source to influence the police and thereby establishes the nexus.

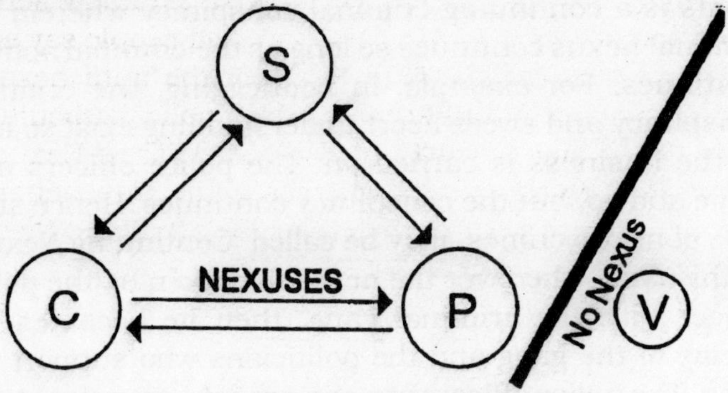

A Triangular Nexus

S = A common source C = Criminal

P = Police V = Victim

The nexus is established in the indirect way and therefore it is also called the indirect nexus. The common source can be a local level politician, a social higher up, an affluent in society, a departmental superior or a friend of the policeman/officer. The source has an influence on police and therefore he is able to see that the nexus is established between the C and the P. The nexus established here between C and P is not long lasting. It is over as soon as the purpose for which the nexus is formed is actualized. In such triangular nexuses, the S (Source) plays at times the role of a *dalal* (agent) and thus the police may be humoured by corruption money, illegal remuneration, graft, etc. The small-scale politicians or political workers in villages often work as the S (Sources) and do the job of *dalals* (agents) which helps them to make a living by their 'service' to people. The effect of the triangular or indirect nexus is miscarriage of justice or injustice.

Syndicate Nexus

Unlike the mini or simple nexuses, the syndicate nexus is a continuing criminal conspiracy wherein the criminal nexus continues so long as the criminal activity continues. For example, in bootlegging, the criminal conspiracy and sweet-heart understanding exist so long as the business is carried on. The police officers may come and go, but the conspiracy continues. Hence such type of nexus crimes, may be called 'Continuing Nexus'. In this type, whenever the nexus is broken by the police officer with the criminal gang, then he becomes the enemy of the gang and the politicians who support the gang. The police officer then can expect a transfer at any time.

Commission Nexus

In a large-scale purchase of computers, suppose the Home Minister, Police Chief and the Home Secretary establish a nexus with the computer manufacturer supply firm and resultingly an understanding is reached to make exorbitant profit by such a deal, then such crimes come in the category of *Commission Nexus* and it is so because in such unholy relationship among the politician-bureaucrat-businessmen, the role of the *dalal* is important. He receives the commission in the deal and distributes it to the members of the criminal nexus. The criminal conspiracy seen in the deals lasts only so long as it does not affect adversely the special interest which each one in the nexus has. The commission nexus may be seen in all purchases at any level ranging from purchase of safety pins to helicopters for preventive patrolling.

Organized Crimes and Nexus Crimes

"What is the difference between organized crime and nexus crimes?" The characteristics one may see in organized crimes are mainly present in the 'Continuing Nexus' and not at all in mini or simple nexus or the *commission nexuses*. However, in certain places and situations, one and the same police officer becomes a part of all the above mentioned *nexuses*. What worries the people today is the existence and prevalence of continuing and commission nexuses in police service. It does not mean that the people are not worried about the mini or simple nexuses.

The Criminal Fence

In United States, the 'criminal fence' is a notorious organized syndicate. 'Criminal fence' is intended for disposing of stolen property. Thieves, particularly professional ones are afraid of keeping the stolen property with them unless it is money or money like things. The main objective of these criminal fences is to get the stolen articles and find a way to dispose them off. More often than not, those who indulge in legitimate business enterprises do cater to this sort of illegitimate activities as well. They may encourage underworld criminals to break into houses and steal articles for promoting their business enterprises. Studies have proved that some of the automobile graveyards in United States are notoriously establishing linkages with law enforcement officers to carry on their business without fear and with legal immunity. Likewise, second hand stores are also found to have unholy nexus with police functionaries. In India too, such or similar criminal fences are in operation, but the nexus between the police and the proprietors of criminal fences is not researched into.

Emergence of New Patterns of Organized Crimes in India

Smuggling into and out of the country is recognized as an organized crime. The drug trafficking has got national and international linkages. The drug syndicates too need police support. Production of illegal and poisonous alcoholic beverages, their storage and sale and bootlegging activities are notorious. In some States in India, liquor tragedies do occur causing the death of a number of people. Gambling houses, roulette, poker and disc, etc., gambling machines, slot machines, the Numbers, Policy and Bolita, the Book-Maker or Bookie, etc., are in vogue. Loan sharking and the ruthlessness/ violence with which the sharks run the business, extortion, protection rackets, counterfeiting of nationally famous products, production of blue films, stealing of intellectual property, copy right violations, video piracy, computer crimes, telephone rackets, etc, are indicative of the emergence of new patterns of organized criminality in India in these days.

Nexus Crimes: Explanations

Why do some police officers associate themselves with organized criminals and establish a sort of nexus. The problem has not been studied in depth in India. According to studies one of the reasons is that the nexus ensures exorbitant profits for the police functionaries.

"What is the prospect of ascending in life?"–asked a sub-inspector of police. According to him, a sub-inspector has a status and he cannot sacrifice it. A clerk in government service or in a bank can do many things which a sub-inspector cannot do. For example, a clerk can travel in a public transport bus whereas a sub-inspector, inspector or a deputy superintendent can't. They need money to maintain their status in society. The salary they get cannot meet their social requirements and as such they are forced to associate themselves with organized criminals–with nexus criminals or become corrupt. Whether or not he has a status which he thinks that he has is worth debating. It may be an assumed status which has no basis in reality and a person who has such assumed status experiences an identity crisis. The social status is linked to one's reputation and character and what is the nature of character if one is corrupt? What is the reputation if one has nexus with organized criminals? When people come to know that a particular police officer is corrupt or is having some unholy relationship with nexus criminals, then he ceases to have any social status. Contrary to common belief, travelling in a public transport omnibus is not below one's status and should not be the reason for the police to enter into nexus with corrupt elements so as to fulfil their unending desires of luxury and fantasy.

Once an additional director general of police was travelling in a second class compartment in a train. A friend of mine who travelled in the same compartment asked him: 'why are you travelling in second class'? His reply was: 'the factors and reasons which make you to travel in this second class compartment force me too to do the same? This assumed status consciousness has caused many to become nexus criminals. People having unrealistic and imaginative status consciousness become more nexus prone and corrupt. What is his status in committing nexus crimes and showing others that he is a nexus criminal? He projects a poor status! If he lives honestly, then he has little or no prospect of ascending in life! This may be another outlook and way of looking at the situation.

Observations of family backgrounds of nexus criminals give evidence to affirm firmly that many of them have a *wife-based* household. The wives make many demands and they point out the lifestyles of their friends and relatives. This sort of family atmosphere–always accusing the husbands as inefficient, good for nothing, ineffective, etc, make them to search for additional income and they find nexus criminality and corruption as sure sources of income generation. In a wife dominated family, as a rule in Indian culture, the life is filled with frustrations and anxieties about money making. In many cases the husbands at home are assaulted by verbal assertions that they are useless and from this situation, there follows a desire to become an affluent man as quickly as possible by short-cut methods. They make their authority and power to become sufficiently rich in life. Those who have a relatively peaceful family life are found to be less nexus prone or not nexus prone.

The *focal* concern of nexus criminals is to become richer and more powerful. One can not become richer and more powerful overnight. Hence, he establishes contacts/associations with people who can make them richer and more powerful. Politicians, criminal businessmen, underworld criminals, and so on can make them richer and powerful. The nexus prone policemen want them and the nexus prone politicians/businessmen and underworld criminals want the policemen/officers. The relationship is mutual and the reciprocity makes them richer and richer in life. As a result of this clandestine criminal conspiracy, the policemen/officers are necessitated to violate laws and become a part of the criminal nexus in syndicate criminality.

No doubt, in nexus operations, there is risk taking–i.e., the policeman/officer takes some risks when he associates with nexus criminals. Whenever a policeman/officer receives money or favours from a nexus gang, he knows that there is a fair chance of him being detected. People around him and his associates in the department talk about it. Yet he takes it, for the advantages outweigh the disadvantages. And the chances of detection are not very certain. "It at all caught, the illegal earnings will protect me"—this feeling overpowers some to take the risk. Honest and straight forward people suffer a lot when they are suspended from service, whereas *nexus* and corrupt personnel do not face serious financial problems. On the contrary they may even get financial and other supports from the *nexus* operators or get all kinds of assistance from them. They are inclined to believe that there is no success in any business unless one is prepared to take some risks. They take precautions so that they are not caught. They act as good, docile and submissive men before their superiors. They work hard to please their superior ranks and often humour them with pleasures, luxuries and cash if they are susceptible to them. The nexus crimes rarely become a matter of public knowledge until they are caught. How much nexus crimes take place in India? How much money is earned by these nexus criminals? There is no accurate account on such issues. Unofficial estimates of liquor nexus-bootlegging shows that an amount of 5000 million rupees is earned by officials annually in a south Indian State. The officials include many from the Excise, Sales Tax, Police and Motor Vehicles departments. The amount is computed from figure (Rs. 20,000 million) calculated to be the amount spent by the liquor Mafia to import illicitly manufactured alcohol to the State and to manufacture illicit alcohol within the State. In other words, one-fourth of the total amount goes to the bureaucrats and another one-fourth goes to politicians. Out of the remaining amount, half is to meet the actual expenditure for the manufacture, sale, transportation and feeding of the gangmen *(goondas)* and the remaining half is the profit earned by the nexus operators. As far as the self esteem of those involved in the nexus operation is concerned, they consider themselves to be honest and upright officials. They do not think themselves as nexus criminals, nor do they exhibit other sorts of deviant self image patterns. They are psychopaths who do not experience guilt feelings. In conversation, private and public talks, they verbalize sentiments signifying that they are opposed to all kinds of nexus operations and the attitude is to compensate their otherwise illegal connections and nexus relations by white-washing their dishonesty. Once an individual becomes a member of the nexus, he cannot/does not get out of it. He frequently engages in repeatitive acts until he is caught. Most of the nexus criminals are married people and are having family responsibilities-majority of whom belong to the age group of 40 or above.

Reports about police-politician-criminal nexus appear in the press and media in these days quite frequently. Criminalization of police is an expression of recent origin. Criminalization of politics is older than criminalisation of police or criminalization of police is older than criminalization of police? People talk about such issues in bus stands, railway compartments, parks, restaurants and family gatherings. The term *criminalization* in criminology is a process by which a person becomes a criminal. How do the police become a part of *nexus* criminality? Criminalization in common parlance was nothing but criminal activities by policemen/officers in collaboration with nexus or organized criminals. If criminalization of police is a process by which the policemen/officers are made criminals, then certainly the process has something to do with nexus criminality as well. Nevertheless, the nexus criminals are classified as *career* criminals. Any bureaucrat (here, the policeman) who establishes a nexus with such career criminals–recidivists–is also known as a career criminal/recidivist by criminologists. Nexus crimes have a drug effect on the criminals as they have some psychological dependence on the commission of crimes. Their mind becomes restless if they do not commit career crimes/nexus crimes. Prostitutes, drug addicts, people who conduct gambling clubs, nexus operators and career criminals, generally, do not have a direct victim to make complaints against them. Those involved in crime syndicates are big guns so much so that an individual policeman is often helpless before them. This being so, the fragile policeman does not go for an attack, rather he reconciles with the situation. 'Swim along with the current and not across the current' - this seems to be the practical strategy for the helpless policeman. Wisely enough, he shows an inclination to join the nexus which certainly is welcomed by the 'nexus sharks'. Doubtlessly, these powerful people create obstacles to efficient police work. Hence some think: "It is better to wink at the nexus criminals than wipe them off".

Traditional criminals are of a different type and the policeman can take a wipe off policy with them. They are, as a rule, poor people and the traditional penal laws have many sections to book them, prosecute them and put them behind bars. But, as far as the nexus criminality and crime syndicates are concerned, the museum piece legislation (IPC) of 1860 is of no earthly use. One should not take it for granted that the penal laws enacted at a time when nexus crimes and organized criminality were not visibly in existence can do nothing much to control or put down the 21st century crimes. The police and law are gearing up its machinery to look into the recent developments in crime. People operate nexus crimes with the help of computers, e-mail and internet connections. In such an organized criminal world, the police cannot fight with arrows, bamboo sticks and black magic or occult practices. They must have professional training and adequate expertise to deal with the emerging pattern of new crimes which include nexus crimes as well. More over, the human elements in enforcement and the formation of conscience in an upright and correct way become all the more essential when police morality is given today relatively a low priority in police work. If police officers are morally legal, then nexus crimes can be controlled and I have discussed it in detail in my book on police morality I think that a solution to the emerging patterns of nexus crimes lies only in the inculcation of moral and legal values to policemen from the constables to the directors general of police.

Reference

Don. C. Gibbons, 1968, *Society, Crime and Criminal Careers: An Introduction to Criminology,* New Jersey: Prentice Hall.

2

POLICE : NEXUS CRIMES AND WHITE COLLAR CRIMINALITY

When Edwin H. Sutherland spoke about white collar crimes, he never imagined the existence of nexus crimes. He said that fee-splitting was a white collar crime. Doctors do so. Two doctors enter into a secret understanding that the patients coming to one's clinic will be sent to the other for consultation and in return, the other must direct his patients to the first one for consultation. This arrangement ensures income for both of them. He called it 'fee-splitting'. The question is: Can corruption money be split? Today, one notices corruption-money spliting! In other words, officers who deal with the files send people to different levels of officers with instructions signifying the motive 'humour him/ them' properly. As corruption money is split, the corruption too is split and it can rightly be called corruption money splitting.

White collar crime, according to Sutherland is a violation of criminal law by a person of the upper socio-economic class in the course of his occupation. It is a crime committed by a person of respectability and high social status during the course of his profession/ occupation. In the earlier days no one knew anything about nexus crimes although the nexus criminality was in existence even then. It was not as visible or conspicuous as it is today. While studying the characteristics of the white collar crimes of Sutherland and the nexus crimes that we see in society today we notice that both involve people of respectability—i.e., the white collar criminals and the nexus criminals (leader, *babu, dalal* and so on). Are the criminals respectable people? Certainly, not; yet they consider themselves to be so! Both white collar criminals and nexus criminals commit crimes during the course of their profession/ occupation and they make money or obtain privilege out of the crimes they thus commit.

Nexus is a link with other people. If so, whenever a police officer registers false cases, manipulates records, concocts evidence, employs torture, etc, as a result of an understanding with others for an ulterior motive during the course of his job/profession, then he can be called a nexus criminal. In the previous chapter, organized crimes and nexus criminality were discussed and the relationship between the two exposed. Organized criminals can not survive in society unless they get the full and willing support and cooperation from the law enforcement machinery and political parties. Those nexus operators who do not get such enduring support from police and politicians will certainly have to face premature deaths.

Police is a monopoly service and they alone are authorized to do certain things under law. Imagine that one is beaten on the road and he approaches the police to initiate an action on the crime committed against him. The police refuses to register a case, for they do not want to take additional work. This is miscarriage of justice, but it does not fall within the definition and meaning of *nexus* crimes. For there exists no secret understanding with police for not initiating an action. Instead, suppose that there was a political riot and the police registers false cases against certain members belonging to a particular party and they do so because there exists a sort of nexus between the police and the political party in power, then it is called a *nexus* crime.

The unholy relationship among the leader, *babu, dalal, dada* and the nexus criminals has already been discussed earlier. The *nexus* can be many ways and the nexuses which the police establish are drawn below:

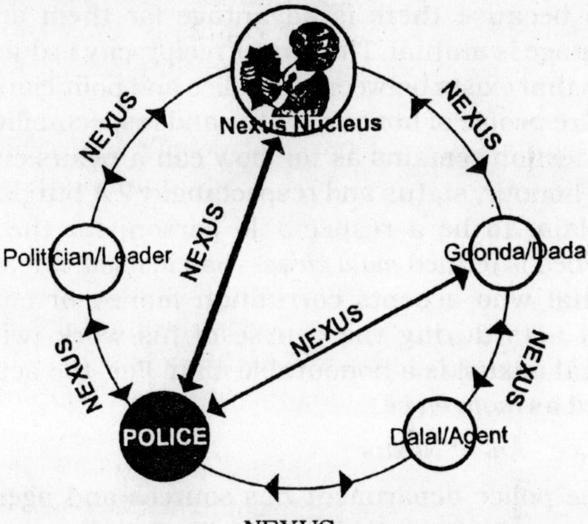

POLICE NEXUSES

Police Nexuses and Crimes

1. *Police-Nexus Operator Nexus*

Here the police establish their link with the nexus operators as one sees in syndicate crimes. For example, the bootlegging or gambling syndicates and their nexus with police may be taken. Here the police do not arrest the *nexus* operators during the course of their job/ profession. They do not initiate action against the criminals. They can not, for, there exists a secret understanding. There exists legal immunity for what the nexus operators do.

2. *Police-Politicians Nexus*

During the course of police functioning, the police will be able to do many things for politicians. But, there must be a politician-police or police-politician nexus for the same. Politicians go to police stations. Why? Politicians of the ruling party go to police stations as invitees. They are listened to and treated well. The police do so because there is advantage for them and the advantage is mutual. The proper reciprocity is due to the nexus that exists between the police and politicians. And both are people of honour, status and respectability! Yet, the question remains as to: 'how can a nexus criminal claim honour, status and respectability'? A burglar does not claim to be a respectable person, for the crime described is termed *mala en se*—bad in itself, but a nexus criminal who accepts corruption money or commits illegal acts during the course of his work (with his political nexus) is a honourable man! For, the act is not treated as *mala en se*.

3. *Police - Agent Nexus*

The police department has sources and agents for collection of information and intelligence. But, in nexus crimes, the agents are for violating crimes by police for the advantage of some vested interests which are interested in the commission of acts which are *mala prohibita*. Commission agents, nexus brokers, go-betweens come under this category. Small-scale politicians, businessmen, struggling lawyers, yellow journalists, trade union local leaders and so on may work as nexus brokers. They may collect money from people and pocket a share for their use and give the rest to the police. They make a living by their job and make the police happy for getting things done in the way they want. The police may manage and manipulate things during their work to satisfy the brokers. This sort of nexus brokers work more at the lower levels and middle levels whereas at the higher and highest levels, it is the commission agents who work profitably. They involve in the commission of illegal and unethical acts as a result of the unholy nexus established between them and the police. These *dalals* (brokers) may involve in corruption–money splitting and embezzlement of public money.

4. *Police - Dada Nexus*

Some police officers establish nexus with *goondas* and underworld criminals. They share the booty. Once a police officer got an envelope containing some money through a courier. He was asked the source of his income by his friends and he was candid enough to confess that he got it from a *goonda* gang with whom he had a nexus.

5. *Leader-Babu-Dalal-Dada-Nexus Gang*

All agents in nexus crimes may join together to commit nexus crimes. The leader will do his work, the *babu* will do his, the *dalal* will do his, the *dada* will do his and the Nexus Gang will do its work.

The label Nexus Crime can be put into all categories of crimes enumerated above. The nexus criminals are enemies of justice administration who exploit their position, misuse their power and abuse their authority to administer wounded justice, miscarriage of justice spreading injustice among people and society. They contribute nothing to the legal health of the society and people, instead they deviate from providing law and order in society. Nexus criminals are not respectable people, rather are condemned ones by the public. They are called respectable people not for committing *nexus crimes* but for performing their duties as per law and procedure established by law! It is amazing how a nexus criminal can be called a law enforcement officer? - a leader? and so on!

The nexus crime is one in so far as it violates the law and the nexus crime as far as the police is concerned is one in so far as the law violation takes place as part of the police job and during the performance of doing the police job–committed by a police functionary as a result of a criminal nexus between him and others for mutual benefits. By this definition, commission and omission to do any legal duty by police is a nexus crime if such commission and omission results from a nexus established between police and others. Acts of torture, acceptance of corruption money, registering of false cases, uttering filthy words and epithets, informal arrests, illegal detention, misappropriation of seized articles, manipulation of records which may take place in police work and if they are not the result of an unholy nexus by police with others, then they do not come under the label *Nexus* crimes if at all they are otherwise crimes of heinous nature. They are not *nexus crimes* by police, for, they are not law violations which have come out of the nexus established. As a result of the nexus understanding, the police may commit/omit several acts utilizing their professional skills, but are occupationally deviant and are often committed for satisfying the self interest. The *mahazar* written by the head constable about a ferocious dog with no teeth is a cliche, but is often quoted to show how nexus works even in such a simple case of dog biting.

Nexus Criminal Role in Police Career

Illegal/criminal acts in which the police functionaries, as a result of a nexus established by them with others, violate the laws for their benefit and for the benefit of the *nexus* partners are included in the category of nexus crimes. The law, people and society do not sanction such criminal acts, but helplessly tolerate them as they have no options but to suffer. The nexus criminal category is comprised of those policemen from constables to the directors general of police who violate the law as a result of the nexus formed by them with others. Many of their nexus crimes are complex in character and it is often difficult to expose them to the public.

The nexus criminal policeman knows that he is committing crimes by becoming a member or partner in the nexus family. Ignorance of law is not at all an important factor in nexus crimes. A constable who worked as a carrier of *ganja* knew very well that he was involving himself in illegal activities, but he was a member in the *nexus* family. They know fully well that they are doing a moral wrong as well as an illegal act, but they do it as they lack moral sense and legal mindedness together with a lack of an upright conscience formed in the right way.

Development of Nexus Criminality

Nexus criminality as a career has started developing after India became independent in 1947 as the politicians who got power and authority came into existence only afterwards. In the recent past, the nexus crimes assumed a lot of importance particularly after Vohra Commission made the observation of criminal nexuses among politicians, bureaucrats and businessmen. Hawala cases and many other transactions, of late, stimulated further interest in nexus crimes. The interest has been further generated by recurrent reports in the mass media regarding criminality and unethical conduct by businessmen, bureaucrats and politicians. Many raids conducted against crime syndicates and organized criminality have brought to light the involvement of police officials in the criminal nexus. Political interference in police work and subsequent police activities to please the politicians complicated the issues. The activities of the police and their connection with nexus criminals, in the meantime, became matters of serious discussions and adverse criticisms. Some courts including the Apex Court made few observations against the police. Corruption became a social cancer and nexus crimes were found to be one major cause for the extent and intensity of corruption in society.

The Ethics of Nexus Crimes

Criminologists always ask a question: "Is white collar crime ethically accepted?" Opinions vary, but opinions may not differ on the question: "Is nexus crime morally accepted?" Nexus crime is a moral evil and immorality proper. The policeman/officer who commits nexus crime is an enforcement officer and he knows well that what he is doing is illegal and immoral. Studies on police nexus criminality give ample proof that morality is not a major concern or consideration of police officers involved in nexus crimes. Nexus crimes in different forms and varieties are committed by many in all ranks in police and they do not have any prick of conscience for what they do during their work. Mini nexuses are found more among the lower and lowest level in police hierarchy than what they are at higher levels. One time nexuses are seen more among the middle levels than at higher levels. Nexuses with organized crime syndicates may be seen in all ranks and there exists no ethical code to control the behaviour in this area. It is firmly believed to be a transitional stage in police to be succeeded by an ethical code. It is found that a lot of the policemen/officers is also genuinely verbalizing their sentiments for ethical police behaviour and some of them condemn the unethical nexus crimes and criminals. They believe that police work must be concerned more with goals to administer justice than anything else. In a person to person talk with police functionaries, it is found that many of them do profess a high level of ethical aspirations and conduct for themselves. The behaviour of superior ranks in police is probably the most important factor in police morality. If the superiors are immoral or having connections with nexus criminals, then the subordinates follow them.

Is Nexus Crime a Crime?

The question itself is out of question. It is a crime in every sense and meaning. But, the policemen/officers involved in nexus crimes do not consider themselves to be criminals. Their group forming the nexus does not consider them as criminals, but they are regarded as criminals by the society and people. The community's law enforcement officers and responsible civil servants must not become its criminals. The low visibility of nexus crimes, lack of social condemnation and the ability of police functionaries to maintain positions of social prestige must not be made a ground for mitigating the gravity of the moral and legal evil committed by policemen/officers during the course of their work as policemen. Every policeman (Director General of Police included) must examine the problems of value deterioration/value conflicts and the formation of an ethical mind in himself.

Nexus Crimes and Public Opinion

No doubt, the public do not approve of nexus crimes in any government departments including the police. People and the press react against any kind of nexus transactions from sweet-heart dealings by policemen to international Mafia operations in which the policeman may be a member. Nexus policemen are looked down upon by the citizens and treated as enemies of justice administration. The secret and surreptitious transactions with nexus criminals—including those in mini nexuses, if and when known to the public, become a news item in the media and an item of debate in the Legislature/ Parliament, etc. Such allegations are heard time and again and these nexus policemen/officers are very much responsible for damaging the police image among the public.

Accusations Against the Police

After going through press cuttings of ten years relating to police involvement in nexus crimes we find a lot of accusations against the police and they include:

1. Accusations against policemen/officers who violate the positions of trust. After reaching an understanding with people who matter in society, the policemen misuse their power/abuse their authority for helping the nexus partners usually through manipulating some records or destroying some documents, etc.

2. Accusations against policemen/officers who ostensibly perform a conventional police job while, in secrecy, they engage in nexus criminality. In one instance the police officials seized a vehicle carrying illicit liquor and registered a case and while they were doing so, many lorries carrying illicit liquors were taken through another route to destination. Here the police officials take great pains to keep their nexus activities minimally visible.

3. Accusations against senior level police officers for directing the subordinates to wrong paths so that the *nexus* partner gets an undue advantage.

4. Accusations against police functionaries for their active role played in *nexus* crimes. Corruption, corruption-money splitting, corruption-money fixing, pay off, etc., come under this category.

All these show how the public, press and media view nexus criminality in police service. Only a few police functionaries having nexus transactions are exposed and in many cases they are persons coming from relatively comfortable middle-class backgrounds. In very few cases only, they were found to come from very affluent backgrounds. It has been noticed that the policemen/ officers having nexus dealings have special likings to money, wine, women, song, food or luxury. It has also been observed that many *nexus* contacts develop as a result of attempts to sustain a standard of living and to live according to a pattern of expectations for which legitimate income is insufficient. They have an assumed status consciousness in them. One thing quite clear with nexus criminality is that it is a form of illegality which rarely results in criminal prosecutions. In reality not even (0.1) per cent of the nexus criminality is prosecuted.

Nexus Criminality and Permissiveness

Corruption and corrupt practices may be seen in police service. Why? There exists a subculture which permits corruption in the department! If that is so, there will be corruption-money splitting as well. One reason, for the permissive subculture to prevail is that there is too much scrutiny of the *nexus* behaviour among the police functionaries which creates an undesirable atmosphere for many to work. In a democracy, everybody is important and opinions of all count. It may not be difficult to bring to light many dark corners of police activities and the evidence of even peccadilloes by the one who shows intolerance to nexus crimes may be brought to book.

Some officials/men accept *nexus* crimes as desirable within the organization. Their logic is: "how can a police officer meet the unforeseen expenditure which he has to incur while he performs his police duties?" Here, he finds out a source of income by way of extending his service for the promotion of nexus operations. It means that law enforcers become law violators when they conceive of themselves as having unforeseen expenditure and financial problems which are nonshareable. They want to solve the issue by establishing secret ties with nexus criminals. Some police officers complain that they face a plethora of difficulties from superior ranks when fund is requested for meeting unforeseen expenses / expenditure while they perform police duties. As they can not resolve their difficulties by legitimate means, they go after illegitimate means and methods which include nexus crimes as well. No doubt, it may be a reason for searching for alternative sources of income. At the same time, one may have to accept and acknowledge the fact that such explanations and rationalizations are often cover-ups for their many kinds of illegal activities in uniform. Many nexus criminals in police adopt a style of living for which their 'incomes' may not be adequate. Most of the nexus crimes relate to the status seeking and status maintaining attitude of police functionaries who want to earn illegitimate income through short-cuts.

Organized Crimes, White Collar Crimes and Nexus Crimes

All of them— organized, white collar and nexus crimes— belong to the same family. Why nexus crimes take place in police? Do they willfully decide to become a member in the nexus? Are they driven into nexus criminality by psychological urges, forces or disorders? Are they impelled towards nexus criminality by adverse social circumstances? Some studies and observations prove that the nexus criminality like organized crimes and white collar crimes often remain as covert or hidden in society. It is more so if done in police department. Moreover, nexus crimes get a distinct identity only in these days. The fear that the police will apprehend the *nexus criminals* is not much in police department, and indeed it may be a more important factor in nexus recidivism than many other variables in police. Mostly in nexus crimes, it is found that there may not be any complainants against the police. Hence the higher authorities too wink at the nexus criminals if that is possible. Policemen become targets of public and media criticisms and there exists a good deal of public hostility. The superior ranks do not want to complicate the issue by exposing the extent and intensity of nexus crimes within the department. This cold attitude too is a cause for the commission of nexus recidivism.

Police Hostility Towards Police Nexus Criminality

The police is of different types and most of the studies are conducted on the police in the general executive branch of the police. They alone have authority under law and therefore, they alone can involve themselves in the commission of most of the nexus crimes. Even in the general executive branch of the police, there are many units and wings other than the Thana Police. They too can not be blamed for involvement in the participation/ commission of nexus crimes. A major reason for the involvement/participation of Thana Police, Circle offices, sub-divisional offices, district police office in nexus crimes is that they are primarily responsible for arresting people, patrolling the jurisdiction, maintaining law and order, controlling, preventing or suppressing crimes, dealing with *goondas,* and so on. On a scrutiny of Indian police history, one may see that the police has been frequently linked with organized criminals and white collar offenders. The same allegations and accusations are heard or levelled against the police even in developed countries. To quote Gibbons, "City police have often operated as regulators of prostitution, gambling and other forbidden activities, and have shared in the division of spoils from these enterprises". He continues: "Although prostitution and gambling depend for their support upon a public which presses for provision of illicit services, this fact has not prevented a good many citizens from venting their indignation upon the police, particularly on the occasion of recurrent exposes of police corruption reported in urban newspapers". On an examination of the newspaper reportings on police activities in India, it is seen often that the police are criticized for their unholy relationship with organized criminals of every description.

Criticisms are also levelled against the Thana Police and the upward hierarchy in police from the Thana by the policemen/officers working in other units, wings, armed reserves and armed batallions of police for involvement/participation in *nexus* criminality. Thus the policemen/officers working in Thana and upwards in the ladder in the general executive branch become targets of negative responses from policemen/officers in uniform. They express their dissatisfaction with the thana police (upwards) in many ways especially against their various or questionable enforcement procedures and involvement/participation in *nexus* criminality. The use of third degree methods as a consequence of a nexus understanding is not favoured by policemen themselves. Some show resentment to suggestions by superiors and some react against. Whatever that be, the police department has an unenviable image among the people. The negative criticisms which the policemen/officers themselves level against the police functionaries in their private talks and discussions have, doubtlessly, contributed much to the low esteem in which the policemen/officers are held today in society. The policemen/officers themselves do not have trust/ confidence on policemen/officers working in Thana Police and upwards. They accuse them with corruption and *nexus* practices.

Elements of White Collar Crimes and Nexus Crimes

Edelhertz has brought out certain elements in white collar crimes and it can be seen that they are found in the *nexus* crimes as well. They are:

1. Intent to commit a wrongful act or to achieve a purpose inconsistent with law or public policy. In nexus crimes too, the partners have an intent to commit a wrongful act and thereby they want to achieve a purpose inconsistent with law and public policy. The purpose here is to have mutual advantages in cash, friendship, position or otherwise.

2. Disguise of purpose or intent. In nexus crimes, the purpose or intent is disguised. The purpose may be to help the nexus partners, but that is not projected out. Everything done is given a legal colouring.

3. Concealment of crime by (a) preventing the victim from realizing that he has been victimised (b) relying on the fact that only a small percentage of victims will react to what has happened.

For this, the nexus partners manipulate records to disguise the true nature of what has occurred. The police may exercise their authority and power and sometimes their pseudo-authority and power. They are expected to arrest the culprits, but because of a nexus understanding, they refuse to exercise their power and authority. Instead, they may exercise pseudo-authority and power. The police have no unlimited powers, but they have the muscle power which they can abuse/misuse for the actualization of the *nexus* objectives. For this, the police can use their discretion.

At present, there exist no laws defining *nexus* crimes, yet the police can have recourse to some laws which are in existence if they want to put down *nexus* crimes. But, they do not do so and it is because there exists some nexus understanding. They go about selective enforcement of criminal laws and that is done to save the *nexus* criminals. For example, the police can enforce the provisions of the Gaming Act/Gambling laws. But, they do not enforce them, because they can not do so as they have established a sort of *nexus* with the proprietors of gambling houses. At the same time, there is the differential application of gambling laws to different individuals. The police may apprehend some, but not all, of the persons whom they find violating the same laws. This is because there exists some nexus with those who are spared by the police. In recent years, the criticisms against police of their involvement/participation in nexus crimes have been very apparent in newspapers, public speeches, street corner meetings and debates in legislatures. While some of these recent charges may have been exaggerated, there can be little doubt that some police officers and policemen are associated closely with the nexus operations.

Nexus in Disciplinary Proceedings

Disciplinary actions are taken often against the middle and lower level functionaries in police department. There is widespread allegation that some of the departmental inquiries are the result of nexus operations among the controlling authority, disciplinary authority, inquiring authority, and so on, and in some cases owing to some political interference as well. All want to punish the official under inquiry and they manage and manipulate everything in such a way that the official under inquiry is somehow or other punished. Cases are reported that some lower level functionaries are proceeded against for their refusal to support the *nexus* activities of their superiors. In cases when the superior authority finds a subordinate not susceptible to his nexus desires, then he waits for an occasion to fix him and proceeds against him by conducting inquiries through his 'Amen' men in the department. Senior level officials contend that no disciplinary action is generally initiated as a result of any *nexus*. The subordinate and lower ranks maintain that *nexus* works powerfully in departmental inquiries. It seems apparent that the senior levels choose not to give an impression that such nexus inquiries do take place or acknowledge the unpleasant facts about the department. The higher ranks can do so during the course of their job and in the pretext of administering disciplinary justice. It is probably true that the lower level functionaries - particularly the constables — are somewhat more hostile towards departmental actions than officers at the higher echelons in the hierarchy. The hardening of 'a constable afterall, sentiments in both society and department in the past decades has probably heightened the antagonistic views towards disciplinary inquiries and nexus actions.

Nexus Crime as a Way of Life

Grifters, boosters and carnies—all are termed professional thieves in criminology. Professional thieves make a living by their activities. What do the nexus criminals do? What do the syndicate criminals do? What do the white collar criminals do? All of them are in every sense professional thieves who commit crimes as a way of life— a luxurious life. A professional thief has received a long period of training, complex occupational skills and special attitudes and approaches. Likewise, a *nexus* criminal, organised racketeer, a white collar criminal too may have special training, skills and attitudes. Like a professional thief, the nexus criminals do not experience guilt feelings, instead they exhibit a pride in their success in life.

Among the policemen/officers, there is a sort of race to go to *thana* police and upwards in that ladder. Some do not show any such over-enthusiasm and they are found to be less nexus prone or not nexus prone. On the other hand, there are officers/men who can not feel at peace if they do not go to serve the people in police stations, circle offices, sub-divisions, districts, ranges, zones, etc. and this is seen in constables upwards to the director general of police. There is ample evidence to show that such restless officers are *nexus* prone. They have an excessive desire to earn more and have material success. Moral values and legal sense do not have greater significance in them. They have received definite teaching or coaching in the art of cheating people and betraying others. They have the development of verbal facility, social charm and ingratiating ways of behaviour. Most of the *nexus* prone policemen/officers are found to possess above average intelligence and see that they are not detected easily. Indian society exhibits a cultural climate in which profit motives stand out and if the police uniform can be misused for that purpose through the nexus operations, then they feel that there is nothing wrong in doing so. A nexus prone policeman/officer turns his job/profession to his advantage.

Nexus Crimes and Victims

Who become the victims of police nexus? Many policemen take a comfort in the view that they do everything for the good of the people–and precisely therefore they do not view nexus crimes as crimes. They do not think that the police nexus has victims. Once a police officer said: "I did many things for him and all were for his benefit. He offered me some money and he gladly offered it to me. If I did not accept it, then he would become desperate..." and he gave the impression that he did everything for the greater glory of man and humanity. He committed a nexus crime and the victims suffered the consequence of his nexus. Once a police officer was asked: "If the victims of the *nexus* crimes rise up to prosecute you, how many of you will be convicted?" A meaningful smile on the face gave the answer. However, no study has been conducted on the extent and intensity of *nexus* crimes in police and their impact on the victims. An enormous variety of acts which police do today make up the nexus crime problem in society. Crime is not just a poorman stealing a coconut, it is a professional thief stealing cars; a policeman accepting monthly pay off; a constable keeping his eyes shut to bootlegging, to cite a few, which make the crimes today. It is a well dressed policeman helping a smuggler to carry on his activities or helping a politician to commit atrocities on people which makes the crimes of today. No single formula, no single theory, no single generalization can explain the vast range of nexus crimes committed by men/officers in uniform–said a sessions judge in a casual talk while talking about nexus crimes in law enforcement. The victims are a legion.

How to control the nexus crimes among the policemen? Nexus crimes can not be controlled unless the policemen are at it. For, the crimes are committed by those who are to control, suppress and prevent them. It is difficult to control nexus crimes because, the crimes ensure money, fortune, position, welfare, promotion, status, name, fame, pay-off and what not? Policemen/officers know fully well the existence of nexus crimes at every level in the hierarchy. They talk about them, but they are not afraid of them because they know that they are safer in their own hands. Some stay in the commission of nexus crimes because their uniform and authority offer an assurance that they can well continue in the job without being afraid of others. Prof. Sutherland says that no index or rate of white collar crimes has been officially constructed, but their prevalance has been shown abundantly in many industries. Likewise, the index or rate of nexus crimes is not officially constructed, but heir prevalance is well recognized.

Extent and Intensity of Nexus Crimes

The President of India in a recent telecast to the nation on the eve of Independence day (2000) cautioned the country about the extent and intensity of nexus crimes. The financial loss to the country and to the victims of nexus crimes is probably greater than the loss caused by traditional crimes by burglaries, thefts, robberies, etc. In a nexus crime, a single individual in India made an amount of Rs. 950 crores. The financial loss to the victims of property offences in the country is estimated to be less than Rs. 1000 crores during an year. In an ayurveda medicine deal, the nexus criminals made profit of Rs. 5000 crores as it is reported in the press. Two bank officials make a profit of 120 crores and thus goes the list. Financial loss and other damages to human rights and dignity caused by nexus crimes in police department are not subjected to any research studies. A nexus crime in police department may cause violence and massacre in the State and sometimes in the fall of a democratically elected Government in power. The damage caused to public trust on police and to police-public relations is very huge. Nexus crimes in police creates distrust and lowers the morale. People do not tolerate nexus crimes in police, but they suffer them as they are otherwise helpless to fight against the mammoth police machinery and the forces behind it. The members of the nexus crimes are influential people and they work with the strength of the police authority and power. The victims are generally weak and are not organized to declare a crusade against the nexus operations. Despite the seriousness of the problem today and the increasing challenge in the years ahead, there take place no operational and basic researches into the problem of nexus criminality by those who are within and without the police department.

Nexus crimes in any department are generally tolerated by the employees of that department. Police may not be an exception to it. A sort of group support is seen in favour of nexus crimes. As a result, a nexus criminal does not regard himself as a law violator–rather he regards him as a law enforcer in police department. A *nexus* criminal may be free from neurosis, psychosis or mental defectiveness. He is a person who knows what he is doing and the consequence of his behaviour, nevertheless, seems to have no inner feelings of guilt for what he does. He repeats his criminal acts. He evaluates and over-evaluates his advantages in becoming a nexus criminal. Once he becomes a nexus criminal, then he is not concerned with the rights and privileges of others.

Recruitment/Posting Syndicates : A Myth

Where does the nexus crime originate? Some studies show that it originates in the name of recruitment. According to them, the candidates to any service spend a lot of money prior to and during their recruitment. They want to get back the corruption money which they spend as soon as they start working in the department. They search for avenues to make money and commission of nexus crime is a way by which they make money. There are contradictory versions as well. They argue that some policemen/officers who are nexus prone make this social reality— i.e., corruption prior to and during recruitment– as a cover up to involve themselves in the commission of *nexus* crimes. Many policemen/officers have been asked about the corruption money they had to spend for getting police jobs. Honestly, many have disclosed that they did not spend any huge amount for their recruitment. Studies too show that it is not that easy for many to get a pass in the written test with the money they have. It is not easy to get a pass in the physical efficiency test which is being conducted on open grounds in public's visibility. Though the possibility of some candidates spending money for their recruitment is not dismissed, most probably the corruption money they spend is taken by some middle men who have nothing to do with recruitment. There are recruitment syndicates actively operating in the present day society. In such a social background anything practised and propagated will be sold. *Nexus* prone policemen/officers exploit this situation and cash it for serving their self interests. They spend money to get desired postings and transfers and their eyes are fixed on the commission of *nexus* crimes. They seek for *nexus* relationship and establish unholy *nexuses* with them for trading on the police job.

References

1. Don C. Gibbons, 1968. *Society, Crime and Criminal Careers: An Introduction to Criminology,* New Jersey: Prentice-Hall.
2. Herbert Edelhertz, 1970. *The Nature, Impact and Prosecution of White Collar Crimes,* Washington: U.S. Government Printing Office.

3

POLICE : NEXUS CRIMES AND ENFORCEMENT CRIMINALITY

A comma can hang a man (Hang him, not let him go; Hang him not, let him go)–is a cliche in judicial circles. "A head constable will send a man to jail"- this is another cliche. People see a lot of work connected with crime investigation including the writing of scene *mahazer* which is done by the head constables. The old people, therefore, advise the younger ones to have some sort of nexus with the head constables to see that the criminal case is strengthened or weakened as the case may demand.

Professional "Fringe" violators are respectable citizens who are engaged in law violations in such a way that their professional skills are misused for personal advantages. A doctor-abortionist is the best example. His activities are considered and treated as unacceptable by his own professional colleagues. He moves with law abiding and non-deviant fellow professionals who are themselves loath to commit abortions. Hence they refer such cases to the "fringe" violator. This is a nexus between the non-deviant professionals and the fringe violator.

Concocting Evidence

Forget about the head constable who writes a *mahazer* for getting a conviction or acquittal as the case may be.

A police investigator will be able to manipulate the evidence, contaminate the evidence and destroy the evidence in crimes. .He can plant a strong evidence to the scene of crime and in one instance, it was proved that the investigator, after a nexus understanding, poured human blood on a knife that was made at his request and sent to the forensic science laboratory to get an opinion whether or not the knife had human blood. The police investigator expected a positive expert opinion confirming the presence of human blood, but when the report was received, he became disappointed as the report did not confirm the presence of human blood on the knife. Did any nexus take place between the experts in the forensic science laboratory and vested interests?

Fringe violators are described as members of legitimate professions who misuse/abuse their professional knowledge for committing crimes. Their activities are not regarded as legitimate and ethical within the profession. In police too, an enforcement criminal is one who misuses/abuses his power and authority or professional skills for commission of crimes. In the above case of concocting evidence, a crime investigator involves himself in a *nexus* understanding between himself and his victim. The victim may be the victim of offence or the accused in the offence. The victim of offence is involved if the case is weakened by the introduction of fragile evidence. The accused is involved if the case is strengthened by introduction of strong evidence. In both cases, miscarriage of justice takes place. A police officer who has an upright conscience formed in the right way and who possesses a moral sense can not and will not concoct evidence whatever may be the advantage he gets by doing so.

Forcing a Non-deviant Police Officer to Submit

There are cases in which politicians may be interested. If the case is investigated by a police officer who is honest in his conscience, the politicians may not be able to establish a *nexus* with him. He will not manipulate evidence and will object to any such movements. In such instances, the politicians may see to it that the honest police officer is transferred or the investigation is entrusted to someone who may not be hesitating to enter into a *nexus* with the politicians. Certainly, such *nexus* investigators–enforcement criminals–are regarded by others in police department/ government as engaged in nexus behaviour which is objectionable. The superiors and top level of the hierarchy know it well. But, sometimes they too enter into a *nexus* with the politicians/vested interests and do abet the enforcement/*nexus* criminal investigator to continue his investigation ensuring miscarriage of justice.

Allegations are sometimes heard against senior levels that they misuse their subordinates to employ torture on suspects or abuse their authority to force the subordinates to commit illegal acts on others. Such officers may be unwilling to do such immoral/illegal activities eventhough they are bound to do so as a result of their *nexus* with vested interests.

Enforcement Crimes and Nexus

Lawless law enforcement is notoriously known in police circles. Police officers are bound by law to enforce law; nevertheless, some, owing to a *nexus* understanding, violate the law and commit crimes. Police have virtually unlimited powers which they can misuse/abuse if they want to. Some powerful people want the police to harass their opponents and see that the police are pressured to do so after a nexus understanding. Some police functionaries bitterly resent the *nexus* dealings- they are non-deviant and do not see or want to see themselves as craftsmen skilled in using/misusing their power and authority to the benefit of vested interests whatever may be the advantages for them.

A citizen in Indian democracy enjoys fundamental rights and freedom from improper police actions by virtue of the Constitution of India. The laws are framed to protect the citizens from illegal arrests, detention, searches, etc, and there is no justification for the police to violate such laws whatever may be the temptations offered by the *nexus* operators. There are any number of instances to show that the police have employed third degree methods on the suspects to coerce confession from them or on the innocent to ruin him as a result of the unholy nexus with interested people. Researches have proved that policemen have engaged in searches without warrants, suspects have been detained and interrogated for unduly long periods of time, detinues have been forced to remain under starvation in short loin clothes, etc. Historically too *nexus* criminals have misued police to commit illegal acts circumventing or ignoring the procedural rules and legal requirements which are supposed to control their activities. Over the past fifty years or more, i.e., after India became independent, there has been constant attempt to make police partners in political activities. The politicians wanted to establish a politician-police *nexus*. Each policeman/officer then had to make a choice. Some resisted, some became indifferent and some surrendered. Those who surrendered became *nexus* criminals and the politicians saw that they managed everything with their policemen with their hands up.

Selective Enforcement of Criminal Laws

Although the police may or can often claim publicly that they everywhere enforce all laws equally, the fact remains that they go about selective enforcement of criminal laws. Why? It may be due to a nexus that has been created by them with vested interests. They resort to differential application of laws to different individuals. The police may apprehend some people and not all and this they do sometimes owing to their affiliations with vested interests. The exercise of discretion is sometimes guided by pressures from many quarters and when they do so, the selective enforcement deteriorates into police abuse of their power and authority. In the past, the discretionary treatment of people has resulted in carving out an unenviable image of the police in public. Politicization of police has caused serious damage to the police image. The differentials in handling people having political affiliations is fairly complex in character. Politicians belonging to the opposition apprehend that they are being harassed more by the police than those belonging to the ruling front.

Police officers who use their discretion and abuse their power do acknowledge the illegal nature of their actions, but make some explanation or rationalization by which they attempt to square their criminality with their non-criminal self-image. They may even say that their acts are not justified in law, but are necessary for their survival in the department in the existing political scenario. They maintain that a proper solution to the problem is to see that political interference in police work is stopped forthwith. It has been observed that the *nexus* with politicians work with policemen/officers who are senior in service more than the fresh ones to the service. The occupational deviations during enforcement of law by police have been little studied in India and particularly it is so in the areas of nexus crimes and enforcement criminality.

Studies prove that a policeman can complicate an issue if he does not want to solve it. To an innocent suspect brought for interrogation, a police officer, if he wants to do so, can adopt strategies calculated to unsettle, frighten or degrade him. He can deprive him of adequate food, water, medical attention, rest or other physical necessities. Once a woman who was interrogated had to suffer extreme humiliation as she was not provided with sanitary napkins to attend to the special needs of women during their mensural periods. This is an enforcement crime and if it is done as the result of a nexus entered into by the police officer with some vested interests for mutual advantages, it becomes a nexus crime. Enforcement crimes have been defined as crimes committed by the enforcement machinery while the law is enforced. The enforcement criminal violate the laws when the laws are enforced.

Coercive and Improper Investigation Techniques

A police officer, for instance, attempts to induce an arrested person to make a statement by questioning him of such unfair frequency, length or persistence as to constitute a sort of harassment to him and if it is done for making a gain after entering into an understanding with some vested interests, then it becomes a *nexus* crime during law enforcement. What is the meaning of pressuring the interrogated by any methods which, in the light of his age, intelligence, mental and physical conditions, unfairly undermines his ability to make a choice whether or not to make a confession to the interrogator? In some instances, the police do so with an ulterior motive. Before the enactment of the Protection of Human Rights Act - 1993, such cruel methods were frequently employed - that is what studies and paper reports show. What was the outcome? The output was zero as the conviction rate was found to be deplorably low even when such enforcement criminality was practised.

Detention and Presentation of Arrestees

Enforcement criminality may be rightly called "hidden crimes" during law enforcement and the *nexus crimes* may also be "hidden crimes" as they are not very conspicuous to the people. How can the public know about the use of drugs on the suspects to elicit information from them? How can the public know that the interrogated was coerced to make a confession by indicating that such person is legally obligated to do so. What is the motivation of interrogators when they use such obnoxious practices? The investigating officers are bound by law to produce the arrested persons without unnecessary delay. Of course, the Indian laws permit the police to detain the arrested for 24 hours in their custody without producing him before the magistrate. In some cases, the arrestees are detained for days together and the purpose of the investigators is quite obvious which can be anything other than respecting the law they enforce. Prompt presentation of the arrestees before the court is a law recognized by international community and it is regarded as very necessary for minimizing the opportunity for coercive or otherwise improper interrogation techniques.

Enforcement-Nexus Role Career

Police officers who commit enforcement crimes during interrogation do violate positions of trust by society by abusing/misusing their power and authority. If they do so for making advantages after entering into a *nexus* with vested interests, then they ostensibly perform their duties statutorily conferred on them, while in secrecy they engage in the commission of crimes.

Nexus Searches

A search in a house has its humiliating effects and damages the reputation of a person. Politicians and the police can cause it to be done with an intention to deflate the image of a person for some reason or another. The law permits police officers to conduct searches and that can be done only after presentation of proper credentials and it must be done at reasonable times for performing the duty imposed upon them by law.

Unwarranted Publicity to Searches and Humiliation

Search warrants are issued *ex parte* for obvious reasons without giving notice to the party whose arrest is sought or whose property is to be searched. If the search is done by police after a *nexus* understanding with vested interests, the police party may misbehave with people with an intention to humiliate them in front of others. Naturally an impartial onlooker, a neighbour or the community may disapprove of such filthy police behaviour. Hundreds of policemen, weapons, police vehicles, etc, are brought in such situations to give publicity to the search. The press men and electronic media may be contacted to publicize the search. The motives are very clear in such cases and after the search a press release is given to further put him down in public's eye. Fairness and justness in searches may be overlooked if they are done as *nexus* crimes during the enforcement of law. Police behaviour and actions at the scene of searches have very serious consequences. After a search, a wife in the house committed suicide as she could not face the people around her. The conduct of the *nexus* offenders at the scene of search sometimes shocks the conscience of mankind.

Once in a south Indian city, political tensions broke out. The political party in the ruling Government had a nexus with the police and they together arranged house searches to arrest the culprits belonging to their opposition political party. The action of the police was criticized by the press and people alleging that the searches were nexus operations. In nexus searches, the police may not adhere to legal principles that must guide them during search operations.

What is wrong with nexus searches? Usually, a search warrant is issued upon presentation of true information believed to justify the arrest and search. In nexus searches, the facts may be exaggerated or distorted and that itself makes it an enforcement crime. People enjoy privacy and liberty and *nexus* police officers generally do not show due respect to people's privacy and liberty when they zealously organize *nexus* searches. For, their objective is not law enforcement but making some advantages by their nexus.

Pre-Search Proceedings and Establishment of Probable Course

Law enforcement officers or the police must be neutral and detached when they organize a search. But in *nexus* crimes, their neutrality and detachment are of a questionable nature defeating the purpose of justice administration. The privacy and liberty of the citizenry are sacred rights and the police must not play with them after a *nexus* understanding. A person may be a suspect in a crime, nevertheless, he has a reputation which he could establish over a period of time and the police authority must not be abused to damage one's reputation without justifiable causes. A search warrant must be obtained from a court only upon showing of probable cause for the same. Can a *nexus* searcher do so? Sometimes, press reports are seen saying that the nexus police get search/arrest warrants against citizens without showing probable cause for the issuance of such warrants. This is of bad taste and it often results in the search/arrest of people after a communal/political riot. The media, sometimes, accuses the police, in such situations, of showing reckless disregard for truth and perjury and is of the opinion that the police officers do deliberately falsify allegations to demonstrate a probable cause in such circumstances. This is a case of a lawless or reckless misconduct showing misuse/abuse of authority. The pre-search proceeding is necessarily *ex parte* since the victim of search is not heard before the search/arrest warrant is issued. In the adversary system of justice followed in India, an *ex parte* inquiry is likely to the vigorous. A pre-search proceeding is frequently marked by haste. There is an understandable desire to act before the evidence disappears and the urgency does not always permit a court to make an extended–independent examination of the *nexus* understanding between the police and vested interests. In *nexus* searches/arrests, the police functionaries are blamed for deliberate filing of wrong statements and for showing reckless disregard to the citizen's dignity.

Nexus and Arrest of Citizens

In nexus arrests and searches, enforcement officers may not be very much concerned with the requirements of law and procedure. In connection with or after a sensational case (like arson in a city, communal tension, political riots etc.) there may arise the necessity to conduct searches and seizure of many things. In other words, the police may have to conduct warrantless searches and seizures. However, in such instances, there is the likelihood of establishing *nexuses* with vested interests. It may invite severe criticisms from the press and well meaning citizens. The *nexus* arrests and seizures may be called enforcement crimes with ulterior motives. It must be remembered that the right of the people in a democracy ensures them to be secure in their persons, houses, papers such that their effects are well protected under law. Hence the people have a right against unreasonable searches and seizures. In *nexus* crimes, this right of the people is violated.

Honouring Sanctity/Privacy of a Man's Home

Sanctity of a man's home and privacies of his life are honoured in all civilized countries. A senior police officer once stated that the police will have to conduct indiscriminate and warrantless searches for the interest of administering searches/seizures and in such situations, the sanctity of one's home and his privacies of life can not be honoured. In some such situations, there may be nexus understanding with vested interests. Police can not be blamed for what they do, for, they are helpless in such situations. *Nexus* becomes inevitable in such cases. Warrantless searches, for whatever purposes, are viewed with suspicion if they are the result of *nexus* understanding. Such practices may be in existence, but any longstanding or widespread practice is not immune from Constitutional and legal scrutiny. There must be reasonable and probable cause and justification to do any searches/seizures. In the absence of reasonable and probable cause, everything is viewed with scepticism. The zealous officers, their nexus understanding, the citizen's rights for the sanctity of his home and privacies etc., are mixed in such cases and the refusal to show reverence to man's rights is not tolerated in civilized law and practice.

Some police officers argue that the people are more concerned with the safety and protection of the suspects in crimes and are not so much concerned with the enforcement of law and administration of justice. This is in bad taste and the concern for over-protection ensured to suspects defeats the end of justice. They argue so because they do not know the ends of justice in the true sense. Nexus searches/seizures cause abusive or arbitrary enforcement and ensure to administer only wounded justice to people. Every arrest, search and seizure may cause fear, humiliation, harassment and embarrassment to the citizens unless there is justification to enter into the home and privacies of citizens. In fact, the reality is that *nexus* arrests severely hamper effective law enforcement; and go a long way in damaging the reputation of the police department.

Nexus and Electronic Surveillance

Interception of Oral Communication

Allegations are sometimes raised against *nexus* surveillance and sometimes, the law enforcement agencies make use of electronic devices for surveillance. The surveillance of spoken words is of great importance. Surveillance of telephone conversation comes under electronic surveillance. Electronic surveillance constitutes a *search* under law and necessarily therefore the principles applied against unreasonable searches and seizure apply in the case of electronic surveillance. Any person who makes a telephone call reasonably expects that the words he utters in the mouth piece of a telephone must not be heard by others. He has his own privacy interests and therefore the use of recording or listening devices for the purpose of surveillance is to be scrutinized under the rule governing searches and seizures. Laws in many countries prohibit interception of a wire communication or an oral communication. The laws also put many restrictions upon the use and disclosure of information obtained by an interception of a covered communication. Nevertheless any communication involving conspirational activities/ strategies threatening the national security interest stands at a different footing. Interceptions under a court order too stands at a different footing. In the latter case, the principles applicable for reasonable and probable cause as in case of searches are relevant and important.

Psychological Interrogation and Enforcement Crimes

Allegations are sometimes heard about *nexus* interrogations by the use of psychological methods. The interrogation is usually done in a room where interrogated person is cut off from the outside world. It is accepted that an incommunicado interrogation of a suspect in a police dominated atmosphere makes the suspect confused resulting many a time in making incriminatory statements. The *nexus* officer may exploit the situation to the maximum level possible. There are any number of study reports and police commission's observations that police violence and use of third degree methods are in vogue during in-custody interrogation. In newspaper reportings one may take note of a series of instances in which the police are blamed for resorting to brutalities, beatings, hangings, whippings, etc, and to sustained and protected questioning incommunicado for extorting confessions from the suspects. Sometimes, even witnesses make such complaints and this malpractice is seen throughout the country.

Today, the people, press and courts insist for an in-custody interrogation which is psychologically rather than physically oriented. *Nexus* understanding with vested interests may make zealous police interrogators to have recourse to any fair or foul methods. Privacy matters a lot and as the police interrogation is not transparent, a nexus law enforcement officer is free to do many things in the privacy of a police station. It is not possible to know what is going on inside the police stations. The penal laws, procedure laws, evidence laws and police manuals speak against police torture and muscle display in in-custody interrogation. In a recent film it was shown that some police officers joining in hands with criminal politicians and underworld criminals used brutal methods on people who were brought to police custody in the pretext of enforcement of law and justice. Although the film makers may not be fully right in showing the police in bad shape as pictured in the film, but the reality cannot be dismissed in toto and there is some truth in everything that is shown in film or fiction. In the film, the police torture of the suspects lasted for 17 minutes and the impressions such films might cause in juvenile minds is a matter of concern for many. The impressions people make about *nexus* operations during crime investigation is also a matter of worry.

In *nexus* interrogation, creating a psychological atmosphere may not be considered by the police. The arrestee is questioned in isolation and the police interrogator, in that isolation and unfamiliar surroundings to the suspects, assumes an air of confidence in the suspect's guilt. The police interrogator is interested only to get a confession from the suspect. He may not be interested at all to know the truth of the case! The interrogator does not ask whether the suspect committed the offence but questions the reason why the suspect committed the offence. Of course, the interrogator may apparently show patience and perseverance if he has moral values which quite often he may not.

During interrogation it has been observed that the interrogator gives too much weight to his own personality and a near total neglect of the personality of the suspect. The suspect is just a suspect and nothing more. The interrogator may make some emotional appeals in the beginning and if they do not work well, he may rely on an oppressive atmosphere of dogged persistence. He tries to dominate over the suspect. He interrogates him steadily and without relent. He overwhelms the suspect with inexorable will to obtain a confession. He interrogates the suspects for several hours–and sometimes not offering him food, water or rest. Sometimes, the interrogated may charge the interrogator of duress. He makes all attempts to induce the suspect to talk–to make a confession.

Confession by Trickery

The method, *Unfriendly-Friendly* tactics offered good results in police interrogation, especially with first offenders. American police officers called it "Mutt and Jeff" act. This may be wrong as it may simply be used as technique to obtain a confession out of trickery. It was not a psychological method, rather a crude method which only nexus interrogators may resort to. What is the meaning of getting a confession by trickery? Nexus interrogators, sometimes, keep the suspect in a line-up. A witness or complainant (who is tutored earlier in some cases) comes and confidently points out the suspect exactly as the guilty. Then the actual interrogation starts and the suspect undergoes the ordeal. The nexus interrogator is a dangerous man who has no respect for human dignity. He may make use of a technique called the "reverse line-up" in which the suspect is asked to be in a line-up. Several fictitious witnesses or victims who associated with him with different offences may be brought. They will identify the suspect as the real culprit. The suspect as a rule, becomes desperate in such situations and makes a confession of the guilt as he is afraid of the evil consequences if he does not make a confession.

All these techniques are said to be psychological methods and they are complex in nature. The police interrogator creates a situation and the suspect is expected to confirm to the preconceived story which the interrogator seeks to have him to agree. *Nexus* interrogators want it and they employ relentless questioning for the purpose. In certain films such wrong methods have been shown in such a way that the methods are rated to be highly psychological. Trickery is not psychological interrogation. Deceptive stratagems are not psychological tactics. Giving false promises, false legal advice, and using coercion, third degree methods, etc, are considered on a par with the use of trickery during interrogation. If making of false promises is an undesirable act during interrogation, then employment of trickery too is undesirable in every sense. All these are calculated to keep the suspect off-balance and in every sense creates insecurity in the suspect about himself and his isolated surrounding further aggravate his submission. This is nothing but persuading or cajoling the suspect out of exercising his legal rights. A *nexus* interrogator may resort to such methods and when he does so, he is exacting a heavy toll on individual liberty. He trades on human weakness.

A *nexus* interrogator creates an interrogation environment for subjugating the suspect to his will. It carries its own badge of intimidation. This is a dishonour shown to human dignity. Incommunicado interrogation is disfavoured by the Supreme Court of India and in *D.K. Basu Vs. State of West Bengal,* the Apex Court has held the view that a lawyer must be present during the interrogation—though not throughout the process of interrogation. The incommunicado interrogation is against the cherished principles of Indian democracy. No individual must be forced to incriminate himself and every facility must be provided to have adequate protective devices for a suspect during interrogation and such protective devices are essential to dispel the compulsion inherent in custodial surroundings. Every confession must be the product of the suspect's free choice. In *nexus* crimes, vested interests play an important role and in such types of crimes, it may be noted that the suspects are coerced, pressured or tortured to make confessions. The *nexus* interrogator does not have any respect for human rights and dignity. Citizens have dignity and integrity and necessarily the suspects too have them. A police interrogator must prove a crime by his independent labours and not at all by applying cruel, compelling, pressure tactics and trickery. Therefore, an individual taken from his familiar surroundings into police custody and surrounded by policemen with their peculiar looks and language, covered by a police sub-culture of behaviour and antagonistic forces and then subjecting him to techniques of persuasion, coercion and compelling is not by any means a psychological interrogation. It is nothing but obtaining a confession under compulsion to speak. This is particularly so when there is no one to guard against intimidation and trickery.

Undercover Investigation

Police may have to conduct undercover investigations like electronic surveillance in some situations and certainly, the vested interests may exploit this too. People perceive deception inherent in such undercover investigations as they say that such investigations infringe upon the citizen's right to secrecy. No doubt, undercover investigations are of inherently covert nature and they involve 'low visibility' to the public.

As a result of establishing unholy *nexus* with vested interests, some police functionaries involve themselves in undercover investigations. It goes without saying that undercover investigations infringe upon a subject's interest in his privacy. By this, the vested interests bring the law enforcement agency into public disrepute. It has been noted that undercover investigations stimulate criminal acts. This has been seen in cases of entrapment where the law enforcement officers instigate criminal acts by people in order to lure them to the commission of crimes and thereafter to punish them. Some overzealous law enforcement officers commit certain acts and put the blame on others. In one such instance, a police officer places some drugs in the scooter of a person and later caught him as a carrier of drugs. Unscrupulous policemen/officers may do many such things to prove that they are very smart so that they can establish a good relationship with the nexus partners.

Studies show that the *nexus* may start from simple and small things. Syndicate criminals and bootleggers establish unholy *nexus* with many law enforcement officers by doing small favours and they do it with a hook. In some instances, they play diabolical games too. In one instance a senior police officer who occupied a senior position in the Excise Department was invited to spend a holiday at a tourist resort. He was a corrupt man and had some sexual weaknesses. The Abkari contractors made arrangements to see that he was humoured by call girls and they saw to it that photographs of the events in the privacy of the hotel were taken in a clandestine manner. Afterwards, the Abkari contractors used to threaten him by showing his naked photographs with the call girls in different postures and the nexus thus established paved the way for them to obtain immunity from law enforcement and free access to the officer. The Abkari contractors saw to it that he was compensated with sufficient amount of money - pay off–every month for his wholehearted support for continuing their illegal activities, illicit manufacturing and bootlegging.

Reference

Don C. Gibbons, 1968. *Society, Crime and Criminal Careers: An Introduction to Criminology,* New Jersey: Prentice-Hall.

4

POLICE : ORGANIZED, WHITE COLLAR, ENFORCEMENT AND NEXUS CRIMES

In the report of Vohra Commission, one takes note of the unholy relationship among the politicians, bureaucrats and businessmen. The President of India, as stated earlier, in his telecast to the nation on the eve of the Independence day (2000), exhorted the nation to be conscious of and cautious of nexus crimes. In the meantime, a number of reports appeared in the media about the nexus operations. People are now aware of the simple nexuses to complex nexuses in Indian society. Nevertheless, no serious attempts have been made to give a proper definition of nexus crimes. This necessitates proper description of nexus crimes. Many things are treated as mere instruments of gain, profit, advantage and status by unscrupulous people who do not consider their acts and nexus operations as illegal acts. They poison human society and they do greater harm to people and society. It is most unfortunate that the nexus crimes, far from decreasing, are expanding. With the new prospects opened up by urbanization, industrialization, privatization, liberalization, etc., there arise new forms of nexus operations. The nexus criminals justify their unholy relationship and claim immunity from punishment. For example, a highly placed bureaucrat once mentioned that big business firms offer huge amount by way of commission when they enter into a business deal. What is wrong in accepting the commission amount when they offer it with pleasure? When the bureaucrat was asked as to: "What is the meaning of pocketing the commission by the bureaucrats and politicians?" He waivered his answer and justified the act by his argument that the politicians want money to promote their political interests. Who would finance them if the bureaucrats did not offer their wholehearted support to the politicians? Yes, the bureaucrat too gets a share of the cake or is placed in an advantageous position when he supports the politicians in their nefarious activities. It is a nexus for mutual benefits. Choices which the people unanimously consider criminal and rejected by the moral sense values of the common man are becoming administratively, politically and bureaucratically acceptable for the pro-nexus people. Through establishing a nexus they get involved in a trade to make profits and have people by their calling who are responsible to administer justice willing to carry out nexus operations for their benefits and self-interests. In this way, the very purpose and nature of bureaucracy, political service, administration are distorted and contradicted and the dignity of those who commit nexus crimes is degraded. In such a political, business and bureaucratic situation, values get lost and are left open to false and deceptive solutions opposed to the good of the larger sections of the people and the nation as a whole.

Nexus Crimes Described

It is indeed a very difficult task to define or describe various types of nexus crimes which are seen amidst us and around us in society. There are numerous types of nexus crimes seen in all sections of administration. We concern ourselves in this study only with the nexus crimes seen in Indian police.

Simple and Triangular Nexus

In the Oyster Bay definition of organized crime mentioned earlier, we may find the expressions 'self-perpetuating' criminal conspiracy. 'Self perpetuating' means that the organization or syndicate continues to function if at all any of its leaders dies. This characteristic of organized crimes is applicable to nexus criminality which becomes a part of the crime syndicates. For example, in gambling or in bootlegging syndicates, we may observe that the self perpetuating criminal conspiracy continues even when a particular bureaucrat (law enforcement officer) changes, is transferred or dies. This characteristic may not be found in simple nexuses. For example, a revenue officer once sent a middle-man *(dalal)* to negotiate with a person who wanted to get a decision from the revenue officer. The middle-man conveyed that the revenue officer was constructing a house and he was badly in need of money. He communicated the purpose of his visit and said that the revenue officer would make a decision in favour of him if he offered Rs. 20,000. The person who needed the revenue settlement urgently thus agreed and the nexus began. The nexus concluded when the decision was made in his favour. There was a conspiracy in that case, but certainly it was not a perpetuating one. Such types of simple nexuses which consist only of one transaction may be called a triangular nexus , i.e., the nexus is among the babu, dalal and the victim. In simple or one time nexus transactions, it is not necessary that there must be a *dalal* (go-between) in every case. Some *babus* enter into direct negotiations to come to a nexus understanding and in such cases, the nexus is direct or face to face. Hence such nexuses are called direct nexuses or face to face nexuses. If the 'services' of a clearing agent are not available, sometimes, the customs officers negotiate matters directly. In nexuses formed as a part of organized crimes, several people are involved and some *babus* may not have any direct nexuses with the top level of crime syndicates.

Organized syndicate is said to be a malignant parasite which fattens on human weakness. In nexus crimes too, one may see this characteristic. The one time nexus or in simple nexus, the *babu* fattens on human weakness. He knows that he can cash the helplessness of his victim as he takes a decision for him. When nexus crimes take place as a part of organized crimes, then the *babu* fattens on the weakness of the syndicate criminals. He knows well that he can exercise his power and authority in favour or against the syndicate at his discretion. He does not exercise his power and authority as his inaction and support ensure many advantages for him. In turn, the organized criminals make exorbitant profits by such a nexus.

The nexus bureaucrats and their nexus friends may resort to fair or foul means; or legal and illegal means to accomplish the terms and conditions of the nexus to satisfy their self interests. The nexus survives on fear and corruption. For, the *Babu* and beneficiary at the end want to keep the clandestine nature of the nexus. For this, they want to keep the press and politicians in good humour. Resultingly corruption becomes an essential ingredient in nexus criminality. Without political support, it is difficult to occupy a particular post in a democracy. Hence the *Babus* and their beneficiaries together please the politicians and thus the nexus becomes a nexus of bureaucrats-politician and businessmen.

Maintenance of Secrecy in Deal

In simple nexuses, politicians may not be there. However, they need middle-men to transact smoothly in the business of nexus. Familiarity breeds contempt is a well known saying and is well followed by the bureaucrats who want to keep a safe distance from the businessmen in the nexus. The unholy relationship between the bureaucrats and the criminal businessmen must be a well guarded secret and its visibility must be minimum. If not kept in strict confidence the people come to know about it and the unholy nexus may become very conspicuous. In order to maintain the secrecy of the nexus transactions, the bureaucrats want middle-men *(dalals)* who play an important role in the nexus crimes. As the nexus among the partners is strong formed by influential people (politicians and bureaucrats), the nexus criminals get a high degree of immunity from law. If the immunity from law is not very strong, even then the partners have scope for a high degree of the probability of immunity from law.

Organized Crime Vs Nexus Crime

According to the Oyster Bay definition, organized crime is a totalitarian organization; a way of life that imposes rigid discipline on underlings who do the dirty work while the top men of the organization are insulated from the criminal act and the consequent danger of prosecution. As compared to this, Nexus crime is not a totalitarian organization. There exists a sort of partnership-sharing of the profit or accepting kickbacks or pay off in the deal. The bureaucrats get their share from the nexus operator (businessman). Once caught, all of the partners in the nexus become the co-accused in the nexus transactions and the bureaucrats face a vigilance probe and subsequent prosecution. This risk element is there only if the bureaucrats are caught. A particular nexus works till such time the nexus bureaucrats and the politicians can exercise their power and authority. The nexus operator (businessman) needs the support of *dadas* (*goondas,* gang men) for the smooth running of his trade. The bureaucrats may or may not have any relations with such gangmen.

White Collar Crimes

In this context the functions of white collar criminals in organized criminality will give clarity to nexus crimes. Edwin H. Sutherland offered several accounts of what he meant by "White collar crimes". Once he said: "White collar crime may be defined approximately as a crime committed by a person of respectability and high status in the course of his occupation". At another time, he specified that "The white collar criminal is defined as a person with high socio-economic status who violates the laws designed to regulate his occupational activities".

The Respectability Factor

The ingredients of these definitions are not fully found suitable to describe nexus crimes. For, the partners in the nexus family are not respectable people. How can we give respectability to syndicate criminals (who conduct gambling dens, houses of prostitution or bootlegging) who poison the society? How can we give respectability to politicians who patronize crimes in society? Let the politician be the minister of the State, but he is a nexus criminal and not by any means a respectable person. How can we give respectability to bureaucrats who become partners in the commission of nexus crimes? They may be officers from various positions ranging from the chief secretary of the State or the village officer or a sub-inspector. They may be surely occupying posts which carry respectability, but they are not respectable people. High posts are occupied by unscrupulous bureaucrats who are corrupt to the core and do anything to serve their self interests. They do not have any respect for human values. They may be rich as they make money through their nexus transactions.

In the Course of their Occupation Factor

Prof. Sutherland's definition is applicable to the extent that the nexus partners commit the crime in the course of their occupation. What does it mean? It means that the nexus operator (businessman) has a legal enterprise and he commits nexus crimes during the course of his business transactions. A person who runs a liquor shop may commit bootlegging after establishing a nexus with other members in the nexus family. A bureaucrat has power and authority. He commits crime by abusing his power or misusing his authority. He makes a profit out of his nexus transactions. The politicians too do it in the course of their career as politicians, whether they are taluka level politicians or State level politicians or ministers of the State. The middle man too does the job in the course of his job as a nexus broker. He may be a commission agent. The gang men or *goondas* are criminals of the underworld and they make a living by their criminal activities. All of them have no respect for laws designed to regulate their occupational activities and the *goondas (dadas)* are criminals themselves. Why say that the *dadas* are criminals? All in the nexus are criminals and that is the reason why they do not have respect for laws.

Description of Nexus Crimes

To these two definitions, add the ingredients of the definition given by Dr. Vadackumchery to enforcement crimes. The simple description for enforcement crimes, according to Dr. Vadackumchery, is law violations by enforcement personnel during the course of law enforcement. In the nexus family, a bureaucrat alone is the enforcement officer and as such he violates the law by abuse of his power and misuse of his authority. Thus a nexus crime can be well described as under:

A Nexus Crime is the product of a 'one time conspiracy or a self perpetuating conspiracy entered by bureaucrats with people who are the beneficiaries of bureaucratic decisions or exercise of their power and authority. By this, both the bureaucrats and their people at the other end of the nexus are benefitted'. In nexus crimes, the profit is exorbitant. Together they resort to fair and foul means; to legal and illegal strategies to fulfil the terms and conditions of the nexus for satisfying their self interests. Secrecy is maintained or an attempt is made to keep the clandestine nature of nexus transactions. For this the services of middle-men *(dalals)* are utilized, if found necessary. Owing to the nexus among the partners among whom the bureaucrats too are involved, there is immunity or high degree of immunity or probability of immunity from law. There exists a sort of partnership and here is the sharing of profits or acceptance of the pay-off or kickbacks. Once caught for nexus dealings, then all partners face criminal prosecution and the bureaucrats have to undergo a vigilance probe and subsequent ordeals.

A particular nexus works only when the nexus bureaucrats and the political power continue to exercise their power and authority. For the smooth functioning of the organized crime, the nexus operators need the services of *dadas* (gang men) and the bureaucrats may or may not have relations with such *dadas/ goondas*. The nexus bureaucrats are not respectable people, but they occupy positions having respectability. All are unscrupulous partners who have no respect for values. The partners to the nexus commit crimes in the course of their occupation. All in the nexus family are criminals and they do not have respect for laws. The bureaucrat alone in the family is an enforcement officer and he, as a member in the nexus family, abuses his power and misuses his authority for the benefit/advantage of all in the nexus family.

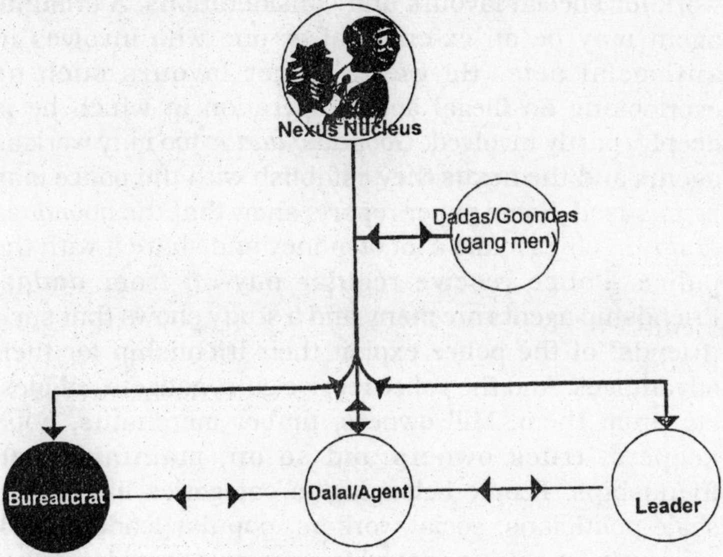

ORGANISATION OF A NEXUS FAMILY

Police and Nexus Crimes

So far, we have seen the nexus crimes outside the police department and the discussion that follows is about police and nexus crimes. In the previous chapter, police, enforcement crimes and nexus criminality have been discussed to some length. Here the nexuses which the police may establish are discussed first. They are—

1. *Police - Agent/ Source Nexus*

Police need collection of massive data for their work. For this they employ sources and agents. There are informants/agents cultivated by police. They are also called the confidential agents of police. Section 125, Indian Evidence Act-1872 gives some protection to police to keep the secrecy of the sources of information. Among the agents so cultivated by the police, there may be paid agents, criminal agents, agents whose intention is to establish friendship/link with the police or agents who work for special favours and considerations. A criminal agent may be an ex-criminal or one who involves in antisocial acts. He wants to get favours such as overlooking an illegal act or operation in which he is deeply/partly involved. *Goondas/ dadas* too may work as agents and the nexus they establish with the police may be misused. Some paper reports show that the *goondas/ dadas* in cities make a lot of money and share it with the police. Police receive regular pay-off from *dadas*. Friendship agents are many and a study shows that such "friends" of the police exploit their friendship for their advantages. And the police receive gifts/gadgets/edibles, etc. from them. Mill owners, timber merchants, hotel keepers, truck owners and so on, maintain such friendships. People belonging to categories like small-scale politicians, social workers, popular leaders work as agents for getting special favours and considerations. Some of them make money for the service they render and they get it from the party for whom they take small favours from police. They also collect money from them for handing it over to police or instruct them to humour the police. These agents are people who work for police as corruption and collection agents and the nexus ensures them some favours from the police as well. In a casual study, it has been observed that there exists the police-agent nexus at all levels.

2. *Police - Police Nexus*

A police officer once said: "I wanted to see that so and so was harassed. I had my batch mates working as sub-inspectors in the city. I told each one of them to see that my target's vehicle was caught and he was chargesheeted under some count or another. There came a situation that he could not take his car in the city".

This type of behaviour was a *nexus crime* otherwise called abuse of power/misuse or authority. Thus the police fraternity could be shown in that way too. Police fraternity *Nexus* is as dangerous as other nexuses and leads to miscarriage of justice and damage of police image.

A police officer/policeman instructs the people to humour other police officers/men to have a favourable attitude to them. The superior officers too may do the same thing. This sort of cooperation-nexus may be seen in many other areas too. For example, a subordinate officer may see that people give costly gadgets to his superior officers through his intervention. Some senior police officers ask their juniors to arrange vehicles for their personal use and the subordinates sometimes do so. The personal vehicles are repaired through subordinates and the superiors do not show their willingness to pay for the repairs. When superiors construct houses, they may manage to get building material through the subordinates at lower costs or without paying anything. The subordinates see to it that many things are provided to their superiors in lieu of remaining in their good books and having a favourable attitude towards them.

When purchases are made, those responsible for the purchase make profits out of such purchases. Purchase-bribery and kickbacks, purchase-adjusting, contract-adjustments, sweet heart contracts entered by those who purchase things, etc., are examples in point. In order to do so, police fraternity and sharing of profits become necessary. It has been taken note of that some police officers see to it that secret service fund is embezzled. False travel or *per-diem* claims are made out of fraternity. When senior officers go on tour, the juniors see that their boarding and lodging are arranged in star hotels on the basis of some nexus understanding with the hotel owners. The intradepartmental nexus is a menace if it exists.

3. *Police - Politician Nexus*

Politicians play an important role in democracy and they together with the police can manage and manipulate matters to their mutual advantage. Allegations are heard that politicians interfere even in recruitment. In States where the recruitment is done by the department, allegations are often raised against police-politician nexus. Politicians are extensively misused for getting priced postings and transfers. Though some police officers complain of political interference in police work, studies show that some other police officers seek for it and go after it. They take decisions after consultation. They think that they are safe with political support and patronage. Some police officers go to politicians just to impress others that they have good nexus. These 'fiat men' dance according to the tune of the politicians. Instances are reported that the police have taken false cases at the instigation of politicians and sometimes damaged the proper investigation of crimes owing to political interests. The police may, as the allegation goes, delay, deny or refuse their services on the basis of political interference/ interest in the matter.

4. *Police and Sister Departments Nexus*

Forests, Excise, Motor Vehicles, etc, are said to be the sister departments of police. Sales tax, Forest, Excise, Motor Vehicles and Police Department have to work in unison and cooperation in certain areas. Sometimes, allegations are heard that the nexus they form in check-posts makes corruption money splitting flourish in State boundaries, etc. Sometimes, the money is collected at one point and then is equally distributed. At other times, the corruption money is collected individually and then distributed among the members of the same department. Even superior levels too get a share. Some Abkari contractors say that the Excise personnel see to it that their brethren in police departments are humoured. Likewise, some forest contractors complain that the forest officers force them to split corruption-money with police officers. Whatever may be the truth behind the allegations, it may be noted that there exist such allegations of interdepartmental nexus.

5. *Police- Bureaucrats Nexus*

Bureaucrats have an affinity among themselves. But, some police officers complain that they are handicapped to enforce law because of the bureaucratic nexus. Any crime-doer has some connection or the other with bureaucrats who in turn have connections with some policemen/officers at some level. For example, a police officer working in the traffic unit in a south Indian State said: "Many of the autorikshaws in the city are owned by some bureaucrat or his/her relatives or friends. When the autorikshaw gets involved in traffic violations, invariably some policemen/officers come to the picture pleading for the autorikshaw. They pressure their subordinates to have a lenient approach in the matter which in other words tantamounts to ignoring the violations."

Equals establish nexus among the equals and precisely therefore, it is very difficult to overlook the bureaucrats-police *nexus* in law enforcement. If not abiding to orders there may be rupture of relations among the police functionaries. The higher ranks can always cause hardships by way of initiating departmental actions against the lower levels at a subsequent time if they choose to do so. The *nexus* among the higher levels may be able to direct the disciplinary inquiry in a particular direction. The officer under inquiry may be punished as a result. A *nexus* between a director general of police and a superintendent of police, once, resulted in the suspension of a helpless subordinate. They together caused harassment and hardship for him which resulted in filing a writ petition before the High Court. The ill effect of the nexus thus cost the suspended as good as Rs. 10,000 and that was the real motive of the nexus operation.

6. *Police-Witness-Lawyer Nexus*

Touts of police or tutored witnesses of police–both have some *nexus* with policemen/officers. In some cases, the touts get money and favours from the accused in crimes and share them with the police. The cases in such situations may end in acquittals and the police lose nothing by that - rather have a gain. The police are sometimes blamed for their secret arrangements with lawyers. In motor vehicle accident cases, the police may direct the victims to get in touch with some nexus lawyers and the police and the lawyer split the fees. A head constable was once found carrying the *Vakalathnamas* of some lawyers to get them signed by the clients to the lawyers. For each case, the policeman gets a share. Some lawyers go to police stations to get the arrestees released on bail. Invariably, they see to it that the police functionaries are humoured. There exists some *nexus-understanding* between the lawyer and the police so much so that all cases sponsored by him are duly attended to and the arrestees are released. They also make arrangements with people who come to police stations for bailing the arrestees out.

Witnesses are very important in criminal cases and the touts can play diabolical role if they are properly tutored. Anyone in the world can be convicted of a crime based entirely on the evidence of an eye witness. The defence lawyers know it well. Hence, they make attempts to win over the witnesses. Sometimes, the witnesses may be reluctant to become hostile to prosecution as they are afraid of the police. In such cases, the defence lawyers themselves get the cooperation of police officers/men to see that the witnesses are won over. For offering this service, the police resort to several strategies and pocket a good amount of corruption-money through the intervention of defence lawyers.

7. *Police - Prosecutor - Defence Nexus*

The police can also have *nexus* relations with defence counsels and prosecutors. This can be done even at the time of granting bail by the court. The *nexus* policeman tells the suspect to humour the prosecutors so that they do not object to the granting of bail. In a recent case, a group of men (bail syndicate, if it can be called in that way) was detected to have been involved in a bail racket sponsored by lawyers. In this racket they used to come to court for getting bail granted to anyone who paid them a fixed amount which would be divided among the police, prosecutor, defence and the members of the racket. A suspect in a bailable offence can get bail, but a situation is created in the mind of the suspect that he will not get bail if the prosecutor objects to it. At that particular moment and mental state, the suspects normally surrender to any suggestions made by the police. The *invisible prosecutor* is kept away during the deal. No doubt, the system of bail is intended to enable the suspect to stay out of jail until a trial finds him guilty. He needs it for preparing his defence. It also serves to prevent the infliction of punishment prior to conviction. But, all these arguments have no weight or relevance to the *nexus team*. During the trial too, the prosecutor can play games 'this way and that way', but he needs a nexus with the police officers who investigate the case.

8. *Police and the Press Nexus*

The press makes trial of a case prior to actual trial by a court of law. It gives news mixed with views and creates confusion among the public. Investigative journalism is one method adopted by widely circulated national dailies and yellow journalism is another method followed by small-scale papers whose sole intention is to make a profit out of police stories. The policemen come to know of many things and they transfer the information to the yellow press. They yellow press gets in touch with people affected by such news and negotiates with them. The profit in the deal is shared. Some unscrupulous policemen leak out very important cluses in sensational crimes to the press and make an income from such acts. They may as well make use of the press for a media wash.

Some local level journalists just like local level politicians keep liaison with the police and some of them work as agents/sources. The *nexus* with such journalists is a powerful source to twist the investigation to wrong directions. They also work as middlemen between the police and their vested interests. They make money and share with police officers/men having lust for making money through wrongful means. Some yellow journalists sometimes bring out special editions on police officers. They give the photographs of police officers and a brief/detailed biodata of them. They project them as efficient and effective police officers and thus they begin a *nexus* for future transactions. A few copies of the paper are printed and circulated. The contact thus established becomes a source of exploitation. The yellow journalists make propaganda of their contacts with policemen/officers and attract people to them. They involve themselves in corruption-money fixing and corruption-money splitting.

9. *Police-Politician-Bureaucrat Nexus*

The police-politician-bureaucrats nexus is seen in all democratic countries and recently a new phenomenon has developed in India and it is called 'politicization of police and politicization of bureaucracy'.

Some critics think that the police in India has emerged as an organised group to support politicians and the bureaucracy has emerged as a power to execute the politicians' whims and wishes. This means that the police are unwilling or are simply refusing to accept being controlled by policies of the society in which they work.

After the institution of police associations at various levels, one may see more and more politicians coming to police with many promises. The history of police in India shows that they conduct raids and strikes with political patronage. When the policemen go to the streets with lathies and rifles and tear-gas shells for strikes, their actions leave the protest citizens marchers exposed to injuries, stampedes and deaths due to police action. In such cases, the police may be responding to their private codes. *Quis Custodiet Opsos Custodes?* (Who guards the guardians?)–this comes from Latin and it means that there is no one to guard the guardians. If the guardians of law, law and order, law enforcement enter into nexus with politicians and other bureaucrats and then violate the law - or- commit nexus criminality, then there will be no one to control them. What will be the net outcome?

Nexus criminality comes into being when it ensures some privileges or advantages for the partners of the nexus family. The policeman, being or becoming a member in the nexus family when he administers or dispenses justice to people, commits himself to miscarriage of justice or injustice proper. At the end police abuses defeat the very purpose of maintaining the police at a heavy cost. Unholy police-politician-bureaucrat nexus injures people and destroys people's respect for the legal processes.

10. *Police - Politician - Businessman Nexus*

Politics has *strange bedfellows* as they associate themselves with people of all kinds in order to get advantages for themselves. They associate themselves with businessmen and encourage them to do illegal business for which they ensure that they get adequate support from police functionaries.

Bootlegging

A case in a south Indian State where prohibition was enforced is a good example of the nexus operation. Some politicians advocated strict and stringent action against illicit manufacture and sale of alcohol at the same time, extending their wholehearted support to bootleggers who could profit from illegal sales while legal sales were barred. They managed to get police support and the *nexus* worked very well as the business ensured regular income for the businessmen, police and politicians. The top level administrators of law-enforcement bureaucracy, politicians at the higher level and businessmen join together so that they have muscle power, authority and affluence to do many illegal activities. The businessmen corrupt the police and politicians and are offered payoffs regularly. This corruption in every sense amounts to official licencing of the illegal business. The nexus thus formed is an avenue to live a luxurious life through law breaking and the nexus crime is pursued as a career.

Loan Shaking

There are several ways to cheat the government. The politician-police-businessman nexus can do them successfully. Businessmen do their business, policemen keep their eyes shut and politicians (government) permit them to do so. Loansharking is nothing but lending money at higher interest rates than what the law permits. Some loan sharks get hold of the services of policemen to realize the loaned amount and these businessmen with their political leaders misuse/abuse the police powers for their business advantages. A share goes to the policeman/officer who is a member in the nexus.

The allegation is that the nexus works well at higher levels and top levels in bulk purchases. The commission which the businessmen offer is shared between the politicians and higher ups. They do it after making necessary manipulations in papers. These activities do not greatly disturb most of the public even though the total money value may exceed that of street robberies.

11. *Police - Syndicate Nexus*

No Mafia, syndicate or any combination can survive without police help. And no police will help a Mafia without a *nexus* and no *nexus* will work without mutual benefits. For crime is profession and business for them. It is an illegal commerce and the police, after a *nexus*, may ensure protection to these most successful entrepreneurs in illicit trade. These criminal sellers have a large clientele. Researches on the syndicate operations show that they get popular support. They make money and the money they make tempts the police and politicians to enter into a sort of *nexus* with them. The common allegation is that the politicians and law enforcement agencies patronize the syndicates.

The syndicate criminals and their partners in politics, police and other law enforcement wings enjoy a sort of status–a sort of status which Mafioso, a Sicilian man of honour who exemplified Mafia values enjoyed. Studies show that the police/law enforcement officers are partly or fully dependent on the syndicate criminals for their luxury and lifestyle. Bootlegging, prostitution, gambling, racketeering, loan sharking, etc., are just a few syndicates with which the law enforcement officers establish nexus. To ensure security and enrich their activities, the underworld leaders, sometimes, resort to threats or violence against uncooperative government functionaries including the police. The nexus is based on maintenance of secrecy, providing security, ensuring legal immunity, offering mutual aid and kinship loyalties, etc. All these take place as a result of a conspiracy by extremely evil minded persons in society and law enforcement/politics.

Is Nexus Crime a Crime?

In nexus dealings, there is a kind of contract. The objective of the contract is to defeat the purpose of justice administration. Suppose, the contract is to allow a syndicate to function without police interference for a consideration that the policeman/officer gets by way of a pay-off. The purpose of the organized crime is to commit offences to make exorbitant profits from them with the help of bureaucratic patronage and support from the law enforcement agencies. As such, the law enforcement officers are the partners in the nexus family. They become members of the criminal conspiracy which reads in the Indian Penal Code-1860 as:

"When two or more persons agree to do, or cause to be done–

(1) an illegal act, or

(2) an act which is not illegal by illegal means.

Such an agreement is designated as criminal conspiracy:

Provided that no agreement except an agreement to commit an offence shall amount to a criminal conspiracy unless some act besides the agreement is done by one or more parties to such agreement in pursuance thereof.

Exception : It is immaterial whether the illegal act is the ultimate object of such agreement, or is merely incidental to that object". (Section 120 A, IPC)

Punishment under Sec 120-B of IPC

Section 120-B of the Indian Penal Code prescribes the punishment for criminal conspiracy as under:

(1) "Whoever is a party to a criminal conspiracy to commit an offence punishable with death, imprisonment for life or rigorous imprisonment for a term of two years or upwards, shall, where no express provision is made in this Code for the punishment of such a conspiracy, be punished in the same manner as if he had abetted such offence.

(2) Whoever is a party to a criminal conspiracy, other than a criminal conspiracy to commit an offence punishable as aforesaid shall be punished with imprisonment of either description for a term not exceeding six months or with fine or with both."

The above laws were enacted at a time when no one knew anything about nexus crimes. The laws could be applicable to traditional crimes and not for crimes which are committed by syndicates and the members of the nexus family. The law enforcement officers who are partners in the nexus are not people who are ignorant of the existing laws. All of them know that they are involved in activities which they themselves recognize as illegal or probably illegal. They are certain that gambling, bootlegging, prostitution, drug trafficking, loan sharking, fencing, etc, are serious violations of law and yet they do them, support them and make exorbitant profits. The law enforcement officer, under the colour of his uniform, permits them for a payoff. In spite of the nexus operations, some people become indifferent to them. Nexus crimes are seen in all parts of the country and their practitioners are people of all ages, income and backgrounds. The causes for the nexus crimes are legion and the cures are speculative and controversial. Nexus Crimes raise a myriad of issues of utmost complexity and that is what the criminologists feel about them.

Causes of Lack of Effective Measures Against Nexus Crimes

In spite of the existence and ramification of nexus crimes, as the President of India says, the justice system is not doing much to control or prevent them, Why? There is no law to deal effectively with nexus crimes. No one makes any serious attempts to study nexus crimes. For, the nexus criminals are VIPs and highly influential people. A law enforcement officer registering false cases against people for pleasing his political bosses is and must be a criminal, so is the concoction of evidence in a criminal case to please the victims after accepting a bribe from them. A police conspiracy for corruption–money splitting is a nexus crime–so is the job of a middleman who humours the law enforcement officer. The embezzlement of department's travel fund, secret service fund, *per-diem* fund by people who manage them is a crime–so is the nexus formed by businessmen and police officials. These crimes can no longer be dumped together with traditional crimes for the purpose of analysis. If that is done, then it becomes like, dumping together lung cancer with common cold or brain tumour with ordinary fever.

Abetment to Crime

If nexus crimes are not crimes, then what are they? In order to call an act to be a crime, it must be legally forbidden by law. All the nexus crimes are legally prohibited. There must be the intention to commit the act. In certain types of nexus crimes, there will be only abetment. An abetment is defined under Section 107, Indian Penal Code as:

"A person abets the doing of a thing, who:

(i) instigates any person to do that thing; or

(ii) engages with one or more other person or persons in any conspiracy for the doing of that thing, if an act or illegal omission takes place in pursuance of that conspiracy, and in order to the doing of that thing;

(iii) intentionally aids, by any act or illegal omission, the doing of that thing.

Explanation (i) A person who, by wilful representation or by wilful concealment of a material fact which he is bound to disclose, voluntarily causes or procures or attempts to cause or procure, a thing to be done, is said to instigate the doing of that thing.

Explanation (ii) Whoever, either prior to or at the time of the commission of an act, does anything in order to facilitate the commission of that act, and thereby facilitates the commission thereof, is said to aid the doing of that act.

Sometimes, abetment may be committed as a result of a nexus understanding. A police officer may abet a suspect to humour the prosecutor for not objecting the bail or after a nexus understanding may abet a person to consult a lawyer whom he suggests. Abetment is an offence in law, but the question is: "can nexus crimes be treated as abetments?"

The nexus criminals have the required *mens rea* for committing the act. Moreover, there exists a casual relationship between the misconduct and the legally prohibited harm. In other words, it is necessary to show that the harm caused by the nexus criminal is a direct consequence of the misconduct. Nexus crimes do carry legally prescribed punishments, but criminologists do not think that the punishment is sufficient or adequate in most of the nexus crimes. For, the justice system does not look at nexus criminals in the way it must. Nexus criminals are men of affluence, position, power, authority and influence. The approach is lenient and tolerant. Nexus criminals are not very much afraid of legal actions against them. Dealing with traditional offenders and nexus criminals alike by applying the same standards are found to be inappropriate. If the nexus is among top level politicians and bureaucrats, then the matter may be inquired into by commissions or joint parliamentary committees. Otherwise, they are dealt with by policemen/officers of the regular service.

Corruption is institutionalized and its magnitude can be well estimated by the fact that if all the corruption-money put together can pay-off the foreign debts of India and free India of its financial liability in one or two years. Ignore the corruption at the bottom level. Take the corruption in nexus crimes alone and calculate it. How many robberies, burglaries, thefts take place in India? The exact figure may not be available. How many are reported to police? National Crime Records Bureau provides the statistical data. How many nexus crimes take place in India? No one has any idea, for, they are committed by people who are to execute the law along with people who are otherwise powerful and influential.

The risk of being attacked by a stranger on a road is far less than the chances of being subjected to/being made a victim of nexus crimes. Nexus crimes may be seen in the adulterated rice/wheat flour we purchase everyday, the patrol/diesel we use everyday and controlling nexus crimes presents a number of problems. While talking about white collar crimes, Sutherland said that the manufacturers of practically every class of articles used by human beings have been involved in legal difficulties with these commissions (he was talking about Federal Trade Commission and other Commissions which have the responsibility of regulating business) with more or less frequency during the last thirty years, including the manufacturers of the surgical instruments with which an infant may be assisted into the world, the bottle and the nipple from which he may secure his food, the milk in his bottle, the blanket in which he is wrapped, the flag which the father displays in celebration of the event and so on throughout life until he is finally laid away in a casket which was manufactured and sold under conditions which violated the law". All the nexus crimes happen under conditions which accept and promote nexus criminality. At every stage of manufacturing, transporting, storing, selling, purchasing, one may see nexuses in some form or another. A point to note is that in spite of the enormous scale in which they are being carried out, they are carried out under cover and very few are detected. Not even a small fraction of nexus crimes is detected - only a handful of nexus criminals may be arrested– and just a few may be convicted. Are the nexus criminals psychopaths? No studies have been conducted on this area. To study them need research patience and resourcefulness. Moreover it calls for courage and commitment. For, the life of the researcher becomes a question mark then so much so that many are not prepared to take up the risks. Certain films show enterprising researchers or a journalist doing the same and finally facing his/her premature death. Ironically enough, the film which depicts such researches on *nexus* crimes had been made under conditions which were pregnant with nexus understanding. There exists no clear information on the extent and scale of embezzlement, fraud and other forms of thievery from government funds which is committed by nexus criminals. We also seem to be in the dark as to how much price-rigging, tax evasion, bribery, graft and other forms of thievery is being carried out by nexus offenders. Proceedings may be conducted against constable who pilfers the fuel from the departmental vehicle, while a senior police officer who misuses his official car for his personal use with the understanding of many in the department may be just praised for his honesty and uprightness. A peon who received a bribery of Rs. 15 or

Rs. 50 may be chargesheeted in the vigilance court while a nexus managing director of a firm who amassed ill-gotten wealth by his nexus transactions might be blessed with awards by vested interests. The economic losses these nexus transactions cause during an year are far greater than those caused by the traditional criminals against property for several years. For example, a single nexus criminal caused a financial loss of nearly Rs. 950 crores to the public exchequer. In another deal on fertilizers, the estimated loss was over one hundred crores of rupees. Almost all nexus crimes get lost in the complications and convolutions of administration and business procedures. The Politician-Bureaucrat-Businessman nexus is indeed very powerful.

Nexus crimes are most damaging and threatening to people, for their corrosive effect and impact on the moral standards by which Indian administration, politics and business are conducted. Businessmen who defraud consumers promote cynicism towards social values and show a total disrespect to the law. The crime syndicates are widely involved in various types of criminal activities with the assistance and willing cooperation of bureaucrats, politicians and *goondas*. White collar crimes and nexus transactions are areas about which the society as a whole has little or no knowledge. Nexus criminals argue that the their nexus transactions do not affect the people directly or may even say that they do not have victims. Of course, their crimes provide people with goods and services which are in high demand. Gambling, bootlegging, narcotics, loan sharking, fencing–offences and their like make the bureaucrats especially those in the justice system, richer and richer. Such crimes and the nexus understanding are certainly are in bad taste. They promote out - and - out corruption in society. Nexus offenders are incurable law breakers and recidivists. The society is tolerant to nexus criminals.

The rebelliousness of people does not express itself in the form of warring violently on nexus family or any of its partners. A nexus criminal is often almost invisible and precisely therefore incapable of being controlled by many in society.

"If nexus crimes are not crimes then what are they?" Are the existing laws powerful enough to fight with nexus criminals? Now a days the criminal laws are becoming weaker and weaker. The programmes and activities of almost all bureaucrats with whom the citizens come in contact are predicted on the assumption that they get their rights established only through nexus dealings. The *dalals,* brokers, agents and go-betweens or whatever way they are named play an important role to settle the nexus dealings. The pickpockets, burglars and thieves are likely to be conspicuous under the surveillance by people and therefore are under their control to some extent. But a middleman- *the dalal-* is generally invisible and therefore not controlled. He has more opportunities for committing nexus crimes or participating in them. He lives his life with the support of bureaucrats and politicians and his hopes thus get fulfilled. It is a tragedy that the common man is left with little or no chance of escape from nexus criminals.

People affected by common cold are several millions in this country and those affected by blood cancer are a few lakhs. Likewise, people directly affected by nexus crime by way of corruption-money splitting or instigation to offer corruption-money are many millions whereas people directly affected by crime syndicates or sweet heart dealings or kickbacks may be few lakhs. Eventhough Prevention of Corruption Act is in force, how many cases are registered under the said Act in the whole country? They are handful and it means that the victims do not make complaints of their victimization. They are helpless. In corruption cases, there must be the demand

and acceptance whereas in *nexus* crimes, one does not find any demand from the erring bureaucrats. Everything is done by the *dalals*. Likewise, in corruption-money splitting, everything is done by the instigators and the bureaucrat who accepts the corruption-money is safe. What to do then?–How to go about then? It is with these nexus criminals who have been blessed by these social situations that the justice system and law must deal. The man on the street, the so called citizens of this great country are embittered by these painful social realities today. The justice system operates on the assumption that individuals are responsible for criminal acts. But, in nexus crimes, it is the criminal family which is responsible for the criminal acts. The justice system has not effectively designed anything to eliminate nexus criminality and the conditions inducing such criminality. Unless there is a widespread ethical motivation to establish an administration which deserves credence, respect, appreciation, upright conscience and loyalty, no bureaucracy—no political system-however well staffed and organized—can rid a society of nexus crimes.

With respect to the nexus crimes in police service, one may accept fairly the fact that many major crimes which are committed in society may be reported to the police. But, the nexus crimes that take place within and outside the police department are rarely reported. There exists a sort of consensus to tolerate nexus crimes and accommodate with them. Don't the police functionaries know the nexus dealings that take place right under their nose? They do, yet they tolerate or encourage them as the case may be. Thus, the number of nexus crimes annually taken up by the police may be very small–invisibly small.

No doubt, the policeman sees first the crimes that take place in his department. He sees the violence, torture, concoction and what not that take place in police stations. Sometimes, they may be the result of some nexus understanding. The major task of a police officer is to track down and arrest persons who commit crimes and if so, he is bound to initiate action against his own people if they violate the laws. It is discouraging indeed for a conscientious police officer to tolerate or encourage nexus crimes or any other criminality among his own men working under the same roof. Precisely therefore, the policemen/officers are attacked by the press and the people as being insensitive to the crimes that take place amidst them.

Certainly, the aim of the police department is to protect the society from crime and criminals and this aim extends to the protection of people from nexus crimes that take place within the four walls and outside the police offices. The eyes of many in society intrude into what is taking place inside the police department. For example, the gratuitous use of force by policemen after a nexus understanding with politicians/political parties on people who demonstrate their protests, entrapment of certain people, man-hunting, simulated encounter killings, etc, encourage the spread of public notion that some policemen/officers engage/encourage nexus crimes and operations. Though the National Police Commission: 1977-81 does not speak plainly about nexus crimes, it brings to light the nexus and dirty relations which some in police keep with unscrupulous politicians and underworld criminals. It shows that some threats to proper law enforcement come from the police department itself, but they are made worse by the culpable negligence, indifference, tolerance, support and encouragement of those who can remedy them. The scandalous nexus criminality within the police department spawns many crimes both inside and outside the department.

It is difficult to catalogue completely the vast array of crimes that may result from nexus criminality. Most frustratingly, some policemen/officers simply refuse to accept nexus criminality. Paradoxically, they consider it as their right to commit nexus crimes. It seems that there exists a profound crisis of culture for them to think so. They lack knowledge in ethics and law and they find it extremely difficult to grasp clearly the meaning of what a policeman is for the society, the meaning of his rights as a law enforcing policeman, his duties as a uniformed servant of the public, the negative implications of promoting and propagating nexus crimes within the department. Human conscience does not cease to function when one puts on a police uniform! Some conscientious policemen/officers tolerate nexus criminality under the pressure of real professional difficulties which nonetheless can never exonerate them from warring against such obnoxious practices.

References

1. Sutherland Edwin H. 1941 *'Crime and Business*, The Annals of the American Academy' of Political and Social Science, Vol. 217.
2. —, 1967 *Challenges of Crime* in a *Free Society*, U.S. Government Printing Office, Washington, 1967.
3. —, 1969, *Our Criminal Society*, Prentice - Hall, Englewood Cliffs: Presidents' Crime Commission.

5

POLICE : NEXUS CRIMES AND CAUSES

Origin of Nexus Crimes

Nexus crimes may be as old as humanity - Yes. "Then the serpant said to the woman. No! You will not die! God knows in fact that on the day you eat it your eyes will be opened and you will be like gods knowing good and evil. The woman saw that the tree was good to eat and pleasing to the eye, and that it was desirable for the knowledge that it could give. So she took some of its fruit and ate it. She gave some also to her husband who was with her and he ate it" (Old Testament). The devil and the woman had established a nexus to which Adam was brought in by Eve. There was temptation and instigation from the devil who appeared in the form of a serpent. The demenological theories advanced by the Biblical author to explain criminal behaviour can also be brought to explain the etiological factors of *nexus* crimes. As scientific criminology does not accept demenology as an explanation to crime and criminal behaviour, the Biblical approach is of no use except to show that criminal nexus to make advantages for people was in existence right from the beginning of humanity. In the history of man, one may see the *nexuses* which people had established to make advantages or to ruin people. Many a time, the nexuses were intended to commit crimes.

Formalized police agencies came into existence from the beginning of 1800's. The London Metropolitan police force was created in 1829 and the professional police force in the United States originated in 1844 in New York City. Indian Police Act came into force in 1861. According to the said Act, the police were Government servants. There is evidence to show that the police had the nexus with the white Government in London to retain the English rule in India and there is no evidence to say that nexus crimes were in existence during the colonial rule. Of course, corruption and corrupt practices were in vogue during the British raj. Again, there is no evidence to show that police corruption was due to any nexus between the police and others.

The Police Politician Nexus

After India became independent, the administration was passed on to the people and thereafter the politicians in large numbers started coming to the public scene. A humourist once said about the transfer of power from the British to Indians as "from the *vellakar* to *kollakar*" which meant that the transfer was from the whites *(vellakar)* to dacoits *(kollakar)*. Whatever that be, the politicians wanted police help to actualize many of their self and political interests. The police also wanted political support to actualize their self interests. Thus started a nexus which was called the Police-Politician Nexus or Politician - Police Nexus.

Politicians had the authority and power in a democracy and they wanted the muscle power and authority of police to employ them against many. The police had the muscle power and also the authority to exercise the muscle power. The politicians' power and the police muscles become more powerful if they have the money power. Businessmen and Mafias had it. Police is a statutorily constituted authority or force which the politicians and the businessmen can not utilize as and when they want. Hence, they developed *goondas*. In order to coordinate the various activities, they wanted brokers and thus emerged the *dalals*. Thus came into being the nexus consisting of *Neta-Babu-Dalal* and *Dada*.

Etiology of Nexus Crimes

How do the policemen/officers become a part of the criminal nexus? Certainly, it is not the demons who make a policeman/officer a part of the *nexus*. It may also not be right to think that the director general of police of a State has an inferiority complex or that the constable is a sadist or that the superintendent of police has an abnormal chromosomal pattern to become a *nexus* criminal. Most of the traditional theories dealing with criminal behaviour and explaining the etiology are found to be of no use to explain *nexus* crimes. When a poor man committed theft, it was said that poverty was the cause. When an affluent man committed theft, the same people did not say that it was due to the affluence or due to poverty he committed theft. Beccaria's hedonism and free will and Bentham's explanations of criminal behaviour are found to be of not much value in understanding nexus crimes. Bentham-Baccaria views which were seen in the classical school of criminology had their influence in Anglo-Saxon criminal laws and procedure. Indian Penal Code - 1860 did not contain nexus crimes and the Code which was drafted with information essentially consistent with the classical arguments could not speak anything about the etiology of nexus crimes. Bribery was seen during the British rule, but corruption-money splitting was not heard during 1860 when the Penal Code was enacted.

Motivating Factors of Nexus Crimes

Money making—exorbitant profit making—becoming rich overnight, etc, may be the motivating factors in nexus crimes, in organised crimes, in white collar crimes or in enforcement crimes. Quetlet in Belgium and Guerry in France who gave the cartographic explanations to crime during 1800-1850 never wanted to explain *nexus* crimes although one of their interests had centered about the relationship, if any, between economic conditions and fluctuations in crime and delinquency. They did not see bootlegging in such a large measure either in Belgium or in France. The business is carried on with the willing cooperation of the law enforcement machinery including the police. Organized police system, as said earlier, has come into being only after 1800. Thermal theories or crackpot approaches in criminology were formulated at a time when nexus crimes were not visibly conspicuous to the people.

According to William A. Bonger (1876-1940), a Dutch sociologist, the capitalistic economic system by its very nature encouraged egoism. According to him, an egoist had an unrestrained pursuit self interest. Similarly in nexus crimes, all the partners— the *neta, babu, dalal, dada* and the nexus operator— have self interests behind their actions. Economic influence on criminality has been widespread. None of the studies has been undertaken on *nexus* crimes in a democracy, nor are there any studies on police and nexus crimes so far. According to criminological studies lower economic class groups have much higher rates of crime than the upper class. Trends show that the crimes of the poor are highly visible as they effect the common man, therefore they are reported to the police— are investigated, etc. The crimes which the higher ups commit are settled and not reported to police as they ought to be. Crimes by the poor people are known and the same by the rich people are hidden. If crimes are committed by a nexus family, then they become quite invisible to the people. If statistics were available on nexus criminality and the varieties of enforcement criminality, then the socio-economic picture of crimes might well be quite different.

Can we think that people, especially the politicians, bureaucrats and businessmen commit crimes just for money and economic prosperity? Economic needs may be a factor or I may say that economic greed is a strong factor. The causative factors for nexus crimes are too many and too complex to be easily measured by economic needs and greeds. The nexus family is rich and the law enforcement officer who is a member/partner in the nexus is well employed. Yet, they commit crimes! Traditional explanation about the etiological factors of crime may not be of much value to understand the nexus crimes. It is not always found that all bureaucrats, policemen/officers are nexus criminals. Certainly, they are not born criminals. They also do not have any peculiar features like facial asymmetry, eye defects, ears or unusual size, excessively long arms and other physical peculiarities. They can be found out in many ways.

A visit to the Abkari contractors, forest contractors, mill owners, politicians, journalists, victims of crime, suspects, lawyers, and so on, will open up the paradigm of the nexus operators. They may be asked to speak openly about the nexus operations of the police functionaries in their locality. Other policemen/officers too may give out information and from what one gathers from all of them, he will be able to make a reliable and valid inference about the nexus relations.

Nexus Criminals and Body Types

Hooton said in 1939 that the primary cause of crime is biological inferiority. Certainly the policemen/officers identified as nexus criminals do not suffer from biological inferiority. On the other hand and contrary to Hooton's observation, they have been found to be very robust people having good physique. They get unaccounted money by way of their nexus transactions, so much so that they can spend any amount of money for their health care. The same physical shape is enjoyed by the *goondas*, leaders and *dalals*. In face, all in the nexus family are healthy people.

"Beware you Cassius for he hath a lean and hungry look, such men are dangerous, they think too much"- said Shakespeare long back. Kretschmer developed on it and studied to show that human behaviour and physical structure were related. While observing certain nexus criminals who had no difficulty in admitting that they were offenders, the Kretschmerian body type approaches did not yield any good result. So was the case with Sheldon's endomorphic, mesomorphic and ectomorphic classification and the viscerotonic, somotonic and cerebrotonic temperaments in understanding nexus criminality. The hypothetical temperament relationship to body structure had nothing much to do with nexus offenders who were identified. *Goondas*/Gang men could be very robust people, strongly built individuals. But, the *Dalals* were not. Bureaucrats who belonged to the nexus family had no specialities of a particular body type, and the leaders didn't have different body types and temperament. Hence the somatotype arguments were of no use in understanding nexus criminality.

Feeblemindedness Negated

It was Goddard who said that feeble mindedness was the cause of criminality. This view may not applicable to nexus criminality. Nexus criminality is an organized crime. It needs coordination and cooperation among the various partners. It needs execution neatly done. It is of a clandestine nature and done in the course of one's legitimate business/occupation. Thus Goddard's statement that "it was no longer be denied that the greatest single cause of delinquency and crime is low-grade mentality, much of it within the limits of feeblemindedness may be rejected. Nexus criminality consisted of the characteristics of various crimes. It included features of organized crimes, white collar criminality and also of enforcement crimes apart from other characteristics of the nexus. It is not possible to visualize the nexus if the partners are mentally retarded! At the top level, the nexus criminals are highly placed bureaucrats who have come to service after a competitive examination, are highly placed politicians who have proved their worth as leaders etc. How can they be feeble minded? Similarly a constable who belongs to the nexus family is not visualized as being cerebrotonic or vicerotonic in temperament. The temperaments of a director general of police who belongs to the nexus family likewise cannot be as sheldon said. Same nature holds good for the political leader– a minister of the State– who is a nexus offender. In the same way there is no hereditary inheritance of criminality among the businessmen who belong to the nexus family. The *Jukes'* and *Kallikaks'* family history studies and the presumption of a long family line of social misfits produced by their ancestors have nothing to do with the nexus businessmen. "Structure determines functions"–this may be a proposition of biological theories, but is not applicable to the criminals belonging to the nexus family. Thus the biogenic explanations have little or no relevance to nexus crimes. "What really causes nexus criminality?"

Neta, babu, dalal, dada and nexus Businessman-crimes are of recent origin in Indian democracy. Nevertheless, we cannot simply dismiss the truth that nexus crimes were not in existence earlier. They were in existence, but in different forms and magnitudes. Can the psychogenic approaches of criminologists give a good causal analysis of nexus criminality?

Causal Analysis : Psychogenic Approaches

Psychologists and psychiatrists long ago proposed that it was the critical causal factors or variables confined to personality problems to which the criminality was presumed to be a response or reaction. August Aichhorn, in his book *Wayward Youth* said: "There must be something in the child himself which the environment brings out in the form of delinquency". The criminals are thus 'sick' or 'maladjusted' people. According to him, the environment might act as a precipitating factor–and never as a predisposing or primary force in criminal behaviour". Later studies conducted in this direction too subscribed to the view that criminal personality developed owing to an interaction between the hereditory potentialities and environmental forces. How far is this approach valid in understanding nexus criminality?

All leaders do not become nexus criminals. Likewise, all bureaucrats, all businessmen and all police functionaries do not become partners/members in the nexus family. Environments do play an important role here. It cannot be said that all businessmen, bureaucrats, leaders have personality problems making them nexus criminals. At the same time, it may be agreed that those who suffer from personality pathologies may become nexus criminals provided they are put in facilitating environments which promote the development of nexus crimes or nexus personality structures. Personality problems are also not class-concentrated. The interaction of heredity and environment must be given due weightage in analysing nexus criminality. It could be seen that some bureaucrats/leaders simply refuse to participate in a nexus network.

Mental Disorders and Nexus Crimes

Do the nexus criminals suffer from any mental disorders? No one has made any indepth research on the issue, yet, at the same time, the researches which were conducted during the early part of the 20th century categorically stated that all sorts of criminals who suffered from psychiatric abnormality–were diagnosed as psychopathic. Such sweeping generalizations of overenthusiastic psychiatrists and other diagnosticians are of not much utility in understanding *nexus* criminals. Studies on nexus criminals give no evidence to show that all of them are psychotic or psychoneurotic. At the same, most of the nexus criminals do not feel guilt for what they do in the wrong way. They are found to be normal although many of them exhibit some kind of mild personality problems.

Psychoanalytic Explanations of Nexus Criminality

Observations have shown mild personality problems in many *nexus* criminals, therefore it is pertinent to study the problem from a psychoanalytical angle. The nexus criminals show a lack of ego formation and also display symptoms of possessing no conscience whatsoever. This is why they indulge in nefarious activities without pricking of their internal guilt and conscience. Though some psychoanalysts believe that law breaking is "unconsciously motivated" it need not be true. Generally, the nexus criminal's behaviour is not influenced much by the unconscious elements of personality or serious personality aberrations of any kind. The *nexus* criminals, are found to be normal and well organized in many areas. Nevertheless, they are characterized by egocentricity, socially deplorable behaviour and insensitivity to others, etc. They do not generally suffer from neurosis, psychosis or mental defectiveness and know the social and legal consequences of their nexus behaviour, if caught, but do not have any guilt feelings. They repeat their *nexus* crimes and do not conclude it after the completion of an assignment.

Nexus Criminality : A Group Behaviour

If a particular person is corrupt, no doubt it is known to others. This knowledge is necessary for getting more and more money to him. If a particular police officer has *nexus* dealings with politicians, underworld criminals or criminal businessman, then it becomes known to many others including his associates, superiors, subordinates and colleagues. The nexus group depends upon the type and nature of nexus crimes. Most of these groups are not large ones—consisting of five to ten persons, though they are often found to be part of larger groups in some cases. In bribery cases and corruption-money splitting, the nexus may be among a few people. But, in abkari *nexus,* these small groups may be a part of a larger group having the characteristics of organized crimes. Sometimes, unusual and sensational news about sex rackets comes in the press. In these there may be larger groups involved.

Media men sometimes raise questions like: "How many criminal gangs operate in the city?" There is no official data to answer their questions. At the same time, it is well-known that the number of criminal gangs is less than the number of *nexus groups* profitably working in the city. Leader-*babu-dalal-dada*-businessmen nexuses are far more than the gang criminality in any city in India. Nevertheless, these nexus criminals are not brought to book or to public views. They live as decent men. In general, the nexus criminals do not experience social emotions. When people in society look at *nexus* criminals, they see them as leaders, *babus*, businessmen, and so on not knowing their reality. They can not and do not look at them as nexus criminals. They look at the gangseters and *goondas* as gangseters and goondas. There are several factors which instigate nexus criminals to involve in nexus criminality. But, the people are not concerned with such insulating situations.

Nexus Crimes and Criminal Subculture

Any vigilance investigation in corruption cases may reveal many nexus operations from simple sweat-heart understandings to complex Mafia networks. Everything takes place in a criminal subculture. In the criminal subculture, the nexus criminals are found to be upwardly mobile, ambitious, oriented towards amassing wealth and fortunes. They accept their high class life and they want to maintain it. The nexus criminal chooses life with other nexus criminals rather than with law abiding people. Enforcement crimes thus become an inevitable outcome of the nexus relations. The nexus world is dominated largely by males and therefore the criminal subculture consists of male activities.

Characteristics of Criminal Subculture

The following special characteristics are found in the criminal subculture of nexus criminality. They are:

(1) Concern over the troubles exists among the nexus. The nexus criminals always expect troubles if and when they are detected. If they get into trouble, certainly they will have to face several problems to get out of the trouble. The *babus* may have to face suspensions sometimes and consequent disciplinary inquiries. If the *Babus* belong to the law enforcement services, then their trouble frequently involves fighting with their own associates/superiors/subordinates. In police, this is more. In a sensational case of bootlegging, police officials were detected among the nexus criminals. They were placed under suspension followed by departmental and criminal actions by police officials themselves. The *dalals,*

netas, dadas and the criminal businessmen have problems and troubles if and when they are caught. Yet, they are involved in committing the criminal acts, thus motivated by considerations and advantages which force them to take the troubles worth enjoying.

(2) Nexus criminals will usually be smart people. The nexus operators– i.e., the criminal businessman, the *neta* and the *dalal* want smart *babus* and they go after such *babus*. Those who demonstrate competence in promoting nexus criminality with smartness earn prestige and a smart *babu* is always sought after. Hence, the personality traits like smartness, readiness to associate with nexus criminality, susceptibility to corruption or corrupt practices, etc., are treated as good characteristics. Early home life, early childhood training, early personality development, etc., have some etiological connection with nexus criminality.

(3) For the nexus criminals, the rhythm of life fluctuates between periods of nexus activity and situations of great stimulation. They want excitement, thrill, luxury, pleasure, etc., for themselves and the nexus criminality is a means to this end. They may drink, gamble, play numbers, go for sexual recreation, etc., and thus they release their tension.

(4) All the partners including the *babus* have a feeling of belonging to the nexus family. Everybody is in good standing of the nexus family and that is of vital importance for its members for their existence, survival and flourishing. All of them are the birds of the same feathers and that is one of the reasons for their flocking together. The push factors which bring

them together may be the etiological components in nexus criminality. The in-group feeling (belonging) thus becomes essential. "So and so or such and such police officer hangs with us"–say some *Netas, Dalals, Dadas* and nexus businessmen. It means that such and such officer is a member in good standing in the nexus family and there is a consensus.

The law enforcement officer, by virtue of his authority, power and uniform, enjoys a special status in the *nexus* family. He is respected by *dalals* and *dadas*. The *nexus* businessman too shows some respect to him and so is the one who approaches him with corruption-money.

There exists *status ranking* in the nexus family. The *neta, babu* and the nexus businessmen are superior in status ranking to *dalals* and *dadas*. Depending upon the stature of the *neta* and *babu,* the nexus businessman places him in the ranking. If the Neta is a State level politician or the Babu is a State level administrator, then the businessman (again depending upon his stature in business) may be placed up, equal or down to the Neta or Babu or both.

The criminal subculture of the nexus family is thus a major causative factor for the development of nexus crimes.

Motivation of Nexus Criminals

Motivation is a major factor in criminal behaviour - say psychologists. The members of the *nexus* family and particularly the law enforcement functionaries know that they are violating the legal and moral codes by committing criminal activities by means of a consensus. The nexus family recruits - wishes to recruit— only 'able' law enforcement officers to the family. They are motivated primarily, it is seen, by monetary considerations. Achieving of financial stability and affluence through activities—fair or foul, legal or illegal— may be a quality valued in the cultural milieu of the enforcement department. For example, police officers who accept corruption-money or commit enforcement crimes by nexus understanding may not be looked down upon by the dominant culture of the department. As a result, the dominant component of the motivation of nexus criminals in police is the moving force so as to achieve financial stability or affluence within their cultural milieu. They are to enforce the law, but their enforcement will be money-oriented. Affluence is a means, they think, of acquiring respect, admiration and prestige for them within the department. They become *nexus* members for acquiring respect, admiration and prestige for them.

Branch Nexuses

A *nexus* family has, as pointed out earlier, the *neta, babu, dalal, dada* and the nexus businessman/ operator. Each category, i.e., the *neta, babu,* etc,— has its own nexus understanding. For example, a mini-nexus family is formed within the law enforcement institution to function as an active partner in a major nexus family. This nexus is created for involving in the commission of bootlegging or similar crime syndicates. In the mini-nexus thus formed, one may see the senior, junior, subordinate members working earnestly for the purpose of achieving their nexus ends and the objectives of the major nexus family of which the mini-nexus is a part. The interpersonnel understanding in the mini-nexus of the law enforcement department gives courage, enthusiasm, energy and confidence for the members to extend their full cooperation to the major nexus family and its various operations. The unity and cooperation among the senior, middle, junior and subordinate functionaries are found to be powerful causes of nexus criminology. If the mini-nexus within the law enforcement department lacks unity of purpose, then it would fail to generate confidence among all partners/members in the nexus family. No doubt, there is an element of risk; but one can not have the cake and eat it too.

Alder Jacob (real name concealed), a police officer told the following story:–

> "Shortly after I secured a job in police service, I got married. I was posted in the operational-functional jurisdiction of police. As such I had more than enough chances to come closer with people. Some racketeers approached me. They said that my superiors and subordinates did many things to make their business profitable to them and to law enforcement officers. I too was taken up by their proposals and offerings. They humoured me with a packet and then I learnt that all my superiors/subordinates were getting a monthly pay-off from the nexus businessmen. I became a member in the mini-racket/in the mega-racket because it seemed unlikely that I could see both ends met with the legitimate income I then received from the Government".

Why did young police functionaries become mini or mega nexus criminals? Officers like Alder Jacob would say that the necessities of life push some to become so. The legitimate income from the job would only give him his bare minimums and in case he spent more he would be deeply in debt. Thus he would never be able to meet his necessities in life. The nexus criminals' offer would ensure financial fortunes. Since his superiors and subordinates were members in the mini-nexus/mega-nexus, the chances of detecting his involvement would be very minimum. Moreover if he did not participate in the nexus activities, the chances of his continuing in police would not be bright.

Attitude and Awareness of Nexus Crime Among People

How many people know or can know the activities of the nexus criminals? The activities of the nexus criminals are outside the level of awareness of the larger society except in those instances in which the media makes the activities public. How many people in society know the nexus activities of police —particularly if they take place at the higher levels of police hierarchy? Some people may be worried of the corruption and corrupt practices at the station house level/functional level. For, they affect them directly. Otherwise the people take a tolerant attitude to nexus crimes and criminality. This attitude of the public is a cause for the perpetration of nexus criminality in India.

The nexus criminals protect the members of their nexus family. They do everything in a clandestine way so that the society may not know anything much about what is going on in the nexus family. The members in the society want police and law enforcement support and for that reason, they do not want to displease the law enforcement officers. This does not mean that all members in the society approve of the activities of all law enforcement officers in the nexus family. They disapprove of the nexus activities silently and consequently their behaviour results in failure of effective implementation of law which is a loss in itself and to the social fabric of the country. The law enforcement officers too know it and they know further that the nexus criminality is a group criminality. The detection of group criminality is indeed very difficult, if not impossible. Nexus criminality is committed by many members and this characteristic of it is the cornerstone of the criminality. In fact, this special characteristic of group criminality makes the members to commit the crime without any fear or with a near total feeling of immunity from law. Of 83 nexus crimes which have come to notice, the criminal nexus consisted of collaboration of more than two persons in majority of the cases.

Cohesiveness and Nexus Crimes

Cohesiveness is found to be a factor causing, nourishing and promoting nexus criminality. How cohesive the nexus family is seen in the *esprit de corps* or face to face relationship among the various members of the nexus family. In any case, the cohesiveness is strongly seen among the *netas, babus* and nexus businessman. Low cohesiveness may be seen between the *babus* and *dadas*. The *babus* may know the *dadas* whom are maintained by the nexus businessmen or the nexus nuclei—but not necessarily always.

Studies on nexus criminals have found that increased cohesiveness among the members of the nexus family did lead to increased criminality. Bureaucratic support was essential for establishing increased cohesiveness. Cohesiveness refers to mutual liking or acceptance of shared norms or values of the syndicate by the members of the nexus family. In order to have the cohesiveness, the criminal businessmen and their *netas* (leaders) recruit suitable law enforcement officers to places and posts which they select for the smooth running of their criminality. It is this cohesiveness which makes the nexus operations successful.

Extent of Anomie and Nexus Crimes

Anomie etimologically comes from a Greek word and it means "lawlessness". I find a total lawlessness in administration and I do not see the traditional forms of social control to be effective in Indian democracy. During the British raj, there were several methods of controlling the bureaucrats under them. There were no leaders who wanted to establish any sort of *nexus* with the bureaucrats for lucrative purposes and self advantages. Hence, nexus crimes were practically nonexistent. When the British left India, anomie (lawlessness) started creeping in and the result has been the flourishing of nexus criminality which was invisible immediately after India became independent— and then became partly visible—and now fully visible to people. Today a state of anomie-lawlessness and normlessness rules the country such that nexus criminality gets more and more acceptance now. A police officer notoriously known for corruption and nexus criminality became the head of the Vigilance

Department thus showing the extent of anomie in the present day society— extent of lawlessness and the nexus between politicians and police officers at the top level. Thereafter, the same officer became instrumental in initiating vigilance probe against some of the political rivals of the ruling Government. The support and the encouragement given by the ruling government is found to be a serious and potent cause for the development of nexus criminality.

Victimless Nexus Crime and Public Approval

Whatever may be the causes of crimes, some nexus criminals may argue that nexus crimes are victimless crimes. It is Edwin Schur who defined victimless crimes as "the willing exchange, among adults, of strongly demanded but legally proscribed goods or services". He continues: "crimes without victims may be limited to those situations in which one person obtains from another, in a fairly direct exchange, a commodity or personal service which is socially disapproved and legally proscribed". What do the nexus criminals do? Do they commit any harm directly to anybody? For example, what is the harm the nexus criminals do to others in corruption money splitting? Suppose, a police officer receives a monthly pay-off for keeping his eyes shut for maintaining a gambling house. There are no complainants, no apparent harms to others and there is only low visibility for it and in such a situation, what is the wrong in naming nexus criminality as a victimless crime? Many people in society do not consider the bootlegger to be a criminal and so do those involved in the nexus with the bureaucrat/police officer who has a nexus with the bootlegger. People do not blame a police officer who shows a passive attitude to bootleggers. Some policemen working in a police station situated just in front of a liquor shop were known to have gone there regularly to get their dues from the sale under the direct view of the public. There is no reaction to it from the public as they think that the police activity does not affect them adversely. This sort of public approval of nexus criminality encourages the policemen to continue their unholy nexus with bootleggers.

Police Morality and Nexus Criminality

The police have a duty to preserve the morals of the people, but do they take any interest on this account? Policemen argue: "People engage in violating laws regulating sexual behaviour, the use of alcohol and the gambling. They want to corrupt the police officials and get things done. The existing laws are not capable of frightening people and therefore they continue to violate the laws. What can the police do if the people are not prepared to abide by the laws?" 'Swim along with the current— and not against the current'— is the attitude some policemen/officers take to such violations of people. This attitude may help them to earn many things which they can not otherwise by indulging in giving sanctions to law breakers or becoming nexus criminals.

Nexus criminality exists in society because people want it to be there. All want it— may they be the top level administrators or politicians, the legislators or the courts of law, the high ranking policemen or bureaucrats who control the administration of justice and none of them wants to see that nexus criminality is stopped. They want the ordinary criminal laws to be enforced and that too against a certain segment of the population. 'Let the nexus criminals flourish and let us make fortunes out of such nexus crimes'- appears to be the attitude of the powerful in society. Selective enforcement of law is another cause of nexus criminality—unequal administration of law is yet another cause—lack of an upright conscience and a correct moral sense is a further cause for the existence, promotion and propagation of nexus crimes. The existing laws, morality and legal system may at best control the lower class segment of society. Nexus criminals belong to the higher class of the society and therefore they go outside the scope of control.

Differential Enforcement of Law and Nexus Crimes

Gambling or gaming in a public place is an offence. People play cards and they do it in villages during their leisure time— without harming anyone— and they play the cards under a tree. They are caught sometimes and a case registered against them. Whereas in a gambling house nobody enforces the law and the enforcement officers themselves actively participate in gambling! The law is only enforced against the poor and the powerless. Sometimes, these poor men are brought to police stations and they are forced to offer corruption-money to get leniency in treatment. Once an allegation was raised against the functionaries in a police station for forcing the arrestees to eat human excreta. The reason was that they refused to humour the law enforcement officers!

Nexus Subculture and its Development

The nexus subculture provides contacts with other nexus criminals and the nexus criminals go after strengthening the subculture. The nexus criminals in such a subculture may commit many crimes in order to remain in the subculture which offers them huge profits. The *goondas* play their role and they need police support. The police too become a part of the subculture and they may refuse to suppress the vice. They receive kickbacks and thus receiving bribery becomes common among them. Till now, no one has made any serious studies to learn the subculture of crimes amidst the law enforcement functionaries. Researchers have been studying the crime and delinquency that exist among the lower, upper or middle class people and especially among the law enforcement functionaries.

More recently, the subcultural theories have tried to explain criminality among the higher strata of society. Thus came out the unholy nexuses among the bureaucrats, politicians and criminals. Now it is well accepted that the social class is a relevant variable in explaining nexus criminality. Crimes known to the police do not include all crimes committed by police during the course of their work — and all crimes which they commit after a nexus understanding. If FIRs are registered for the nexus criminality committed by policemen/officers, then how many will have to be recorded during a day? This has not been studied. Resultingly, a subculture of crime continued to dominate the enforcement areas. In the subculture that exists in police, the policemen/officers become reactive to the crimes committed by people and they do not show a similar attitude to crimes committed by them in various forms. In police subculture, torture is permitted, corruption is tolerated, nexus criminality is not reacted against! This approach certainly helps in promoting nexus crimes within the police subculture. Corruption-money fixing, corruption-money splitting, unfair enforcement practices, violation of trust by police functionaries when articles or valuables are seized, financial fraud or misappropriation of secret service funds, various forms of nexus criminality, etc., seen in police subculture were not treated as crimes within the organization. These crimes certainly caused serious damages to police-people relations. The nexus criminality created distrust, lowered the police morale and resulted in severe criticism against the police functioning. But many did not take them seriously.

References

Gobbard, Henry H. 1914, *Feeblemindedness: Its Causes and Consequences,* New York, The MacMillan.

Schur Edwin, 1965, *Crimes Without Victims,* Englewood Cliffs, N.J: Prentice Hall.

6

POLICE : SUBCULTURE OF NEXUS CRIMES

Causative Factors and Nexus Criminality

Why do people commit nexus crimes? There are sufficient causes and necessary causes. Nevertheless, we may say that a crime is not always a necessary outcome of certain situations, forces, characteristics or subcultures. Nexus crimes do not always exist among all bureaucrats—policemen/officers— although they work under the same environment and circumstances. Corruption-money fixing is not always the characteristics of policemen who work in police stations although it may be observed in some police stations. Hence, we see that no nexus crime has both necessary and sufficient causes. Certainly, there are factors encouraging nexus criminality but a single factor cannot be identified as the sole cause of nexus crimes.

Therefore what causes and promotes nexus criminality? What about the economics of nexus criminality? William Adrian Bonger (1876-1940), a Dutch criminologist spoke about a climate of motivation for criminal behaviour. He was not speaking about nexus crimes, but at the same time he said: "Upon the basis of what has gone before, we have a right to say that the part played by economic conditions in criminality is preponderant, even decisive". Bonger's view on the causation of crime may not be fully applicable or valid in understanding nexus crimes, nevertheless, his explanations has some value when it is appreciated with other etiological factors behind nexus criminality. Poverty may not induce a director general of police to have nexus relations nor can it turn some poor constables away from becoming a member of a nexus family. Social and economic improvement can not necessarily reduce nexus criminality, rather, a development in the moral consciousness in the right way can certainly do so.

Social structure exerts pressure on some people to commit crimes—this was the view of Robert Merton and the question is: "How does his approach explain nexus crimes in police?" The structure is pyramidal with the director general of police at the top and the constables at the bottom. The structure is authoritarian in nature such that the superior rank has a decisive say in the behaviour of the subordinates. According to the existing laws, the subordinates are not to obey the illegal orders of the superiors. If that is so, how can the structure - approach explain nexus criminality? Police has a goal and it is decided by the people in a democracy. Commission of nexus crimes— and for that matter any type of crimes— is not the goal of the police department. The structure is not intended for that purpose. The goals of the police department must be achieved through methods/means accepted by law and procedure established by law. Establishing law and order and thereby peace and harmony may be one of the major goals of the police. But, for some in police department, the goal is monetary gain, lucrative benefits and other personal advantages. Policemen/officers who consider money, privilege and gains as values in life have recourse to many means— fair and foul— to accumulate wealth, luxury and position. Becoming a member in a nexus family is an easy cut to reach their destination.

Nature of Police Subculture: A Causative Factor for Nexus Crimes

How does the structure help one to commit nexus crimes? Here comes the relevance and importance of the subculture which exists in police department. What are the characteristics/features of police subculture? Take for instance, the characteristic features of the subculture of police constables. They get poor pay, facilities and working environment. They do not have an enviable social status. A person who joins as a constable retires as a constable or head constable. He has no avenues for promotions. He does not have an upward or vertical mobility. He starts his career with saluting and winds up the career with saluting. He can not achieve anything through approved means. He also cherishes dreams in life. He wants to have economic prosperity and luxuries in life. Thus he resorts to illegitimate means. Nexus crime is an easy way for him. He forgets his role as a policeman and rejects the legitimate means of society. Thus becoming a nexus criminal.

What about the higher levels? - top levels? They too have goals which they know can not be attained through legitimate means. They come from families which may not be affluent. Some may have a lot of liabilities, commitments and obligations. A senior deputy inspector general of police once said: "I have paid my income tax from the peanuts I receive as my salary". This brings out the level of satisfaction among the seniors for their income levels. Thus the higher levels too establish nexus relations to appear bigger than what they are - to be more affluent than what they are. India is a country of unemployment and those who get a government job are treated as blessed people. When one accepts a government job, he comes in a state of transition in his social status and he wants to elevate himself to the new status which he thinks that he has. As a person who joins the police at the middle level as an officer, he assumes a status which he does not have till then. He wants to live upto his expectations and upto the expectation of the society. He thinks that he is a man of authority and power. Surely, he is but for this he should also look like a person enjoying a lot of power and authority. For this his salary may not be enough and thus he becomes a prey to nexus temptations.

Policemen/officers in the past have lived in a subculture .wherein nexus dealings, corruption-money fixing, corruption-money splitting, etc, were in vogue. The new entrant to the police service is put into that subculture to the extent of being devoured by the subculture of nexus criminality. Nexus criminals approach the newcomers and offer them temptations and drag them to that nexus network. The nexus relationship may start in an innocent way and may develop in to nexus criminality. Policemen/officers who resist the subculture and fight against the system can not survive. The survival of the fittest works very well in the nexus world. Once a bootlegger visited the sub-inspector's quarters and he found that the wife of the sub-inspector did not have a mixi in her kitchen. He saw to it that a mixi reached his house readily and quickly. The wife of the sub-inspector felt happy at it. The sub-inspector objected to the clandestine transaction and returned the mixi to the bootlegger who felt insulted. He moved his pressure points in the political hierarchy and saw to it that the sub-inspector got a transfer within 24 hours. The higher levels having nexus dealings with the political higher ups did not want to contaminate their relationship for a sub-inspector who refused to be party to the nexus network. The sub-inspector could not survive in the subculture as he was not the fittest whereas the higher levels could as they were the fittest. The subculture has certain norms and the subculture does not allow anyone to violate the norms. If someone violates the norms, then he is pushed out of the subculture. The nexus criminality permitted and promoted by the subculture in police and outside continues to dominate the policemen/officers and the policemen/officers are influenced by their status consciousness which can be maintained only if they become members in the nexus family. Officers in the nexus family can enjoy luxuries without straining their purse whereas those outside the nexus subculture can not have them even with loans and hardships.

Nexus Subculture and Police

Some constables are seen telling others that they are sub-inspectors in police. What is the reason for this? They want to appear as sub-inspectors. A brown shoe means a police officer and a black shoe means a constable. Some constables purchase brown shoes to look like officers in police department. They feel less to "feel like a constable" - 'to look like a constable'— and they accept middle level police values. Such constables do not make use of cycles as they want to use only motorbikes. They measure themselves with values and lifestyles of middle level police officers and they can not reach their destination with the income they get. They then make money through illegitimate means and one such method is to become a member in the nexus family. A government employee in India means a person with regular income and adequate security and a member in police service means a person who can make illicit income by misuse of his power/ abuse of his authority. The people around him in the society judge him as a person who has legitimate and illegitimate income. He therefore wants to maintain a certain standards which he can not without being or becoming a nexus criminal. He wants to move up in the social hierarchy and for that he finds an easy way out. He becomes a nexus criminal! He knows that he is looked down upon by the people when they know that he is a nexus criminal. He is certain that his relationship in the nexus transactions will remain hidden precisely because of the clandestine nature of the nexus dealings, he therefore fearlessly plunges into the field. He has a low self-esteem and faces many adjustment problems. In spite of them and amidst such problems and difficulties he lives in a subculture/wants to live in a subculture which accepts nexus criminality.

Activities of Subculture

The nexus subculture which exists in police department consists of the following activities:

(a) Examples of Nexus Crimes by Persons Operating on an Individual, ad hoc Basis

1. A sub-inspector has a nexus dealing with a loan shark. The police officer misuses his authority and does a favour to the loan shark. He receives the amount agreed upon.
2. A circle inspector has a sweet-heart agreement with a person to do something as he likes and the police will not entertain any complaint against him.

(b) Examples of Nexus Crimes in Violation of one's duty of Loyalty and Fidelity to the Government/ People

1. Bribery-fixing, corruption-money splitting and payoff.
2. Embezzlement of secret service money by nexus understanding.

(c) Examples of Nexus Crimes Incidental to and in Furtherance of Police work, but not the Central Purpose of Police Work

1. Concoction of evidence, production of tutured witnesses or in touts in criminal cases, etc.
2. Employment of torture, informal arrest, illegal detention and human rights violations.

(d) Examples of Nexus Crimes as the Central Activity

1. Misuse of police vehicles, personnel and Government facilities for personal use.
2. Exercise of pseudo-authority for the benefit of vested interests.

Prof. Edwin H. Sutherland has extensively dealt with white collar crimes and has classified them into many categories. Likewise the nexus crimes too can be classified. A study on the existence of nexus criminality in police subculture gives light to alarming facts. The nexus subculture in police is characterized by activities which offer advantages to the police functionaries. Sometimes, it may be characterized by short-run hedonism (e.g., a lunch at noon, a dinner or a wet party). Instances are plenty to show that police functionaries are entertained by nexus friends who have no lasting interests in them. This may be called a bribery after a nexus understanding. Policemen/officers, after their institutional training immediately after their recruitment, go to police stations where they are introduced into a subculture, usually, contaminated by nexus dealings, transactions and criminality. The subculture exerts influence on the new entrants and affects them. As a result, they too become members in the nexus subculture.

A Subculture without a Conscience

What is the subcultural value of police to crimes? The police are bound to detect crimes, investigate them and see that justice is administered to criminals. This means that the police respond to values which are accepted by the society. For example, a man commits a murder. The police and society view it as a murder. If a custodial murder takes place, how do the police and society view it? How do the police and the society view tortures, abductions, rapes, informal arrests, illegal detentions, Gheraoes, corruption, bribery fixing, etc. If something is viewed as crime outside the police station, it becomes a crime inside the police station too. If forgery is an offence, then manipulating records by police too is an offence. If people join together and make a plot to commit a crime and subsequently commit a crime, it becomes a criminal conspiracy. If the policemen together with others manipulate records, concoct evidence or produce tutored witnesses, then they commit crimes. Nexus crimes are thus crimes committed during the course of the job for the benefit of the nexus partners.

Do the nexus criminals feel shame—feel guilty when they commit nexus crimes? Many policemen/officers have shame/guilt when they are caught for nexus crimes. If they do not, then they are psychopaths. The society has a moral system - has moral values and the policemen/officers have to accept them. Commission of nexus crimes is against the moral values of the dominant normative system of the society.

Policemen/officers are often seen justifying/rationalizing nexus crimes. This rationalization/justification is due to their acceptance of a perverted value. For example, many police officers justify the use of torture on property offenders. Why? Their rationalization/justification itself shows that they do not accept their behaviour as justifiable or acceptable. A police officer alongwith others caused the custodial death of a suspect in a police station. Whatever might be the justifications or rationalizations, both police and society condemned the police act. The subculture in police stations sometimes neutralize the police atrocities to people. The neutralizing subculture of police is said to be the cause of nexus and other criminality.

Neutralization of Nexus Crimes

It is the neutralization of nexus crimes which promotes nexus criminality. Corruption-money sharing, for example, is a nexus crime. But, the subculture permits it- such that corruption-money sharing is not considered as an undesirable act. This is due to the effect of neutralization. Once a policeman was candid enough to disclose that they used to share the corruption money– and another police officer honestly revealed that corruption-money splitting is tolerated and encouraged in police subculture. Police employ torture on suspects and many in police subculture and outside know about it. Some tolerate it - some neutralize it - some react to it. The neutralizing subculture in police had developed, probably, as a result of the limited success rate if and when alternative - human rights friendly - methods are employed during crime investigation.

Police Structure and Subculture

Police have both legitimate and illigitimate opportunities in course of their duty to protect law. They are free to select any one, either they can choose to accept corruption money or they can refuse it. Similarly they can encourage corruption fixing or splitting or they can avoid it. They may or may not likewise use third degree methods. In the police subculture, if a proliceman/officer has little or no opportunity to become a nexus criminal, then he may not. On the contrary, when the subculture provides ample opportunities to commit nexus crimes/ other crimes, then people may be inclined to commit them. Where the means of concocting evidence in criminal cases - manipulating records - producing tutored witnesses are not available in police subculture, a nexus crime-oriented subculture would most probably not develop. But, one sees many kinds of nexus criminality in police subculture and it shows that sufficient opportunities do exist for the promotion of nexus criminality in police subculture.

Criminal Subculture in Police

On going through the judgements in criminal cases pronounced by courts and seeing the judgements in acquitted cases, one may come across a number of observations made by the judges against the investigating officers - against the police department. A casual reading may give an impression that a criminal subculture exists in police. Even the research reports of eminent scholars suggest that there exists a sort of criminal subculture. More so, even the reports of the police commissions give out negative comments made by the commissions against the police such that one is ashamed to see the criminal subculture in police! Likewise, even the press reports relate about the existence of a criminal subculture in police. Look around and see the policemen on duty. What is the impression which the people form about the policeman? While travelling by bus it is common to find policemen checking vehicles on the road. This invites comments by passengers like: "Look at the policemen on duty. They collect money". This shows that it is well known among the common men that there exists this form of the nexus criminality in police department.

A Policeman's Vision

A criminal subculture develops mainly in police stations where the commission of crimes becomes very visible. An inspector of police once stated that: "Many or all in police stations are found willingly associating with the people who commit crimes" - To this, a sub-inspector in low tone reacted: "the criminal subculture develops in the offices of the inspectors, deputy superintendents, superintendents of police and even in the police headquarters. People who live in a criminal subculture and particularly the new entrants to the service do not see role models who have achieved success through legitimate channels."

Policemen/officers including the new entrants to the service see nexus crimes being committed and their accessability to criminal success models induces an idea in them that they too can become successful if they resort to illegitimate means and methods. The policemen/officers who get an opportunity to perform illegitimate roles may not be reluctant to have recourse to such means and methods. If they get support from the subculture or from the superiors/subordinates, then they may involve in committing crimes. They get rewards–monetary or otherwide–and they derive gratifications from such acts.

The police subculture very willingly supports criminal activities. For example, when a custodial murder takes place within the four walls of a police station, it is indeed difficult to get any evidence as everyone in the subculture keeps silence about it - supports the fellow colleague in a silent language. The law on custodial offences has put the burden of disproving the allegation on police functionaries. The law has been enacted because of the observations made by commissions of inquiry against a subculture that supports the crime-doers in custodial cases within the walls of police stations. Criminlogists see "Fencing" by the subculture and the fencing encourages/promotes all sorts of criminality including nexus crimes.

Public Culture and Police Subculture

Ask a man on the street about the police subculture. In a study conducted by the author along with Dr. Alphonse L. Earayil, 4823 people were asked to honestly tell us about the illegal and unauthorized practices in police and the responses were—

(1) 45.82 per cent said that the police coerced complainants and petitioners to provide petrol for police vehicles. Certainly, it is a nexus activity not only between the police and complainants/petitioners but also the policemen among themselves.

(2) 43.87 per cent told that the police asked complainants/petitioners to hire taxi/other vehicles. 23.03 per cent obtained liquor, food or refreshments from complainants, petitioners, witnesses or those who show special interest in keeping the police in good humour.

What is this? Has it become a subculture in police so that the people in such large numbers speak about police practices which are illegal/unauthorized?

(3) 29.37 per cent responded to the question saying that the police got special favours such as modern gadgets, edible things, clothings, repair of personal vehicles, etc., 19.49 per cent reported that the police got rice, firewood, edible oils, etc, from mill owners without paying for them. The list of unauthorized practices in police was very lengthy and it showed the extent and intensity of nexus crimes practised and perpetuated in police subculture.

A Mini-Culture within the Main Culture

The study throws light on the fact that the police 'culture' is really a 'subculture' in the dominant 'culture' of the society. The police subculture responds to values which are not accepted by the dominant culture of the society. At the same time, there are policemen/officers who argue that the police are the very part of the society and precisely, the subculture of police too is a part of the dominant culture. This view may not be true in toto as the subculture means a mini-culture within the main culture. The mini-culture has its own special characteristics and features. The mini-culture/ subculture existing in police may have values which the main/dominant culture of the society does not accept. Corruption may be seen in society, but it does not mean that corruption is accepted in society. People and their culture do oppose corruption although corruption and corrupt practices are seen in society. Likewise, the dominant/main culture of the society opposes corruption in police subculture and therefore the argument that the police subculture is a part of the dominant culture of the society ceases to have any validity. The subculture in police may not accept corruption as a desirable thing. That is one of the reasons why cases under the Prevention of Corruption Act are registered against police officers by police officers themselves.

Police Subculture and Influence of Environment

Psychologists say that the socio-cultural environment exerts influence in the development of human personality. Through the contacts with the subculture, the new policemen/officers learn the practices the seniors follow, the values they believe in and certainly the *modus operandi* of the subculture in committing legal/illegal acts. The subculture existing in a police station teaches its younger members many things which they will not otherwise learn. Such practices tend to make all members in the police stations somewhat alike. Individuals reared among people who commit nexus crimes or in a subculture which promotes nexus criminality are, in all probability, prone to become nexus criminals. Studies show that the more uniform and thorough the education and exposure of the new members to nexus crime prone subculture, the more they take to it. There exists no wide individual differences among them regarding their views on nexus criminality. The values and behaviour patterns they learn depend heavily on whether or not their superiors are nexus crime oriented.

During the process of policing, a certain patterns of behaviour is built into the policemen/officers which becomes a part of them. The subculture is seen as a principal element in the development of the individuals. The functioning is moulded by the subculture within which the individuals have been reared. The nexus subculture certainly provides a pathological social and subcultural climate for the rearing of its members and plays a large part in shaping their attitudes to nexus crimes. Those who have a favourable attitude to nexus crimes soon learn that with the aid of nexus subculture, they can achieve gratifying feelings of adequacy and self-esteem.

Factors in Subculture Perpetuating Nexus Crimes

There are three subcultural factors which appear to lay a decisive role in promoting and perpertuating nexus crimes in police and they are:

(1) The degree of tolerance to nexus crimes and the extent of encouragement to nexus criminality;

(2) The attitude towards nexus crimes and to individuals who commit nexus crimes by the subculture;

(3) The degree to which the subculture provides substitute means of income through nexus crimes and to the satisfaction the individuals derive if they do not involve in the commission of nexus crimes. The more the favourable attitude of the subculture to nexus criminality, the more will be the commission of nexus crimes. Adverse subcultural factors appear to play a major role in the reduction/elimination of nexus crimes.

Prevention of Nexus Crimes—Strategies

It follows therefore that nexus crimes can be prevented only if the subculture favouring nexus criminality is changed. Three prevention strategies are suggested below:

(1) Primary prevention which involves any attempts to reduce/eliminate the conditions promoting nexus crimes;

(2) Secondary prevention which consists of an early identification of all conditions and subcultural factors favouring nexus criminality; and

(3) Tertiary prevention which means correcting the individuals who are involved in the commission of nexus crimes.

Nexus/Consensus Understanding and Differential Law Enforcement

Rather than enforcing the law, the police are committing nexus crimes (as the allegation goes) during the course of law enforcement. The enforcement of law, no doubt, reflects the interests of the enforcing authority. For example, the laws against corruption and bribery are not enforced strictly, because it is to the advantage of the enforcement authorities not to enforce them. Any corruption/bribery is well-known to many in the department concerned; nevertheless no action is taken. This is due to the nexus/consensus understanding to promote and propagate crimes. At the same time, the law enforcement authorities enforce laws on others! There is a double standard in the approach. This is otherwise called the differential law enforcement.

Nexus crimes in law enforcement departments are not treated as crimes though many may agree that the subculture promoting nexus crimes is a sick one and needs treatment. Treatment means initiation of strict legal action against the nexus criminals? Will it be ever possible if the nexus partners are high level politicians, bureaucrats, businessmen etc? The State has three wings: (1) Legislature, (2) Executive and (3) Judiciary. All said and done, the State is a political organization wherein the politicians play an important role. The politicians decide many things in a democracy and they themselves become nexus partners. What to do then? - or what can be done? The politicians, bureaucrats, businessmen, law enforcement officers are motivated by *acquisitive individualism* - they want to make money, position and status and they do anything and many things to achieve their goals. Commission of nexus crimes is just one method to achieve their goals.

If nexus crimes take place at many levels of administration, it means that the higher authorities tolerate such crimes/approve such an atmosphere. Nexus criminality, I think, must be taken as an indicator of the failure of the higher authority to control the subordinates - of the higher authority to see that a nexus crime free atmosphere is created. The higher authority may not have sufficient moral courage to insist morality on their subordinates.

How do the nexus partners respond to the conduct norms? A person must not show duality of conduct norms. If he shows so, then he is criticized and reacted against - sometimes openly and loudly and sometimes silently and vehemently. People react to nexus crimes strongly when they are reported in the press or when they come to know of them by other sources. What types of nexus crimes do take place in police stations and police headquarters? The former may be visible and known; the latter may be invisible and unknown to many.

Nexus crimes in police can be of three categories and they are:

(A) Visible and known to many

(B) Invisible and unknown to many

(C) Visible and unknown to many

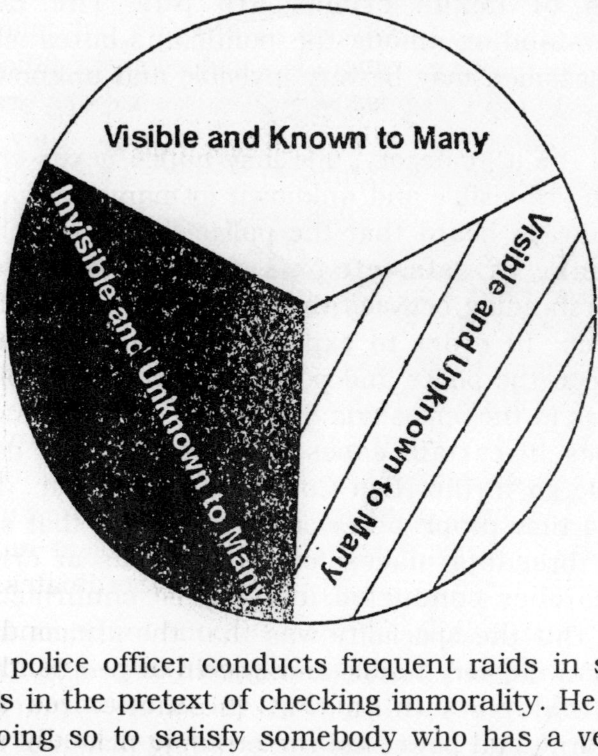

A police officer conducts frequent raids in some hotels in the pretext of checking immorality. He may be doing so to satisfy somebody who has a vested interest in harming the hotel owners. A bootlegger takes 10 truck load illicit liquor through a particular route and one truck load through another route. After reaching a nexus understanding, a law enforcement officer gets hold of one of the trucks carrying illicit liquor. Here, the activities of the law enforcement officer is very visible, but the nexus nature of the enforcement is unknown to the people in society. He commits a nexus crime, but many do not know the nexus nature. This type of nexus criminality is put under (A) in the above classification.

In (B) category, invisible and unknown to many types of nexus crimes are put. The nexus understanding among the politicians-bureaucrats-businessmen may be very invisible and unknown to many.

In the (C) category, one may notice nexus crimes which are visible and unknown to many. Allegations are always heard that the police do certain things or make arrests, etc., as a result of a nexus understanding between them and the ruling political parties. In order to expose the unholy relations between the police and political parties, the political parties in the opposition insist or demand for judicial probes in certain cases. In certain other cases, people go to the High Courts with writs etc. There was a time people and scientists thought that slums were breeding places for many types of crimes. Researches conducted in the area confirmed the fact. But the speciality was that the crimes in the slums were very visible and known to people. Today, criminologists think that the higher places of authority and power are the breeding places of many kinds of crimes including nexus criminality. The speciality here is that the crimes that take place at such places are beyond the reach of the common man and therefore are invisible and unknown to many. Whenever they appear in the press, they make news to many. They become news not because such crimes are not taking place, but because they are not known to many as they are not visible. The media makes the crimes known and visible.

The Study of Nexus Crimes

During 1940s, 1950s and 1960s, etc., students of criminology used to go to jails and correctional institutions to study the personality of criminals and to prepare their case histories. Today, they rarely go to such institutions as they know that such institutions contain people who are convicted because there were no vested interests to defend them properly in the court. Most of the convicts in jails are poor people who are not influential in society. Whatever be the reason, today the students of criminology want to go to the big businessmen, politicians, bureaucrats, or otherwise affluent and influential people in society and learn the pattern of crimes they commit to feel bigger and taller. Nexus criminality can thus be studied. The Chicago School was concerned with the ecology of crimes. The ecologists attempted to explain crimes as a function of social change that occurred along with environmental changes. Burgess's concentric circle theory was well known in ecological theories. He divided the city of Chicago into five major zones. His studies showed that crimes and vices would flourish in the Zone No. 2 which was characterized by warehouses, pawn shops, cheap theatres and restaurants, etc. He further found a breakdown in the usual institutional methods of control in Zone No. 2. In this case he was talking of the visible crimes– the crimes which were traditional in nature and which were committed by the ordinary mortals in the society. What about the nexus criminality? They are planned in the city's best hotels or in the palace-like houses. They plan them with liquor in hands amidst airconditioned surroundings. These crimes are invisible and not known to many. The tourists' resort centres, star hotels, roof gardens in mansions, swimming pools, bars, etc., are the breeding places of nexus crimes–and the technological revolution through mobile phones, e-mail, internet facilities, STD/ISD connections, etc., may aid the execution of nexus crimes in a speedier way. Eventually the invisible and unknown nature of nexus criminality may make everything to appear fine in society.

No Social Stratification of Crime

The subcultural theories of crime explain crimes committed by people in lower economic and social class. In prisons, people from low social and economic strata are seen in plenty. Studies on nexus criminality may reveal that the social class is not and should not be a significant factor in the commission of crimes. The social classes *per se* may not be an etiological factor in the commission of crimes. In current parlance, people classify crimes into two categories and they are: (i) high class activities and (ii) low class crimes. High class activities which are criminal in nature must be treated as crimes and in no event should their sugar-coating into being called high class activities considered right. A gambling in a star hotel is as much a crime as gambling under a tree in a village by the poor people. Describing crimes on the basis of the status and class of the people involved in such activities as crimes or not crimes is not correct. Irrespective of the social class to which an individual belongs, crimes are crimes, no matter who commits them. For, their values do not conform to those of the larger group. They do extensive and lasting damage to many in society. Nexus criminals belong to this category. Nexus criminals just like gang criminals have a criminal subculture— a subculture in which they direct their activities towards theft, extortion and other illegal means of obtaining income. But, the activities they commit to obtain an illicit income may not be called thefts, extortion, misappropriation of property, etc., though on a closer scrutiny, their activities too are coming under theft, robbery, extortion and criminal misappropriation of property. They too involve in violent activities and other illicit transactions.

The Traditional vs Nexus Criminal

'Nexus crime', 'nexus criminals', 'nexus subculture', 'nexus criminality', 'criminal nexus'– are they new words in criminology? This may not be so as they were in existence in an invisible way in the past—unknown to the people. Now, they have become visibly conspicuous. Today, the nexus crimes have become an exceedingly complex problem. It has become a lifestyle for many to be involved in nexus criminality. Non-nexus criminals commit traditional crimes to make money in the quickest way possible and the nexus criminals do the same thing to make money in the safest way possible. Unlike the traditional criminals, the nexus criminals make not only mony, but also status, position, fame and many other things which they can not obtain otherwise. The nexus crimes are well planned and even discussed in depth. Many people think of nexus criminals as new criminals and certainly, they possess a different type of personality from that of the traditional criminals. A nexus criminal commits crimes for making money, obtaining ego-status, position, authority, etc. and he participates in planned activities. Often he is not detected and precisely therefore he himself does not think that his criminal behaviour is a part of a larger pattern of personality maladjustment. Hence, no one including the nexus criminal thinks about the correction of unhealthy personality trends in him. E.A. Robinson in his peom Richard Cory writes

"Whenever Richard Cory went down the town,
We people on the pavement looked at him;
He was a gentleman from sole to crown,
Clean favoured, and imperially slim.
And he has always quietly arrayed,
And he was always human when he talked;
But still he fluttered pulses when he said,
"Good morning" and he glittered when he walked.
And he was rich - yes, richer than a king -
And admirably schooled in every grace;
In fine, we thought that he was everything,
To make us wish that they were in his place.
So on we worked and waited for the light,
And went without the meat, and cursed the bread.

And Richard Cory, one calm summer night,
Went home and put a bullet through his head".

The nexus criminal too is having a personality which Richard Cory had; but the difference is that the nexus criminal does not understand that he is a maladjusted personality. Like Richard Cory, he may not commit suicide, yet he is a person with a maladjusted personality make up.

Reference

Bemmelen, Van J.M., 1973, William Adrian Bonger, in Hermann Mannheim, ed., *Pioneers in Criminology,* Montclair, N.J.: Patterson Smith Publishing Co.

7

NEXUS CRIMES: SOCIALIZATION AND POLICIZATION

Once a housewife committed suicide by jumping into a well. The doctors certified that it was a case of suicidal drowning. The deadbody was buried after obtaining the clearance from the police. If the versions of the relatives of the deceased were true, then they had to spend a lot of money at various stages on different agencies to get a clearance certificate for burying the dead body. The doctor who accepted money and conducted the postmortem knew well that his assistants in the mortuary did accept money for their services. The constable who accompanied the dead body was certain that the doctors and their assistants had a nice harvest on the dead body. The police officer who issued the clearance certificate for burying the dead body knew quite well that the doctors, their assistants, the constables and many officials who rendered services were happy to see that a clearance certificate was issued. He demanded his share and all was well as it ended well! The dead body was buried. In the evening, three constables came in a police jeep and said: "It seems to be a suspicious case. Perhaps, the dead body will have to be taken out and exhumed". The relatives became confused and ultimately they came to an understanding that everything could be closed if the constables were kept in good humour. The nexus crimes have got many faces and dimensions!

The Self Concept Approach

Given the alternatives of law abiding and law violating behaviour, some people turn to violate the law. Walter Reckless and Simon Dinitz said: "We live in a society of alternatives, where the self has more and more opportunities for acceptance or rejection of available confrontations". They advocated that the self-concept was the key factor in explaining the alternatives of behaviour.

In police and nexus criminality, how does the self-concept approach work? The policeman/officer goes through two stages in his personality development which leave a long lasting impression on him: (1) the socialization and (2) the policization. Socialization takes place during the early infancy and policization comes into being when a person enlists himself as a member of the police service. If adequate socialization formed in the correct way with an upright conscience takes place, then the self-concept thus formed will work as an inner buffer or inner containment against deviance, destruction, lure and pressures. As far as the nexus criminality is concerned, it is indeed difficult to learn how the socialization was during the early stages of personality development. As the crime takes place later in life, we may have to look into the effect of policization on policemen/officers. Policization is a process by which an entrant into police service becomes a full-fledged policeman/officer with desirable or undesirable personality traits.

Reckless and Dinitz say emphatically that a favourable self-concept formed during the early infancy directs an individual toward law abiding behaviour and an unfavourable self-concept directs him or her towards delinquent behaviour. They studied juvenile delinquents of the age of 12 years and precisely therefore they could say so, because their samples did not have subsequent socialization. In the case of police officers/policemen who become nexus criminals, one may see the effect and influence of both socialization and policization.

On asking the new entrants to police service immediately after their entry to police service about their attitude to nexus criminality they have replied that they were against any kind of crimes including enforcement crimes and nexus criminality. After 10 years or more service in police, their earlier attitudes and views had changed considerably in favour of accepting enforcement and nexus criminality. After another ten years, it was further found that they often advocated enforcement and nexus criminality. The views and attitudes they had when they were 20-25 years of age get changed when they become 35-40 which again undergo changes when they are 50-55 years of age. They are often heard saying: "I was an honest officer when I joined the service; but honesty did not pay me much. Hence, I changed my attitude and approach".

"My principles and philosophies did not work. I became a misfit in the service. I changed my principles and philosophies and now I am the most wanted man".

"My parents taught me morality. I find immorality everywhere. I am now in a transition stage from morality to immorality".

Behaviour modification takes place in all walks of life. People can be changed; their attitudes can be altered. A director general of police once said: "I was an honest man and my bank balance when I was placed under suspension was zero. During the suspension, no one including those who were close to me extended a helping hand. After the reinstatement, I knew how to make my life safe and secure".

Life experiences and frustrations make the people to change their attitudes and approaches. Specifically, why do some policemen/officers who live and work in law enforcement service commit enforcement and nexus crimes? Reckless and Dinitz would explain the behaviour by their social process theory of self-concept formed during the early infancy. On the contrary studies prove that the self-concept undergoes changes when the individual grows up-when he faces new situations - when he experiences frustrations, etc. People who have good and adequate socialization turn to commit crimes if and when they are exposed to live situations which cause criminality. Policization has many effects in behaviour modification. A nexus crime prone subculture—an enforcement crime prone subculture may effect changes in the self-concept. Thus a new self-concept will be formed and the new self concept will have the components of socialization and policization.

Nexus Crimes: A Good Self-Concept in Police

A child at 2—A juvenile at 15—An adult at 25—A middle aged at 40— A retired person at the age of 60— this is the life history of a policeman/officer too. In spite of many changes, there is an "Iness" in everyone and the "Iness" is created by socialization and policization in a policeman/officer. The principle of socialization may be: "Be honest in life" whereas the principle of policization may be: "Many in police service are not honest then why should I be honest?" These two principles melt together to form a new principle and it may be: "Honesty is good, but in police it is not so always". Here comes a new self concept which will be the product of socialization and policization. In such a new self concept, nexus crimes and enforcement crimes may be accepted modes of behaviour. The dominant culture in the society may call it to be a poor self-concept, but the police subculture may accept it to be a good self concept.

Nexus Crime : A Product of Socialization and Policization

Inadequate Socialization + Inadequate Policization

Inadequate socialization during the early stages of personality development plus an inadequate policization in the police subculture may make a person to commit crimes, enforcement crimes and nexus crimes. The self concept has the components of both adequate socialization and inadequate policization. Here he may not feel the guilt.

Adequate Socialization+Inadequate Policization

Adequate socialization during the early stages of personality development and an inadequate policization in the police subculture may make a person to commit crimes, enforcement crimes and nexus crimes. As the self concept has the components of both adequate socialization and inadequate policization, he may feel guilty when he commits a crime or a nexus crime.

Adequate Socialization + Adequate Policization

Adequate socialization during the early stages of personality development and adequate policization in police subculture will make a person not to commit crimes, enforcement crimes and nexus crimes. If he comits a crime, a nexus crime, then he will invariably feel guilty.

Reckless and Dinitz argued that a good self concept was the evidence of favourable socialization and the development of a strong self concept. On the contrary, a good self concept is the evidence of adequate socialization in early personality development and later policization (here as the concept in police subculture) in police service.

Cultural Norms: Police vs Childhood

Two cultures have a great influence on the personality and traits of a policemen/officer. They are 'childhood culture and police culture'. Childhood culture is one inculcated into a child during its early and later stages of development and the police culture is the culture inculcated into a police recruit after his entry into the service. For example—

1. The childhood cultural norm was not to forge a document to harm a person. The police cultural norm was that one might make manipulations in a document if that was needed. Thus, manipulations could be made in the FIR itself. Here the childhood culture (socialization) and police culture (policization) conflict each other.
2. The childhood cultural norm was not to hurt anyone. But the police cultural norm was that the suspects might be tortured to elicit a confession. The cultural norms and police norms fight each other.

Conduct Rules: Police vs Society

According to Thorsten Sellin: The conduct norms are defined by the groups to which an individual belongs— He continues: "culture conflict is the inevitable result of conflict between conduct norms". In police, the conflict is between the conduct norms of early childhood and the same of the police culture. For example, the police may register a case of forgery against a person outside the police whereas they do not do so if it happens in the police department. Corruption committed by others may be registered as a crime, but corruption committed by the police functionaries may not be registered as a crime. In that way, there may exist a conflict between the conduct rules of the police culture and the culture existing in the society outside the police. In nexus crimes, police establishes a nexus and thereafter it violates the conduct norms of the society. For example, take the case of corruption-money fixing. Here the police responds to the conduct norms prevailing in the police subculture. The conduct norm is in conflict with the same existing in the dominant culture of the society. The same is the case with corruption-money splitting.

Push-Pull Causation Approach

The push-pull causation theory is the result of research on criminal behaviour. The push factors in a man are his attitudes, philosophies, values, visions, etc, on a particular norm. They are inculcated into human personality through the process of socialization and through the process of human formation during the early and later childhood. The value system may confirm to such socialization.

Pull factors are the environmental or situational factors which make a man behave in a particular way. Both the factors are seen to fight each other. The behaviour including criminal behaviour is the result of an interaction between the push and pull factors.

Push factors (pf factors) consist of the superego norms, the values, do's and don'ts, rules, morality, regulations, laws, customs, traditions, etc. A person has the pf (Push Factors) already formed in him when he joins the police department as a policeman/officer. Socialization and the formation of his conscience play an important role in the development of the pf (Push Factors) in a person.

After joining the police, the policization takes place and in that process certain more values will be inculcated in his pf (Push Factors). For example, calling epithets to people is an undesirable act - this is his 'pf' when he joins the police. Through policization, he modifies his already formed 'pf' and thus, he inculcates the value that 'in police, one may use epithets if that is necessary'. For, the police does things for public good.

Hence, after joining the police, the 'pf' will be modified and thus will include the values of socialization and policization. Hence, then

Push Factor = Values of Socialization + Policization

Some psychologists may say that the values are planted in a person during his early infancy. But studies show that the values so formed in the early infancy may get modified by inculcation of new values in later life. Behaviour modification is possible to the right or wrong direction depending upon the values inculcated in an individual.

Pull Factors (PF factors) consist of the pressures of the situation and weakness of the social order/values. The pressures can be anything from financial difficulties to political interference. Weakness of the social order can be anything from law and order deterioration to value decline. Thus, the behaviour of man will be

$$\text{Human Behaviour} = \frac{\text{Pressures of the Situation Plus Weakness of the Social Order/Values}}{\text{Values of Socialization Plus Policization}}$$

The fight here is between the situation and the individual. Applying this in nexus crimes, we may say that a person commits nexus crimes, because he is weak in his values and the situation overpowers him. Examples—

Push/Pull Factors in Corruption Money Splitting

I. Nominator/Pull Factors

(i) Pressures of the situation Plus Weakness of the Social order	Pressures of the situation	1. There is the need for money; 2. Associates, superiors and subordinates insist for it; 3. There are pressures from many quarters to do a particular thing in a particular way. 1. Corruption has become a culture; 2. Corruption-money splitting is encouraged; 3. Corruption-money splitting is a custom and there is no stigma attached to it; and 4. Corruption-money splitting is not treated as a crime and therefore no guilt feeling.

II. Dominator/Push Factors

Socialization plus policization	Socialization	1. Corruption is an evil; 2. Corrupt people are condemned; 3. Corruption is looked down upon; 4. Corruption is not a saviour; 5. Don't become corrupt; and

Policization

6. Corruption is a sin against God.

1. Corruption-money splitting is not an evil. Everywhere it is seen;
2. After all, people give money as I do some special service to him. Everyone in my position may accept it. Then what is wrong in it?
3. Salary is not enough. These corrupt ways of earning some money is the only attraction in service.
4. Who is not corrupt? In fact, corruption-money splitting is not corruption at all. It is only a sharing.

And thus, in the denominator, what one sees are the values which an individual has from his socialization plus policization. The values inculcated by socialization are modified by the values of policization. If the denominator overpowers the nominator, then he does not commit a nexus crime or any other crimes. If the nominator overpowers the denominator, then he commits a nexus crime/any other crimes.

The same principle can be applied in all sorts of nexus crimes.

How Does a Person become a Criminal/Nexus Criminal?

Man thinks - He thinks in many ways - He discovers many things - He designs many things - He manipulates many things - He executes many things and he manages many things. According to Gabriel Tarde: imitation was the process in committing crimes. It might be so in some instances, yet one could not imitate another fully. I think that people commit crimes even when there is no scope for imitation.

Counting the Waves and Corruption

The story about the corrupt man who was posted to count the waves is known to many. The King found a man to be very corrupt. As a punishment, he was sent to a seashore with an order to count the number of waves arriving on the seashore. There were many fishermen who wanted to go to the sea for fishing. They had made small boats which they wanted to take to the sea. But the newly appointed waves-counting officer would not allow them to take the boats to the sea. His argument was that he was appointed to count the waves and he wanted to count them correctly. The fishermen and their boats would disturb his counting and therefore, he did not allow them to go to the sea.

Thus, there arose a lot of law and order problems. The intellectual people among the fishermen started to think independently and jointly. They discovered methods and they started to offer corruption-money to the newly appointed waves-counting officer. So the post became the most attractive one within a short time. This story thus proves that human initiative, wisdom, intelligence, executing power, etc, are very important—more important than anything else-to commit crime. People commit crimes because they are intelligent enough to commit crimes and corrupt people are generally noted to be more intelligent than people who are not corrupt. People who are not intelligent are caught easily.

Theories on Personality of Criminals

(i) Feeblemindedness Negated

Henry H. Gobbard believed that the single cause of criminal behaviour was feeblemindedness. His theory was attacked and proved to be wrong as most criminals were not found to be feebleminded. Studies on the contrary show that every crime is an invention and every invention is the result of intelligence. Every crime is a new crime and in nexus criminality, the newness is seen in many respects. Take for instance, the nexus between politicians and police. They design, devise, manage, manipulate and execute their criminal nexus. The role of intelligence in all the above steps is very important. The more intelligently one designs, devises, manages, manipulates and executes the nexus consensus, the more successful he becomes.

Learned vs Invented Behaviour

Edwin H. Sutherland's Differential Association Theory has little or no relevance in nexus criminality. According to him Criminal behaviour is learned. Observations show that the criminal behaviour - particularly in nexus crimes - is invented. No one repeats a crime. Every crime is unique in nature and is individualistic in character. Every crime is intelligently planned and executed. A superior intelligence may detect a crime, but it does not mean that the crime is not intelligently planned and executed. Although Sutherland's 'learning' may help to intelligently plan and execute the crime but 'learning to commit a crime' does not necessarily result in committing of the crime. What causes a person to commit a crime is different from what he has learnt from his association with others. His learning does help him to devise, design, manage, manipulate and execute crimes.

Intelligence and Nexus Crimes

The overpowering effect of push and pull factors in committing nexus crimes indicate that if the pull factor overpowers the push factors then crime is inevitable. In that case, the question arises: "What is the role of intelligence if pull factors overpower push factors. No doubt, intelligence is the chief determinant of human behaviour and it is so in pull-push factor interaction as well. When intelligent people commit nexus crimes or any other crimes, they commit them intelligently. This does not mean that a superior intelligence will not detect the crime which is committed intelligently. Nexus criminality means the establishment of nexus with many people, agencies, organizations and institutions. Necessarily, they are intelligent people and that is how they can come up in life. If that is so, intelligence plays an important role in nexus crimes.

Animals do not and can not commit crimes. For they do not know the laws. They can not make distinctions between right and wrong. Man commits crimes for, he is intelligent. Nexus criminals are intelligent people. There was a time when scientists thought that criminals were not intelligent and criminal activities did not require intellectual programming and execution. This belief no longer holds good as many of the organized crimes like terrorist abductions, hijackings, murders, etc., or white collar crimes like bank frauds, forgeries, embezzlements, etc, or nexus crimes like enforcement criminality, corruption-money fixing, etc, require extensive conceptualization, preparation, planning, execution and escape. The more intelligent a person is, the more capable he is of committing crimes. In nexus crimes, conceptualization, concentration, compre-hension, memory, critical faculty, judgement, etc, play an important role. Intelligence is required to adapt to changing conditions, to inspire and lead others and to understand many aspects of criminal behaviour in the commission of nexus crimes.

Edwin H. Sutherland further says that criminal behaviour is learnt in interaction with other persons in a process of communication. In reality this is not so. What man does is to understand criminal behaviour through his interaction with other people in a process of communication. Later, he adopts intelligent strategies and thus he modifies his learning. He is not blindly repeating what he has learnt through his interaction. In pure science, a man can learn a theory and apply it to solve the problems. Even there, intelligence plays a role. In criminal activities there is no blind execution of crimes as they are learnt. In nexus crimes, blind execution is not possible.

Role of Intelligence in Fighting Push/Pull Factors

Everybody is intelligent and the intelligence level varies only in degrees. Everyone commits crimes if crime is considered as a mere violation of laws. Laws can be social, cultural, ethical, penal, institutional, etc. What type of crimes a man will commit depends upon many factors. A man in a particular social and cultural milieu will commit crimes which he can in that milieu. The PFs (Push Factors) are important here. A man fights against the PFs by his pfs (Pull Factors). In that fight too, the intelligence has a decisive role. For example:

In a purchase, the nexus is operating for kickbacks. The PFs are very strong and the pfs are weaker. Naturally and necessarily, a nexus crime comes into being. Then the intelligence plays its role and decides the how and the modes of committing the crime - the strategies and methods to escape detection. Intelligence finds out the favourable and unfavourable aspects in the commission of crime and of the escape from it.

Biologically Inherited Traits and Nexus Crimes

Studies on identical twins by the German psychiatrist, Johannes Lange proved that criminality was inherited. His theory is a rejected one today. Nexus crimes are new arrivals and precisely therefore the heredity theories are of no use. Nexus crimes are the crimes committed by two or more people and therefore to have the same heredity for all the nexus partners is just impossible. Take, for instance, the police-politician-businessman nexus or the police-criminal nexus. How can they have the same criminal heredity? Likewise, the XYY chromosomal abnormality explanations of criminal behaviour is of no relevance in the study of nexus criminals. No one has ever conducted any researches on the chromosomal abnormality of the policemen, politicians, businessmen, criminals taken together. In some cases, the politician may be a businessman and also a criminal. A policeman may be a politician as well as a criminal. How can we say that they have inherited nexus criminality? If at all chromosomal abnormality is detected in the policeman - in the businessman - in the criminal, how can we link it to nexus crimes? Human cytogenetics and vague criminological implications of chromosomal abnormality in criminal behaviour can not explain the etiology of nexus crimes.

Body Type Theories and Nexus Crimes

Ernst Kretschmer's body type approaches and his identification of asthenic, athletic and pyknic types have nothing to do with nexus crimes. Similarly William H. Sheldon's classification of ectomorph, endomorph and mesomorph, etc, too have nothing much to do with nexus crimes. The nexus partners are seen to be having different body types and the physique of the nexus partners has nothing to do with the commission of nexus crimes. People with all types of physiques commit nexus crimes.

As far as the nexus crimes in police are concerned, the physique of policeman/officer may be robust and firm whereas the physique of the nexus partners may not be like the physique of the policeman.

Guilt Feelings and Self Devaluation

In nexus crimes, more than one person is involved. The nexus partners should have the same objectives and therefore any theory which explains criminal behaviour from an individualistic point of view may be of no relevance. Hence, biologically inherited or subsequently developed physical abilities or deficiencies can not cause nexus criminality. Some nexus criminals have been noticed to be suffering from guilt feelings and apprehensions of punishment. Hungry for position, status, money, power and authority, some police officers commit atrocities on human beings after a nexus understanding with vested interests. Unfortunately, these clandestine and nexus affairs create distressing conflicts, feelings of guilt and apprehensiveness that they will somehow be caught and punished for their nexus behaviour. Some such people may develop anxiety reactions. Those who have a fairly strong conscience/ superego development by socialization are likely to experience severe guilt and self-devaluation. Inadequate policization may mitigate the intensity of the guilt feelings and self-devaluation. Some nexus criminals find it extremely difficult to tolerate the self-devaluation resulting from their failure to live up to their ethical views and very high opinion of themselves. This happens in the case of people who have a very strong superego. A high ranking police officer committed suicide as he could not think of tolerating his devaluation. It so happened that he was involved in a nexus which operated in connection with the construction of a stadium. This happened to be detected and it was alleged that a group of officers in the nexus had misappropriated a lot of cement iron rods and wealth. There came a situation that a vigilance probe was likely to be ordered. Knowing this, he committed suicide and that was what his kith and kin told about his premature death to people. Some other nexus criminals justify their actions by projecting their immoral desires to others who are making attempts to take advantages of them. False T.A. claims, misuse of government vehicles, manipulation of records are often done only after reaching a nexus understanding.

Some nexus criminals are seen to be exhibiting paranoid symptoms, this may be due to socialization or/ and policization. It is not uncommon for such individuals who commit nexus crimes to become suspicious of others' behaviour and to come to the conclusion that others too are nexus criminals.

Nexus criminals are usually prominent people and they want people's approval, appreciation and admiration for what they do. They do not want any one to know of their nexus involvement. They want to maintain their illusion of a respected man before the people. It is nothing but a show-window display. If they are psychopaths - i.e., people having no guilt feelings - they may not show any anxiety at all.

Nexus Personality

No doubt, the nexus criminals do have many behaviour traits in common. It may not be possible to specifically pinpoint some personality traits which may be characteristic only of nexus criminals or which can be used to predict their behavioural patterns. Nexus criminals are generally found to be intelligent, efficient, energetic, enthusiastic and able to manipulate matters and records. Many nexus criminals openly narrate their nexus activities - and are found willing to narrate them if they do not face any threats. Apparently, the first involvement in the commission of nexus crimes is of very great significance to the individuals who later becomes nexus criminals in every sense. They are found to be sensitive to criticisms and react to failures with a marked feeling of hurt. They rebel against conventional morality. They have a feeling that they can achieve many things in life if they stick to their nexus dealings. Some of them have a feeling of security, adequacy and self-esteem when they involved in the commission of nexus crimes. Nexus criminality is often connected with generation of income in many cases. Precisely, therefore, the nexus criminals feel important and affluent. If their family members, especially their wives, encourage it then it becomes an incentive for them. The wives of such nexus criminals suffer from personality weaknesses. If such nexus criminals hold positions where they can not make nexus income, then their wives are found to belittle them and implore them to strive to prove their efficiency. The comments made by such wives on their incapability irritate them and they take to drinks or drugs to escape themselves from the home atmosphere. Some make attempts to come back to a post which ensures nexus advantages. Some may even take long leave and bribe the forces which may extend a helping hand to come to occupy a post which offers nexus satisfaction.

Can we think of a nexus behavioural therapy? Psychologists admit that maladaptive behaviour, having been learnt, can be modified or unlearnt. Reconditioning or counter-conditioning must be provided to nexus criminals to become law abiding, ethical and honest. No researches have been conducted in this area and therefore, the issue calls for further researches.

Reference

Reckless Walter C. and Simon Dinitz, 1967, Pioneering with Self Concept as a Vulnerability Factor in Delinquency, *Journal of Criminal Law, Criminology and Police Science,* 58 (December).

8

NEXUS CRIMES : PUSH-PULL FACTORS OF CAUSATION

In the previous chapter the Push-Pull theory of crime causation has been introduced and discussed in some detail. 'Push' in dictionary means 'to urge to some action or course' and 'Pull' means 'to take hold of and cause to move toward or after oneself or itself'. The questions here are: (1) 'What are the Push Factors in *nexus crimes*?' and (2) 'What are the Pull Factors in *nexus crimes*?' Why do some people commit crimes? - Commit nexus crimes?

The answers to the above questions will require an understanding of the Push and Pull factors of crime causation. Criminologists admit that the heredity influences the determination of psychological traits in men and provides the potentialities for the development of psychological traits. Today nexus crimes in general are considered as a social problem destroying democracy in India. The existing penal laws enacted in 1860 have proved to be totally ineffective in dealing with nexus criminals. Addiction to nexus crimes and excessive involvement of nexus criminals in the commission of crimes are seen in everyday newspapers and electronic media. No realistic estimate of nexus criminals is available now. Nexus criminals are found to be psychologically dependant on the commission of nexus crimes. They are like alcoholics and drug addicts.

Involvement in nexus criminality may be due to many factors and to enumerate a few, it can be:

(1) to counter financial problems and difficulties;

(2) to please people in authority;

(3) to remain in a desired post;

(4) to feel important;

(5) to have self-esteem etc.

No doubt, involvement in nexus crimes and ensuring of money, position, status and contacts, etc., lead to feelings of adequacy, relief from worries, self importance, etc. Involvement in nexus crimes is thus an ego booster for some and a source of pleasure for others particularly in a democratic set up. What about the psychological vulnerability? Is there a specific 'nexus personality'– a type of personality which predisposes a person to become a nexus criminal?

Push Factors in Nexus Criminals

Nexus criminals have many *push factors* in common. They have unrealistically high levels of aspiration, i.e., they want to become secure in life, economically and otherwise. Typically, they expect a good deal of praise, appreciation, status, position, etc. In police, they want to enjoy power and authority. By the time, a nexus police officer comes to the attention of the people and media, he often shows a number of criminal characteristics such as a tendency to violate laws for his favour - rebel against the moral values and a lack of responsibility as a policeman/officer. Generally, they try to imitate their superiors and associates in committing nexus crimes. They also invent new methods. Sometimes the superiors provide a highly undesirable model and some of them show a tolerating or even encouraging attitude for nexus crimes. This is seen particularly in corruption-money fixing and corruption-money splitting. The work atmosphere may be contaminated with nexus dealings. Almost inevitably a nexus partner has problems in understanding what is expected of him in law enforcement. A potential nexus partner learns that with the aid of nexus involvement, he can achieve many things which he cannot otherwise. By involving himself in nexus criminality, he achieves gratifying feelings of adequacy and self-esteem.

Nexus crimes have become a part of our administrative culture. Most of the policemen/officers are accustomed to seeing their colleagues, subordinates, associates, superiors involving themselves in such crimes. In short our administrative culture is blamed/seen to have become dependent on nexus crimes of various descriptions. They act as lubricants for efficiency and effectiveness of the nexus.

New entrants to police department/any other departments are introduced to nexus criminality by those who work with them. One may observe a nexus culture in such work-environment. Often, they are introduced by their best associates in the work-environment–and they are doubtlessly nexus partners in the commission of crimes. The new entrants thus enjoy nexus benefits and advantages. In the initial stages, they may experience guilt feelings, anxiety, etc., depending upon their socialization, policization and formation of conscience. If they continue to persist in their nexus dealings, some become immune to guilt feelings and anxieties. They are found to suffer from personality deficiencies which predispose them to nexus criminality. Their ability to evade reality by way of a fight into nexus crime-induced fantasy is empowered. Continuing our study on what are the push factors in nexus criminals we see that.

Push Factors

Human Drives

Drives are in every individual and they motivate people to behave in a particular way. Like drives, there are incentives which motivate people to behave in a specific way. A person may become a nexus partner just to earn an incentive or to establish his importance in the professional field. Biologists believe that a man has certain drives which make him to behave in a particular way and they call them instincts. According to them, all instincts are inherited and therefore biological in nature. Psychologists do not accept this view of the biologists and argue that instincts are not biological, rather are psycho-physical. Human drives work as push factors to the commission of any crimes including nexus crimes. Human drives motivate people and every motive has 'need, means and goal'. A goal oriented behaviour is a motivated behaviour. In nexus crimes (all crimes), we may see the connection between 'needs means and goals'. The need may be the nexus partnership and the goal may be the actualization of the need. The motivated (Push Factors) behaviour persists until the goal is reached and for this a nexus criminal adopts several means. He varies his behaviour according to circumstances. Since man's behaviour is the expression of his intelligence, the more intelligent a nexus criminal (any criminal here), the better he is for the purpose of actualizing the need or the goal.

Intelligence

Intelligence is considered to be a push factor. One can commit nexus crimes - the nexus crimes have the characteristics of organized criminality, white collar crimes and enforcement criminality as far as the police are concerned - only if he is intelligent. For, nexus crimes require extensive conceptualization, preparation, planning and execution. Manipulating records, concocting evidence, executing the nexus plans of politicians/criminals, etc, necessitate a lot of intelligent strategies. There is a possibility of detection of one's involvement in nexus crimes. Intelligence of a person works as a push factor in so far as he is able to manage and manipulate his nexus involvement to his advantage without being detected.

Intellectualization: A Push Factor

Intellectualization is another push factor in criminality. A nexus criminal (any criminal) may reduce his guilt feelings over unethical behaviour by emphasizing the subcultural relativity of morality and immorality. He may content himself by saying: "The director general of police involves himself in nexus crimes"; or "How can I live with the salary I get?" Such intellectualizations reduce guilt feelings in him. The less the guilt feelings, the more will be the force of that push factor. Many convicted persons in jails take recourse to such intellectualization for their criminal activities. Similarly, many policeman/officers intellectualize their misconducts including nexus involvement.

Rationalization: A Push Factor

Rationalization is seen to be another push factor in nexus crimes. A normal man with an upright conscience knows that crime is an immoral act and so does a policeman/officer when he commits a nexus crime. It being so, he may rationalize, i.e., attempt to prove that his crime is rational, justifiable and worthy of approval by all. His act certainly helps him to soften his difficulties. A policeman beats a man after a nexus understanding with the victim of offence. Here, he sees the torture of the crime-doer not as a human right violation, but as a noble and just duty. People offer corruption-money for manhandling offenders. The rationalization thus works as a push factor and the corruption money there becomes an incentive.

Insecurity

Insecurity feelings can be push factors. Policemen/officers suffer from a lot of insecurity feelings. At any time a disciplinary action may fall on them. They may be attacked by unprincipled men and terrorists. They may be placed under suspension and thus there exists insecurity. Why do you commit nexus crimes? - the answer to this question by nexus criminals is that they want to make their life more secure. If at all they are caught for their nexus involvement they have nothing to worry if they have sufficient money which nexus crimes can ensure for them. The need for security develops with and is closely related to the need or anxiety.

Identification

Identification is the increasing feeling of worth by identifying self with some person, 'isms' or institutions of enviably illustrious standing. A policeman/officer may compare his position to others similarly placed. The society and people evaluate a policeman/officer in terms of his group affiliation/identification. For example, if many deputy superintendents have motor cars, any deputy superintendent of police may be evaluated in terms of his group affiliation. Resultingly, a deputy superintendent of police sees himself in the light of such luxuries. He may have fantasy identification as well. But how to have the actualization? He can opt for nexus advantages.

People want to achieve many things–namely, name, fame, wealth, authority, position, status and what not? An achievement can come only after great efforts. Many are not prepared to do hard work. They want to get many things through short cuts and in quick time. Reaching a goal through hard work is painful and laborious. Many obstacles may block the progress. Nexus crime dealings can take many to their desired destination without any difficulty. A police officer gets regularly a kickback from bootleggers just for participating in the nexus business.

Emotions

Emotions play an energizing role in behaviour. Commission of nexus crimes is only a means to an end, the end being accumulation of wealth, status, position, authority, power, good will, etc. For example, a nexus partner (here, a policeman/officer) may employ torture on a suspect as a result of a nexus understanding. Fear, anger and anxiety may be emotions. Some police functionaries have fear and anxiety when they deal with powerful politicians and such people will be prepared to enter into any sort of nexus understanding. Anger and hostility are aroused by barriers blocking one's need for gratification. The nexus criminal wants to reach his goal, but obstacles may come in between. He may then attack the obstacles directly and make attempts to remove the barriers. Many nexus criminals have been found to be suffering from excessive anxiety which is aroused by a threat to the adequacy or worth of the self. They experience psychic pain due to the anxiety they have - which operates as a potent driving force towards maintaining the nexus partnership.

Pleasure

Pleasure drives some to enter into nexus dealings. A policeman/officer may be spurred on by hopes of recognition and acceptance. If nexus crimes are helpful for the actualization of his hopes, then he may accede to them. The old hedonistic doctrine that pleasure and pain are important in the commission of any sorts of crimes (In fact, the Indian Penal Code was drafted under the influence of this pleasure - pain theory) may be applicable in the case of committing nexus crimes.

Lack of Ethical and Moral Development

The most outstanding characteristics of a nexus criminal, I find, is a marked lack of ethical and moral development. A nexus policeman/officer may show that he is loyal/very loyal to his nexus partners. But, my researches confirm that nexus criminal maintains no real loyalty to any person. They are found to be unprincipled businessmen, crooked politicians, selfish policemen, and so on. Their inability to understand, acknowledge and accept moral values itself may work as a push factor in their nexus involvement.

A nexus policeman/officer is rewarded whenever he does something towards the actualization of the nexus goals. If a policeman/officer is not prepared to render his services to the nexus criminals, then he is punished. Many policemen/officers are not prepared to suffer the pain associated with the non-cooperation. They weigh the advantages and disadvantages. If advantages are more, then they establish a nexus partnership. They thus become approved members of the nexus groups with which they identify themselves.

Police officers like others want to have feelings of adequacy and social approval. They feel that they are important people and they command respect from people. Usually, they judge their personal and official worth in terms of the values and standards of those working around them. Officers of the Indian police service compare themselves with others in the same service and rank. No constable compares his worth and value with a deputy superintendent of police or with a deputy inspector general of police. They follow the principle - comparables only can be compared. On doing so they may feel relative deprivation and they make all compensatory defence mechanisms to get out of their relative deprivation.

Nexus involvement is thus a compensatory defence mechanism which may be considered as a push factor.

Compensation

Compensation, psychologists describe as an ego defence mechanism which covers up the weakness by emphasizing desirable traits or making up for frustration in one area by overgratification on another. Many policemen/officers working in armed reserve camps/armed batallions have been found to be complaining about their ill-fate. According to them, they suffer from all disadvantages of police and are not enjoying the advantages of the policemen/officers who work at the cutting edge level or in the general executive branch. They point out their inability to go for income generating strategies to which nexus crimes too may be included.

Compensatory reactions may be to the positive or to the negative directions. Nexus involvement, no doubt, is to the negative. The poor police officer by nexus partnership can become rich, the rich police officer can become richer. Likewise, the powerless to powerful and the less powerful to more powerful. Certainly, the nexus compensatory reactions are not desirable ones, yet they are resorted to. Those who resort to such compensatory reactions compare themselves with others and measure their worth, value and importance and the same of others similarly placed by status, achievements, accomplishments, possessions, richness, luxuries, etc. Such values and considerations lead to the development of strong psychological push factors for achieving superior fortunes and nexus advantages.

Ultimately and always such nexus compensatory reactions result in grave antisocial activities and crimes.

Fulfillment of one's strivings motivate many towards nexus crimes. Depending upon one's capacities, values, desires, ambitions, life situations, etc, he may fulfil his strivings. A police officer wanted to own a new car. He entered into a nexus understanding with gold smugglers where he, in police uniform, drove a car containing smuggled gold coins and biscuits. After reaching the smuggler's destination, he drove the same car to his house. Thus, he got the car in exchange of his services rendered while smuggling gold. By nexus involvement, some policemen/officers get a satisfaction of self-enhancement, self-actualization, self-fulfillment. On talking to policemen/officers who were known for their nexus dealings from concotion of evidence in criminal cases to nexus conspiracy to the sale of illicit liquors it is found that each one has the same problem - the same push factors working in varying intensities. Behind the nexus involvement, each person was found to be asking the same question: "Who am I really? He tries to answer his question and finds out means and methods to become somebody enjoying more pleasure luxuries, status, power, authority, acceptance, etc, and ultimately they want to become somebody who is not himself. The actualization strivings make them to commit nexus crimes and thereby to achieve all or many of their desires within no time by easy and short cut methods.

Push factors are drive forces which may lead to homeostatic disturbances if they do not reach their actualization. These drives sometimes involve reasoning, learning and activities and are necessary to restore the mental equilibrium. For this some people have recourse to criminal activities including nexus involvement. When money, status, position, etc, are desired, they may resort to illicit activities as well. It has been found that psychological needs operate even on relatively unconscious levels. In such situations too, one may rationalize his behaviours.

Nexus crimes and involvement in their commission doubtlessly, are in conflict with people's ethical attitude. Nevertheless some people commit them after seeing the success of others who engage in committing the same. This prompts them to involve in nexus activities with little or no conscience prick. If that happens, it is an indication that there was inadequate socialization, conscience formation and policization. They experience little or no conflict when they commit antisocial acts. A good number of nexus criminals may be included in this category. Adequate conscience formation may result in conscience prick and they may find it extremely difficult to justify their acts. They may develop fear which may lead to feelings of inadequacy, sensitivity to criticisms and exhibition of worries.

Existentialism, Democracy, Policing and Nexus Crimes

Existentialism has caused disruption in the value system even to the extent of the loss of traditional values and beliefs. The existential philosophers have emphasized the breakdown of traditional values. After India became independent, many democratic values came into being. Many people became important and the police had to take into account their existence. For example, the politicians became very powerful, they were supported by businessmen and other affluent people. Thus power and money started exercising their powers on police authority. Vested interests wanted to manage and manipulate the police in the country. The vested interests found the pattern of values capable of giving meaning to their lives. This was not viewed as a matter of moral nihilism, for everyone was concerned with his advantages and benefits. The politician, the businessman, the bureaucrat, the policeman - all thought of themselves more than others. From the existential viewpoint, everyone made attempts to actualize his potentialities and well understood that they could make more and easily actualize their potentialities by joining with others who could help in reaching the destination. In a democracy, thus, the power (politicians), muscle (police) and money (businessman) joined together to convert many things to their favour.

The traditional values and ethical considerations were of no use to them - were found to be no longer adequate guides to 'good living'. As a result, the law enforcement officers with upright conscience suffered from value confusion and mental conflicts. The police had no option and therefore some of them made attempts to resolve their dilemma by yielding to the desires of the more powerful and affluent. They found some satisfaction in blind conformity to the views of the people who are powerful and affluent. Thus came into being a nexus subculture. Policemen/officers who had no upright conscience had no difficulty to establish the nexus with politicians and businessmen–with criminals and underworld gangsters, and so on. The values which a policeman/officer should have when he exercises his authority under law were changed thus and became the values which the nexuses had. The nexus partners found their own values and the policeman as a nexus partner accepted such new values.

Existentialism strongly emphasized the individual's responsibility to his fellow men. The existentialists viewed life as an obligation and the most important consideration was not at all what one hoped to get from it, but what one could contribute to. Politicians said it very loudly and there were many politicians who adhered to that philosophy. The policemen too proclaimed it as their philosophy. But, as days went by in Indian democracy, many politicians who had no values other than their self interests - came to the scene. They started to establish contacts with criminal businessmen. The politicians and the businessmen wanted to get police support and they found out that the best way to get police support was to establish a nexus with the police. Unscrupulous policemen who had to push factors for actualizing their vested interests established nexus with them. They did not think seriously about their obligations to society and other fellow men. Such people feel less fettered to their past values and are only concerned about their present and more so their future.

As a result of the nexus involvement, miscarriage of justice takes place. As a result, the police are denied social support for what they do. People look at them with suspicion and people keep away from them showing a positive hostility to them.

Nexus Crimes: A Means to an End

Many types of new crimes are emerging now. These include:

(1) Criminal pollution of air and water and food adulteration victimize the people. The law makers and law enforcers keep their eyes closed! If at all there exist some laws, the law enforcement agency may not be concerned with it. It may be due to nexus understanding or otherwise. If it is due to nexus understanding, then it becomes a nexus crime and the police become a partner to such nexus criminality. Nexus crime then becomes a means to an end - the end being some sort of advantage.

(2) Criminal electioneering is another area of nexus criminality - the nexus is between politicians and the police. It victimizes the general public by forbidding to exercise their democratic rights and privileges.

(3) Criminal invasion of privacy is yet another nexus crime.

(4) Cruelty to wild life becomes a fourth category of nexus criminality.

(5) Illegal selling offences - i.e., gambling, prostitution, sale of government service for bribe, kickbacks, etc are other forms of nexus crimes.

These are only a means to an end. Nexus crimes evoke support from those who benefit from the commission of such crimes. Do nexus crimes pay? Whether nexus crimes pay or not depends on what is gained or lost.

Once a sub-inspector of police came to this author. It was at a time when the general transfer of police officers was being given the final shape. He knew that the officer who was entrusted with preparing the list was closely known to me. He asked: "Sir, will you please put a word to the officer who prepares the transfer list" This author asked him: "Where are you now? Where do you want to go?" He said that he was working in the Computer Centre and he wanted to get a transfer to a police station.

This author further asked: "Why do you want to go to a police station?"

His answer was: "Sir, if you take me to a police station, I know how to make a good living".

The Meaning and Purpose of 'The Police Uniform'

The push factors were active in him and for satisfying these the nexus crimes were the only option as they paid well to a person who had an inclination to make an income out of it. Soon after the author took a class for sub-inspectors where he told them about the push factors in police work and about the fact that he had been in police department for the last twenty years and—

'Knew, the *person* in police uniform

Knew the *power* of the police uniform

Knew the *purpose* of police uniform

Knew the *promise* of police uniform", one of the officers asked him to explain more about the person in police uniform.

The 'person' in police uniform is and must not be an ordinary person. He is and must be a person with legal mindedness and morality consciousness.

Push Factors which motivate him to make a nexus income have no place or space in the person in police uniform. "I know the *person* in police uniform and you too must know the person in your uniform" the author repeatedly told them. For, the uniform has a power. It can be misused or abused for making an illicit income, to commit an enforcement crime or to involve in nexus activities. The uniform has a purpose, the purpose being administration of equal justice under law. Policemen/officers who wear the uniform without knowing the purpose of the uniform are influenced by the Push Factors which lead them to the commission of nexus crimes. Such policemen/ officers do not know the *promise* of the police uniform that it is a symbol of justice, equity and good conscience. The Person, Power, Purpose, and Promise of police uniform are something unique and the push factors in every policeman/officer, must be: "Sir, if you transfer me to a police station, I know how to witness the meaning of equal justice under law" - yes, that is the power, purpose and promise of the person in police uniform. The four 'Ps' in police are of great importance in understanding the meaning and worth of the police service.

Nexus Crimes—Types and Consequences

Nexus crimes are seldom prosecuted - rather usually 'pay' for those who perpetrate them. In police too, the same situation remains and therefore, the offenders do not regard themselves and generally are not regarded by many as criminals. Corruption-money splitting, corruption-money fixing, concoction of evidence after a nexus understanding with the accused/victim, manipulation of T.A. claims, purposeful causing of delay, informal arrests, misuse of departmental vehicles/stationary, pilfering of government supplies by policemen/officers, etc, are just a few among the nexus crimes. Sweet heart dealings, payoff, kickbacks, misappropriation of seized property, etc., may be other types of nexus crimes. How many cases are caught, investigated and adjudicated?

It is accepted by criminologists that a person's crime or restraint from crime is determined to some extent by the consequences he anticipates from it. In the case of nexus criminality, there exists no such anticipation. Expectations determine human conduct - this is a simple theory in psychology and therefore, an expectation of sure punishment will determine criminal/non-criminal behaviour. In the absence of an expectation of sure punishment, pro-criminal behaviour-especially that which ensures some advantages-will be repeated.

Authority - Abuse and Nexus Crimes

In every nexus crime, an abuse of authority/ misuse of power can be seen. Why does it take place? Is it due to the Push Factors or due to Pull Factors or both of them? The next chapter deals with Pull Factors and their interactions with Push Factors. Police can misuse their power and abuse their power, for, they enjoy a lot of discretion when they enforce law, investigate crimes or control crimes and criminals. It is just impossible to remove the discretionary powers of police. So long as the police have the discretion, nexus crimes may be in existence. No bureaucratic/judicial/legislative actions can take away police discretion. Whenever a policeman/officer senses the possibility that an action is going to be initiated against him, he prepares his defence sufficiently in advance to win his case.

The police know very well that they can only use their position and authority in case there are cases of criminal charges against a person hence they see to it that some criminal charges are brought whenever they want to abuse their power/misuse their authority. The policemen have a solidarity nexus within the department and therefore, it is virtually not possible to bring to the attention of the press or people or outsiders of the abuses of power/misuse of authority of one's colleagues, associates, subordinates or superiors. Nexus crimes will not come out of the police department. Everyone keeps silent about nexus crimes as they ensure benefits to each other. The policemen/officers will block the way to make things public. The resourcefulness and solidarity of police in concealing their nexus dealings are something incredible. The police may misuse their discretion, but no one comes to know about it. The police are, it is alleged, free to exercise discretion/judgement without proper guidelines. Canons of human decency can be violated by police for the nexus advantage. A superintendent of police once took action against some nexus criminals who worked under him. The sad effect was that the superintendent of police had to suffer persecution and victimization until at last he got a deputation to an organization where his associates, subordinates and superiors could not do anything much against him.

Push Factors and Abuse of Authority

Non-Enforcement of Laws

The push factors which activate a person to abuse his authority/misuse his powers are found to be the factors which motivate him to enter into nexus dealings. The police are always blamed for their discretionary and selective enforcement of laws. Why don't they enforce the laws against bootlegging effectively? They do not attend to the statutes prohibiting bootlegging. The push factors make them ignore such laws. Laws against various forms of gambling represent another case in point. The police adopt tolerance policies which allow such statutes to be violated with immunity - which allow the policemen to get nexus benefits–which allow the push factors to control police behaviour.

Differential Application of Laws

Why do the police have recourse to differential application of laws to different people? The poor gamblers from the villages are caught whereas the same in the affluent areas are tolerated. Why? It is for making some nexus income and the push factors are powerfully operating here. The police apprehend some, but not all, of the persons who violate the same laws. What begins as selective enforcement invariably degenerates into discretionary law enforcement, abuse of power, misuse of authority, commission of nexus crimes and what not? Illegitimate business and 'dangerous' organizations like prostitution, gambling, traffic in drugs, etc, are activities in which the police can keep their eyes shut if they have nexus advantages/benefits. According to many, they are victimless crimes. There is no one to act as a complainant in such victimless crimes and precisely therefore the police can have nexus understanding and involvement. The police department is placed under the administrative control of the director general of police who is supposed to 'police the police', but the control exercised by the director general of police in the use/misuse of police discretion is often minimal. In most cases, the real authority and power are vested with officers at lower ranks, especially with the station house officers.

Human Rights Violation by Police

One of the chronic complaints lodged against the police in India before 1993 was their gratuitous use of force, muscle power and torture. The allegation was repeatedly being made in the press, media, legislature, etc. After the national emergency, a number of cases in which police had tortured people to death came out in newspapers and an inquiry commission was appointed to inquire into police atrocities at the national level. After 1993 - i.e., the year in which the Protection of Human Rights Act was enacted-the number of police tortures has come up. Till then, cases of police torture were not known to the public. Since 1993, the cases of police torture have been brought out by human rights activists or others. While some of the recent charges are exaggerated or overexaggerated, there is little or no doubt that the police have utilized their muscle power in their dealings with citizens in which torture/violence clearly exceeded the demands of the situation. Now a days we hear allegations of nexus involvement of police with politicians, criminals, gangmen and *goondas,* criminal businessmen, unscrupulous fundamentalists, the affluent, and so on. Why do the people accuse the police of nexus crimes? The accusation was not heard of earlier and now it is heard more and more. Certainly, they cannot be dismissed as being baseless or groundless. No doubt, the police values have changed a lot. The push factors that activate the police now are different from what they were in the colonial past. The Pull Factors in the present day society make the police enter into nexus contacts. Nexus crimes are a reality and the criminologists identify them in all areas. While identifying nexus crimes in police service there is the need for epidemiological data to make a clear and detailed picture about the nexus crimes and police in India. Researches in this area give some information on the Pull Factors of nexus crimes.

Reference

Coleman James C., 1970, *Abnormal Psychology and Modern Life,* D.B. Taraporvala Sons & Co., Pvt. Ltd.

Random House College Dictionary (Revised Edition)

9

NEXUS CRIMES : PULL AND PUSH FACTORS

There is no push factor which does not have a pull factor. If I feel thirsty, there will be something which can and will quench my thirst. McDougall spoke extensively about instincts and accompanying emotions. According to him, the instincts are innate or inherited. These instincts are the Push Factors. McDougall himself says that: "An instinct is an innate or inherited psychophysical disposition which (determines) makes the organism to attend to certain kind of objects rather than others, to experience an emotional excitement of a particular quality upon perceiving such an object, and to act in regard to it in a particular manner or atleast to experience an impulse to such an action".

If that is the reality, they push the organism to some objects and the organism is pulled by Pull Factors. For example, acquisitiveness is an instinct, the accompanying emotion is a feeling of ownership. There must be something which can satisfy the emotions in man. Pugnacity (combat) is an instinct and anger is the accompanying emotion. There must be something to satisfy the emotion of anger. For a Push Factor in man, there will be one or more Pull Factors. In nexus criminality, what are the Pull Factors?

Pull Factors and Nexus Crimes

Criminological forces are in the environment - in the society where one lives. Look around you - amidst you and see the pull factors of criminality. One has to look inside and outside himself to learn the Push-Pull Factors of criminality including nexus crimes. Physical and socio-cultural environments are important. Indians are Indians because they are Indian citizens. Indian crimes are Indian crimes because India is the place from where such crimes emerge. The cartographic school examined the distribution of forms and rates of criminality among special areas. The school spoke about the regional variations in crime. The Pull Factors vary considerably in different parts of the world and precisely therefore there may be variations in the actualization of the Push Factors. William A. Bonger (1876-1940) argued that the capitalistic economic system by its very nature encourages egoism.

While studying the Pull Factors and nexus criminality, let us go to the sale of illicit alcohol. Alcohol is very much a part of our social world. Even in States where prohibition is enforced, one gets alcohol everywhere. How? The bootleggers bring it and distribute it. Dependency on alcohol may be a push factor and availability of alcohol may be a pull factor. In spite of the existence of prohibition on alcohol how can the availability of alcohol be ensured? It is obvious that this is being made possible through full support of police and other law enforcement functionaries to the bootlegger to manufacture, transport and sell alcohol in society. The bootlegger knows that the police will not allow it and therefore he makes attempts to establish a nexus with individual policemen/officers. If he becomes successful, then a nexus crime comes into being.

Various policemen/officers have confessed of their nexus involvement with bootleggers. Why did they involve themselves in nexus criminality? They suffered from inner stresses and tensions produced by several push factors. They wanted money, position, luxuries and status which they could not get easily and through short cuts. They experienced stresses and tension. All of them were found to take a tolerant attitude to nexus criminality fostered by the subculture in which they worked. "After all what is there" attitude was seen in them. The bootleggers are influential and affluent people and therefore 'let me go along with the current and not across the curent'–attitude could be seen in them. They could not find substitute means to resolve their stresses, conflicts and anxieties. The intensity of the tension and anxiety levels of the policemen/officers was directly in proportion to their nexus involvement.

Some policemen found it to be next to impossible to survive in the work environment without maintaining good group identification and *esprit de corps* and precisely therefore one's nexus involvement became necessary to express one's feelings of 'we-ness' in the work culture. For example, corruption-money splitting is an accepted subcultural practice in the work environment. How can one refuse to become a member in that work environment if he wants to work there? In a quiz programme, once a question was asked: "What does the tower of Pisa whisper to Big Ben?" The answer was: "If you have got time, I have got the inclination". Similarly a person who has strong push factors to nexus criminality tells pull factors that if you are there, I am with you. The Push and Pull factors combine together to commit nexus crimes. What is the role of the individual in the commission of nexus crimes? The horse has the thirst and there is water to drink. The horse does not drink it. Why? Likewise, a person has the push factors and there are pull factors, but he does not become a nexus criminal. Why? The answer is that the push factors are not strong enough to activate him to the pull factors. Here comes the role of human conscience which will be discussed later.

On Standing Alone Amidst Nexus Crime

In an age of nexus criminality and in a subculture of nexus crimes, the one who stands alone, is psychologically isolated by the group and he will find it extremely difficult to withstand the stress. In an age of nexus corruption, one may find it extremely difficult to live in that nexus environment without being and becoming corrupt. No doubt, there are people who have swimmed across the current. They had a strong ego strength and upright human conscience.

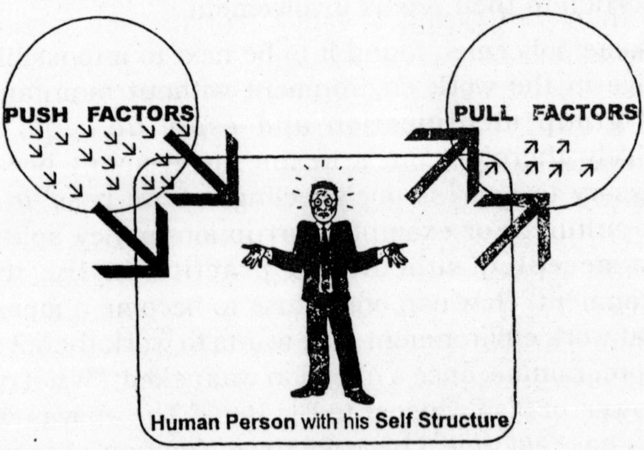

Development of Personality

A man's personality is not decided by push factors and pull factors alone. In a discussion on the development of human personality, scientists speak about the basic sources of personality development. They bring heredity and environment in their discussions. Today it is well accepted that an interaction between heredity and environments decides the personality of an individual. In other words, hereditory potentialities are developed in accordance to the appropriate environments given to him. If this argument is followed, then it goes without saying that nexus criminality will be developed in a person if nexus environment is provided to him. While a child develops into an adult person he goes through many experiences while help him distinguish himself from other people and things. An 'Iness', a 'self' or an 'ego' gets developed in him and this is besides and beyond his heredity and environment. This self structure or ego-structure becomes the integrating core of his personality and that functions as the reference point around which he takes decisions.

In the case of nexus criminals, there is something more than the Push and Pull Factors which make an individual to commit nexus crimes. That is the reason why some people exposed to the same environment (Pull Factors) do not become nexus criminals. A police officer once decided to resign from his service rather than becoming a partner to a nexus crime. Once, some criminal businessmen approached a police officer to establish a nexus partnership to carry on their illicit activities. He refused to become a partner. He was threatened and he knew that his life was in danger. Yet he fought against it and he was killed afterwards. It means that there is a force which works in man and it is beyond and besides the push and pull factors - which is beyond and besides the heredity and environment— which is beyond and besides the subculture and culture in the society. Whenever a man has to take a decision, he takes it in relation to his self.

WORKING OF THE PULL-PUSH FACTORS, EGO STRUCTURE, SOCIO-CULTURAL ENVIRONMENT AND NEXUS CRIMES

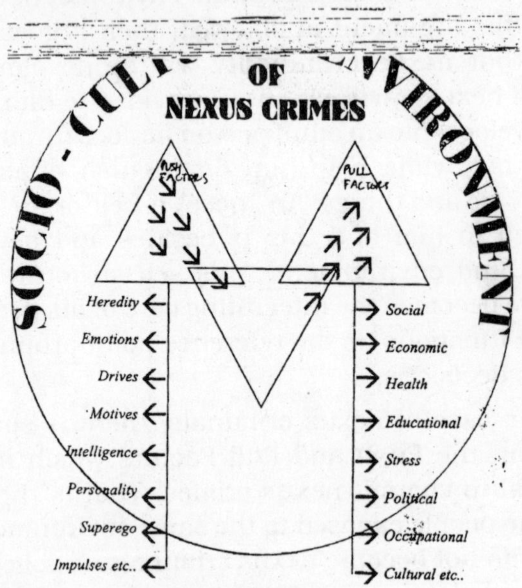

Ego Structure and Push/Pull Factors

The Push Factors, as we saw earlier can be anything from hereditary potentialities to the unconscious drives and they are operating within the individual. The Pull Factors may be anything from social pullers to professional/occupational pullers which work outside the individual. The push and pull factors are seen in a socio-cultural environment of crime (including nexus criminality).

As said earlier, every person has an "I'ness" or self structure with his own assumptions about himself and the world. He has assumptions about: the kind of person he really is; the kind of values he must have; the way things must take around him.

He decides things in accordance to his assumptions which guide his behaviour. A person behaves in a particular way because his ego structure allows him to behave in that way. If a person behaves in a way not allowed by his ego structure, then he may become a neurotic, a psychopath or one who suffers from personality disorders. Self structure gives a man self identity which in turn provides him a self-ideal. The principles in psycho-therapy are based on this principle that there is an ego in every person and it takes decisions amidst the Push and Pull Factors. A man is punished by criminal courts as he is found guilty. The Push-Pull Factors may mitigate the intensity of the punishment, but will never take away the liability of the criminal.

The self-structure, the Ego, the value assumptions serve as guides to one's behaviour. It works as inner controls. In fact, it is these value assumptions which we call the human conscience. The human conscience may prevent a person from committing an illegal or immoral act. It works in spite of the Push-Pull factors operating in and around a man. When the human conscience is not able to take a decision ethically, honestly and justly, then the act may be immoral or illegal.

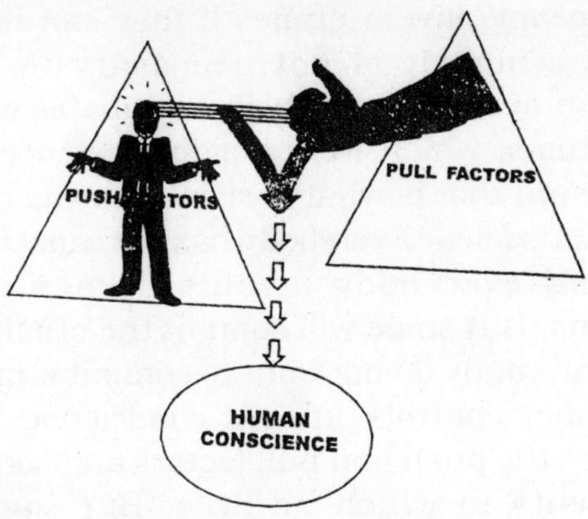

What is Nexus Crime?

The nexus crimes are just a *modus operandi* to achieve a goal (i.e., money, position, status etc) by a motivated individual (Push Factors) in a particular socio-cultural environment promoting nexus criminality (Pull Factors) without proper control exerted by the human conscience formed in an upright way. The individual's conscience is sufficient to direct his behaviour in accordance to human values. A policeman's/officer's human conscience is formed by socialization and policization. Hence, an uprightly formed human conscience by adequate socialization and policization becomes necessary to stop nexus criminality (all criminality) in police service. Nexus criminals in police are found to have developed a conscience which is inadequate. Without the development of proper inner controls to an adequate degree, the police will not get appreciation for anything they do to the people.

Pull Factors and Nexus Criminality

Whenever a policeman/officer involves in the commission of a nexus crime, he is fully aware that he is violating the law. Sutherland spoke about learning crimes, Tarde said about imitating crimes and it may be said that people invent crimes if they can not learn or imitate a crime. It is not necessary to teach the commission of crimes, for they are capable of inventing crimes. Crimes which were not in existence will come into being and that is what is seen in nexus criminality. Who invents crimes? Everybody has the capacity to invent crimes and everybody invents crimes of various descriptions. But some will commit the crimes invented by them, for, many do not want to commit crimes as they possess inner controls/upright conscience. Everybody experiences the push and pull factors and socio-cultural environments in which he lives. But some commit crimes, because people select the messages from the pull stimulations and the messages selected will corroborate their assumptions about themselves and their value system.

Self: The Determinant of Nexus Crimes

Amidst the Push and Pull factors, every individual developes (has) a selfhood. He sees, evaluates and responds to the pull factors in the light of his values - and he achieves on increasing sense of his own 'self-identity' and of self-direction. He is not a passive result of heredity and environment or of a mere interaction of push and pull factors. He is a self with a distinct identity, value system, direction and precisely therefore, it is this self - the human conscience which is the final determinant of his behaviour including nexus involvement.

A New Criminological Theory of Causation

Studies in nexus criminality and enforcement and criminality in police have helped to formulate a new theory on the etiology of crime and criminal behaviour. This theory may be applied to all sorts of crime including nexus crimes. The theory is called Push - Ego - Pull Factor theory which may be put as under—

1. Man commits crimes because he has no inner controls - or the controls outside him are very weak.
2. Criminal behaviour is learned (Sutherland). No. It is invented. If at all criminal behaviour is learnt, the learning is modified by further inventions and innovations.
3. Criminal behaviour is learned in interaction with other persons in a process of communication (Sutherland) and the invention of criminal behaviour does not necessarily require a process of communication.

No two crimes or the methods of committing them are ever identical. Every crime is a new crime and a new creation. People will invent crimes. Who made Eve to violate God's law that the fruits of the forbidden tree must not be eaten? Who taught her to do so? In the Bible, one sees the demenological instigation which is nothing but the Push Factors. Eve had no inner control and she ate the fruit and thereby violated the law. Every time a new law is enacted people find out ways and means to violate the laws. They invent *modus operandi* to commit crimes. Nexus crimes are said to be new crimes and people invented the varieties of nexus crimes and methods of committing them.

When Sutherland says that criminal behaviour is learnt, he does not speak anything about newer crimes. How can a person learn a crime which is not in existence? Nexus crimes are new crimes and there is no question of learning a new crime by association. New crimes are invented and people commit the invented crimes by their own methods. Give a law to a group of people and instruct them not to violate the law. After some days, it may be seen that they violate the law with their own invented methods. Learning, imitation, suggestion, identification, etc., may be mental processes by which people may study to commit crimes. Nevertheless, they are not the causes of criminal behaviour. The cause of criminal behaviour is the "I", the ego which is a strong determinant of human behaviour besides the push (heredity) and pull (environmental) factors. It is this 'I' which makes the people to commit crimes. In nexus crimes, in spite of many push and pull factors, the "I" can take a decision either to commit or not to commit crimes. If the 'I' takes a decision, it will be a decision to create a crime and then commit it.

Criminal behaviour is learnt in an interaction with other persons in a process of communication - says

Sutherland. No process of communication with people who commit crimes is necessary for an individual to involve himself in the commission of crimes. Hoarding, black marketing, share scam, pipe-money, drug sale, international drug trafficking, hijacking, terrorism, insurgency, political murder - and many such crimes are inventions of human intelligence where the role of learning is not much.

Man only can commit crimes; animals do not commit crimes. Hence intelligence is a *sine-qua-non* for the commission of crime. An intelligent man commits crimes because he has no inner control mechanism - no human conscience uprightly formed. Nexus crime like any other crimes is a creation of human intelligence. Today cyber crimes are committed and they are new creations of human intelligence. A question is often asked: "What is the creation in the commission of traditional crimes?" The answer is given by a policeman who investigates a crime. He says that in every crime - traditional and current-one may notice the creativity of human intelligence.

When crime is invented, it includes the techniques of committing crimes which are sometimes very complex and complicated and sometimes very simple. In nexus crimes, the techniques and *modus operandi* are important. If they are not intelligently created, the criminal is invariably caught and easily punished. Politicians create chaos, crimes, law and order situations and they plan them intelligently. The communal fanatics do the same thing and the creativity is shown in fundamentalists' activities which are criminal in nature.

Creativity is the function of the brain. The Stone Age cave man had this idea in him. Half a million years ago, the people had the notion of good and bad. The role of good and bad spirits was accepted as the cause of mental illness including crimes by the early writings of the Chinese, Egyptians, Hebrews and Greeks. In the Old Testament, the Satan who tempted Eve told an intelligent and easy way by which Eve could become like God. The Satan appeared in the form of a serpant and the *modus operandi* too was intelligent. The Stone Age man, probably thought that man committed bad things because he had the evil spirit in his head. By evil spirit, he, probably meant, evil intelligence which was used for evil creations - i.e., the crimes as we understand today. Trephining was a surgery performed by the Stone Age Man with crude stone instruments and he chipped away an area of the skull in the form of a circle. The opening was called Trephine and presumably it allowed the evil spirit (evil intelligence) to escape from the wrong doer. Researches showed trephined skulls of primitive men. Of course, researchers say that trephining was done to cure mental illnesses. Even today people believe the role of evil spirit in the causation of crime.

Role of Moral Force in Committing Crime

The Classical School of Criminology by Cesare Beccaria in Italy (1738-1794) and Jeremy Bentham in England (1748-1832) said that all men, criminals included, acted rationally and deliberately in order to avoid pain and encounter pleasure. Acting rationally meant, undoubtedly, the use of creative intelligence in the commission of crimes. Bentham and Beccaria asserted that a person who made a deliberate, rational and hedonistically oriented decision committed crimes. However, they did not speak anything about the role of human conscience in the commission of crimes. It was perhaps William Bonger who emphasized the role of moral force in the commission of crimes. He said that the social instincts of man were not developed owing to egoistic tendencies. He furhter said that the egoistic tendencies in reality weakened the moral force in man which ought to combat the inclination towards egoistic acts and therefore towards crimes which were forms of these acts. Criminals in general have weak moral conscience and it is seen very much in nexus criminals, naxalites, NOC racketeers, cheats, rapists, adulterators, terrorists and so on.

Creativeness and Crime

Every crime from causing simple hurt to terrorism is a new crime and there is some creativeness in every type of crimes. Creativeness in some crimes may be very visible while in others, it may not be visible at all. The intention of investigating a crime is to find out the creativity in a crime and the creativity may be seen in the design and methods adopted and the goals achieved. In nexus criminality it may be very difficult to understand the design or methods, etc. For, the nexus criminals apply their intelligence to create a pattern of nexus crimes.

Goddard's view that criminals were feeble minded was rejected long back. Embezzlers, abortionists, enforcement criminals, white collar offenders, and so on, exhibit higher intelligence than ordinary people in society. Every crime is a creation and creation presupposes creativeness which in turn presupposes intelligence. Once in a class consisting of policemen/officers, certain sections of the Indian Penal Code-1860 were shown and the officers asked how well they could violate the laws. From the evaluation of responses one learnt that they had designed and devised intelligent strategies to violate the laws. Their strategies consisted of creativeness which had:

(1) *Originality:* i.e., their responses contained novel ideas or at least statistically infrequent ones. They were far beyond imagination. In nexus crimes, one may observe originality in approach and execution.

(2) *Adaptability:* i.e., the strategies were found to be really good to commit crimes in Indian situation. Perhaps, the same strategies could not become successful in a situation prevailing in a foreign country. The creativeness had adaptability. The strategies would thus accomplish the goal - i.e., commission of crimes without being detected.

No one commits a crime with an intention to be caught. People think a lot and devise intelligent strategies to commit crimes and their strategies have creativeness. A creative crime-doer depends more on his intelligence and judgements. Nexus criminals are rated to be creative crime-doers. Their association with criminals, learning, contacts, etc, may help them to apply their creativeness in committing crimes. They are found to be effective communicators. They possess leadership qualities which help them to involve in nexus activities by keeping their subordinates on their side. They are found to mobilize resources for reaching their nexus destination. Nexus offenders are not easily affected by what is going on around them. They are able to think for themselves.

In police where the hierarchical control is intense and discipline is enforced strictly, intelligent nexus criminals show extreme submissiveness to their superiors. They show great respect to authority and their behaviour is found to be polished only at the surface levels.

Surrendering Self Identity to Group Identity in Nexus Crimes

Nexus crimes can never be committed by an individual in isolation. The nexus partners have to work jointly as they are mutually related. Everybody must know the purposes of every other person in the nexus family. Nexus crime is a group behaviour - a sort of criminal conspiracy which works amidst several pull factors. Two or more heads are involved and precisely therefore the creativeness too will be the result of group thinking and action. Every nexus partner shares his creativeness with other nexus partners and the outcome is the product of interaction of the nexus partners. The self-concept, i.e., the ego or human conscience - gets changed as a result of the nexus involvement in response to the expectations of the nexus partners. Whenever a police officer with an upright human conscience establishes nexus dealings with organized criminals/criminal syndicates, then necessarily his ego-concept gets changed in response to the expectations and demands of his nexus partners. The police officer then understands that much of his behaviour is to a large degree determined by forces outside him and beyond him. The Pull Factors become important here. The interaction between the push and pull factors is controlled by the Ego of an individual. As stated earlier, the Ego is the determinant of human behaviour when push and pull factors exert influence on man. A nexus policeman gives up his ego identity in exhange of advantages he derives from his nexus partnership. As a result, the nexus policeman may become richer and richer; may become the blue-eyed son of the ruling politicians; may continue to occupy lucrative positions, etc. In a nexus crime society, the satisfaction of the nexus partners requires collaboration and cooperation - not for law enforcement but for law violations.

A nexus policeman/officer loses a great deal of his autonomy - his right and authority to administer justice to people. He can not ask: "Who am I?" - rather he asks: "Who are we?" He surrenders his self-identity to the group identity. He ceases to be an autonomous law enforcement authority - rather converts himself to be the dependent of the nexus group. The nexus policeman gets a new and an unwanted identity as a nexus partner - an identity that is the logical and necessary consequence of his nexus involvement. Such a nexus identity is something that he probably does not wish to have.

Some policemen/officers are blamed by the press/media as the nexus men of the ruling political parties. The creativeness in them is said to be their contribution to remain in the nexus family of the politicians. Once a leading newspaper blamed certain police officers by naming them as the nexus partners of certain politicians. On observing their behaviour closely one could learn that the nexus identity assigned to them had an unsettling effect on them as it was not keeping them with their individuals' self concept. Many want to reap the nexus advantages, but do not want nexus identity. A police officer who enjoyed a lot of nexus advantages from a crime syndicate did not want to tell others that he was a nexus partner. Society rejects such nexus partners. One day the author asked a senior police officer: "Are you a friend of 'so and so?" (The 'so and so' being a notorious bootlegger). He became wild as he did not want to reveal his connection with the bootlegger. The mind of a police officer who has nexus dealings shows symptoms of unsettling. This is partly so because he thinks that he has a self identity which he likes to have - and partly because others in society perceive him as one possessing a nexus identity–an identity which the police officer does not want at all. On asking policemen/officers simple questions related to the nexus identity of other policemen/officers, most of them disclosed the ways others had nexus dealings and some of them went to the extent of enumerating the groups with whom certain policemen/officers had nexus transactions/affiliations. It thus shows that many people knew the nexus identity of other fellow policemen/officers.

Edwin H. Sutherland in his Differential Association Theory says that a person becomes delinquent because of an excess of definitions favourable to violation of law over definitions unfavourable to violation of law. In nexus criminality, a person is found to get involved in nexus dealings because he finds that it is more advantageous for him to do so and he finds out the means, methods and laws that may help him to do so. Creativeness in man helps him to identify excess of definitions favourable to the violation of law. The pull factors force him to exercise his creativeness for violating the laws and the push factors motivate him. The Ego factors make him take a decision.

Why do People Commit Crimes? - Nexus Crimes?

What is the cause of crime? The question was asked by the Biblical writer when he found Adam and Eve violated God's commands. Ever since, many people asked the same question and today scientists speak of the multiple-factor approach in criminology. The advocates of multiple-factor thinking suggest that the causes of criminality vary from individual to individual-from situation to situation-and there thinking is true to understand the causes of crime. The Push Factors are individual factors and Pull Factors are factors in situations or situational factors. In between the Push and Pull Factors there is a deciding factor which is the Ego Factor in an individual. The Ego is nothing but the human conscience uprightly formed.

Whenever a crime-doer arrives, the first step is usually a diagnosis of the problem. In doing so, one studies the push and pull factors - i.e., the biological, psychological, cultural, religious and sociological factors. For this, a case history is useful. A criminologist studies the nature of the crime, the personal history of the crime-doer, psychological assessment, medical examination, sociological factors, cultural background, the self-structure, conscience formation, superego, etc.

In every person, one sees the push factors. Outside him, the pull factors are seen these are the situational factors. There may have to be compromises between the two factors. For examples:

Push Factors	*Pull Factors*
1. The desire to make money through short cuts;	Financial difficulties, family needs, etc.;
2. The urge to occupy a sought after post;	Non-availability of many sought after posts in the service;
3. The wish to enjoy position and authority.	Competition to get power and authority.

Thus, on one side there may be the psychological pushers and on the other side, there exist the situational pullers. How to compromise? The human mind becomes restless. It makes attempts to resolve the tension through means and methods which are capable of solving the crisis. The creativeness comes into being - and it may be conscious or unconscious. The creativeness may be expressed either by violating the law or not by violating the law. The decision to violate or not to violate the law is taken on the basis of the values which an individual has. If one's conscience has values which do not allow him to violate the law, then he does not indulge in the nexus, otherwise, he does. The conscience becomes the decision maker and that is the reason why individuals are punished in crimes. The push-pull factors may mitigate the punishment, but will never take away the criminal responsibility. In the above example a man may solve the problem by becoming a nexus partner and it shows that he lacks an upright conscience rightly formed. The same principle is true in all sorts of crimes.

Police Conscience and Nexus Crimes

The push-pull factors in a given situation may be perceived by an individual as 'threats' to him. Here, his conscience has to work either against or in favour of the threat created by the push-pull factors. Two cases have been stated in context of people who have and do not have nexus dealings:

When Madhu Alexander opened the *tapal* on Monday morning in June, he found a letter from the Government. He opened the letter and learnt that he was appointed as deputy superintendent of police at Thumpencode. The most predominant push factor in him was to make some illegal income from there and the most prominent pull factor at Thumpencode was that it was a place where illegal *ganja* cultivators offered any amount to police officers who were willing to have nexus transactions. Now Madhu had to take a decision. The values in his conscience were such that he opted to become a nexus partner. He designed and devised means and methods for income generation through his nexus involvements.

On the same Monday morning, Wilson Mathew too received a letter from the Government and he was posted as deupty superintendent of police at Kottarammukk. The most predominant push factor in him was that it was a God given chance for him to make some money by permitting manufacture and sale of illicit liquor there and the most prominent pull factor there was that the bootleggers were prepared to do anything to please the police officers who had nexus dealings. Wilson had to take a decision. But the values in his conscience were such that he did not opt to have any sort of nexus transactions with bootleggers.

Thus there were two different kinds of decisions to the push-pull factors that had certain similarities. When Madhu decides to have nexus involvement, Wilson does not. For both of them, nexus involvement may bring advantages. Both had the same push-pull factors which operated in equal strength. Both of them thought about the push-pull factors and one took a decision not to establish nexus partnership. Here is the role of human conscience. The conscience leads them to conduct an objective analysis and to make plans to cope with the pressures exerted by the push-pull factors. The conscience protects one's self-concept or feeling of self-esteem. The conscience enables them to take a decision. The conscience has a protective function and the one who follows his conscience which is rightly formed feels happy when he behaves the way he does. In nexus crimes, people know that they are doing a wrong thing and this happens because his conscience works well. Conscience-prick disturbs one and it shows that he has guilt feelings.

Police has an immediate obligation to do what is right. To do the right thing, one must have a clean and unspoiled human conscience. Do the police have such a conscience? On asking this question a policeman was candid enough to say that he did not have one policeman, whereas a director general of police said that he did not think seriously about it as he did not get time to think on such issues. On his moral convictions, he had his personal morality and pragmatic standards.

"Do the right thing" - this is a universal principle accepted by the people all over the world from the beginning of humanity. This is the reason why the wrong-doers are punished everywhere. Policemen are there to catch hold of the wrong-doers and to bring them to justice. Precisely therefore the police conscience has this universal and eternal principle. This principle is and should be in the policeman's sense of obligation to do the right thing. The policeman must do his duty—no matter what the consequences are. Policemen moved by this conscience committedly perform their duties and at times they are killed or injured.

The question is: "In nexus involvement, do the policemen perform their duty as policemen?" A police officer recently said that the policing had become impossible now? He showed a newspaper reporting which stated that a group of men armed with dangerous weapons went to a police station to get back their men taken into custody by police in connection with some offences committed during an election to the local bodies like Panchayats and Municipalities. The aggressive people said that the people under police custody were innocent people and they were taken into custody by police as they were instructed by the politicians of the ruling front. In other words, the taking into custody of the innocent people by police was the result of a nexus understanding between the police and the politicians.

On being further asked about the current trend, he stated that the police could not function as they used to i.e. their traditional ways are questioned by the people. Formerly, the police used to get a list of people whom vested interests wished to be accused in crime. This nexus transaction is objected to by the people and policing with a conscience becomes the duty of the police. In other words, the police conscience must be the deciding factor whatever may be the push-pull factors.

Immanuel Kant spoke about the moral imperative, a sense of obligation to do what is right. The moral imperative is an essential part of human conscience - of human reasoning. When the push-pull factors operate, the human conscience which is uprightly formed must take a decision and when the policeman does so, there is no scope for the commission of nexus crimes.

Cognition is a general term that is used by psychologists to refer to such processes as perception, concept formation, reasoning and judging. Psychologists have proved through extensive researches that the ideas of justice are inculcated to the children before the ages of seven or eight. They have further proved that the ideas of justice go deep into their mind irrespective of mitigating circumstances. Hence the idea that a crime is a crime, no matter who commits it - no matter what the circumstances are gets imprinted. The circumstances can mitigate, perhaps, only the quantum of punishment awarded to the crime doer. This idea in children guides them throughout their lives. Policization may inculcate new values to people who join the police. Police is said to be a disciplined service. Studies on policemen/officers reveal that extreme strictness/control can not prevent misconducts among them unless they possess an upright conscience. The fact that nexus crimes take place in police means that the rigid and strict disciplinary atmosphere has no effect upon nexus offenders. Strict disciplinary control may cause fear of punishment among the policemen - and consequently, they become hostile to their authorities. It does not cause the formation of an upright police conscience. That may be one reason why the police employ third degree methods, concoct evidence, manipulate records and involve in nexus criminality. The policeman's misbehaviour may also be the result of the treatment they receive from their superiors. Senior officials have been heard justifying crude disciplinary punishments on policemen on the grounds that they were needed to teach them proper behaviour. The fact that the policemen misbehave in spite of rigid disciplinary controls shows the fallaciousness of such an argument. The superiors and supervisors must, instead, provide opportunities for the formation of an upright conscience among their subordinates. For this, they must set examples. A nexus superior/supervisor can not inculcate such finer values in morality and he may fail to form an upright police conscience among his subordinates. Punishments and frequent initiation of disciplinary actions are sometimes justified on the ground that they serve as deterrents to policemen.

On further analysing it was found that punishments and disciplinary actions have got a deterrent effect only when the subordinates understand and appreciate the justness in action. The superiors' disciplinary actions characterized by an upright conscience and a high degree of justness do help to reduce misconducts. Any nexus understanding by the disciplinary authority and inquiry authority can not help to reduce misconducts. A nexus punishment or an unjust disciplinary action may bring about what experimental psychologists call 'avoidance behaviour' - i.e., avoiding certain misconducts for the time being. The illegally punished policeman regards his superiors with hostility and aggressiveness creaps within him. Excessive punitive attitudes of the superiors aggravate misbehaviour rather than discourage it and further more, the unjustly punished policemen/ officers display to others the same attitudes of hostility and aggression expressed toward them.

Inadequate policization may cause mental conflicts in policemen who have adequate socialization and conscience formation. Law enforcement with a human conscience is a healthy approach while policing the society. Nexus partners lack such a human conscience and as a result, their activities become nexus prone. Men of goodwill do not commit crimes–this is a belief among the people and it follows that men of upright conscience do not tolerate criminal behaviour. Nexus crime is a crime and a policeman can not become a nexus partner if he is a man of goodwill and an upright human conscience. There are policemen/officers who are "underachievers'- who want status, position, money, authority, power etc., but can not achieve them in their profession as law enforcement officials. Those who suffer from a feeling of "underachievement" make several attempts to make as much as they could by several means - fair and foul. Some of them get involved in nexus criminality and they suffer from a lack of an upright conscience. After retirement from police service they feel dissatisfied with their material achievements in spite of their nexus involvements during their service. Thus policing with a conscience is far more satisfying than policing without a conscience. The conscience is the deciding power in a person when he is put between the push and pull factors. A clean-unspoiled conscience is a gift and that is what the little child showed when he saw the King in nakedness. The Malayalam poem in English script is reproduced to show how does a clean - unspoiled-human conscience works

"Rajav Nagnananenna Sathyam,

Rajabhakthanmar Nadungumarutchathil,

Nale Vilichuparayanamennunnikku,

undavatteyavanu Karuthum Sakthiyum"

The story goes as follows. A king once made a proclamation that he would go through the street to see his people and he would be in full royal dress with all ornaments. People who wanted to show their faces came to the street. The King went through the street in nakedness and all the people praised the king and they spoke highly about the royal dress. A child who saw the nakedness of the King uttered loudly: "The King is naked". And that was the truth and only a child could say so. For he made the utterance after taking a decision from his clean and unspoiled conscience. The policemen who possess such a clean and unspoiled conscience only can take just and fair decisions when they are in between the push and pull factors. In such a situation, there will not be any crimes including nexus crimes by policemen/officers.

10

NEXUS CRIMES : POLICE CONSCIENCE IN CONFLICT

An extract from the report of the Committee of Concerned Citizens (1997-2000) on police encounter is as follows:

"The committee has to regretfully point out that despite the Chief Minister's assurance to the Committee of Concerned Citizens that there would be no fake encounters in the State, the policy of extermination of individuals is being relentlessly and unabashedly pursued in utter disregard of law. Any one reading the stereotyped reports of encounters in daily newspapers can not fail to discern that there is something very sinister about these regular reports which have become part of the common lore of Telengana. The fact remains that the police which is the law enforcing agency of the State indulges in killing, plain and simple, even if it is euphemistically described as an encounter. There is little doubt that most of the encounters are no other than custodial and targetted killings. During the last decade, more than 1500 persons were killed in police encounters. An all time record of 275 was reached in 1998, the highest number in the decade. During the year 1999, more than 229 persons have been killed in the encounters. The Committee has been repeatedly highlighting this issue of encounters, precisely because it relates to extinguishing of human life and right to life by the Government itself - a Government which is expected to protect life and liberty under the Constitution - and for which no recompense is possible. Such killings have become part of the administrative practice of the State, consciously pursued and encouraged".

"Such fake encounters can no longer be considered as isolated aberrations or administrative miscalculations or termed as excesses or unintended transgressions of law by individual police personnel. They can only be perceived as the calculated and deliberate system response of the State which is adopting a policy of annihilation of individuals, unable to comprehend a complex problem which is the result of inequity and denial of justice.......The system of huge rewards or what is termed as price on the head is serving as an added incentive to the killings by police".

What is seen in the above report is that the police can not convince the people of their activities as right and justifiable. The people see nexus actions in all fake encounters - and the committee accuses the police and the Government by blaming that a military solution is no solution for a complex societal issue - that a policy of extermination, in the false belief that eliminating individuals will eliminate the movement, can solve the issue.

The report of the Committee of Concerned Citizens brings out the dilemmas faced by the police particularly when they face issues of similar nature. Their life presents them with many choices. They have no option but to take decisions and act upon them. The fake encounter cases and nexus operations are certainly provocative situations. One question in point is: "Are the policemen bound to obey the illegal orders of their superiors?" Police action must be based on legality - must be based on morality - must follow from an upright human conscience rightly formed. Any action done by police disrespecting the law, human rights and humanity is bad in itself. Fake encounter killings result not only in the death of other human beings, but also in the diminishment of the killers' integrity.

Decision Making in Police: Conflicting Situations

Policemen/officers take many decisions. Some decide to become nexus partners while others do not. Some are in real conflict with themselves when they are put under temptations to become or not to become nexus criminals. The policemen in conflicting situations have three options and they are: 1. Teleological, 2. Deontological and 3. Discerning.

Teleological Option

In Greek, Telos means *goal* or end and therefore teleogical centers around the goal or end. The policeman/officer in such conflicting situations takes a decision after looking at the end or goal. Commission of nexus crimes and thereby accumulating wealth or status can not become the end or goal of a police officer who has an upright conscience formed by adequate socialization during the initial stages and by policization during the subsequent periods of the development of his human personality.

Deontological Option

Deon in Greek means duty or obligation and therefore deontological approach makes a policeman/officer to see the basic values of human life such as justice, right, truth, etc. He knows fully well that he can not act violating the fundamental human values. He does his act according to his conscience and does not bother about the consequences, because he concentrates on his duty and obligation as a police officer. Commission of nexus crimes or killing people through fake encounters is not a policeman's/officer's duty or obligation.

Discerning Option

Blind obedunce to law is not what is expected from a dutiful policeman/officer. He must have responsible obedience. Therefore, the discerning approach in police combines human values and the wisdom of law in a particular situation. 'Nexus crimes are wrongs'–this is a value. What is the law on nexus crimes? The law is that nexus crimes, though not defined as such in penal statutes, are crimes in every sense. What is the concrete situation in which a policeman/officer commits nexus crimes? The situation is that the policeman/officer is in an advantageous position to make nexus benefits and advantages. Since the approach combines fundamental human values and the wisdom of law in a given situation, it recognizes the responsibility, dutifulness and complexities of police life. A movie showed a police officer employing third degree methods on a person to please a nexus partner in business. In the same film, the same police officer was seen committing atrocities on human beings for gaining nexus advantages. Anybody who saw the film would say that the police officer's act diminished/ destroyed the humanity of police profession. Thus nexus crimes had very bad social implications. They put the entire department in bad shape.

Conscience and Authority in Police Work

Police job demands mature responsibility. People in a democracy place a lot of trust on the mature responsibility of their police functionaries. Involvement in nexus crimes means that the officer does not have any respect to people's expectations. He is a man with no conscience. He has authority, but exercises it without a human conscience. Conscience, as understood is a word much used and abused in police subculture. The most unscrupulous policeman/officer may speak about his conscience to justify his otherwise illegal act. One is unclear of the word 'conscience' and what it means when police are often heard saying: "I have accepted corruption-money. But I have done it only when I did something to the party which offered me the money. I have a conscience and I do everything according to my conscience". But is it possible to convince yourself that you are doing a good thing when you accept corruption-money? The little voice inside one's mind tells him the right and wrong in his actions. The conscience is the inner policeman within a policeman. The conscience in a man is really the personal self in him. Conscience is a man's most secret core and he can not cheat his conscience.

Dimensions of Police Conscience

Earlier, we saw the role of socialization and policization in the formation of police conscience. The police conscience thus formed has three different dimensions. The first dimension of police conscience is the general sense of values which is the characteristic of all human beings. The mere fact that one is a police officer does not mean that he is devoid of human values. He is very much a human being and precisely therefore he knows fully well that he must do the good and shun away from evils. As a police officer, he must be just and not unjust when he enforces law. Since time immemorial people are in the quest of justice. There will not be any fight for getting justice if people are just and honest. The policeman has the responsibility to choose between just and unjust decisions - between good and evil. People's urge and uncontrollable desire to do the right thing and receive the same are reflected in their general sense of value. That is the only reason why people speak against the police when they see injustice done by them - when they see them involved in the commission of nexus crimes. After a nexus understanding with the director general of police, a superintendent of police initiated disciplinary action against a subordinate. He was placed under suspension. The people, policemen and the press resisted the unjust action thus and showed the general sense of value in human beings.

Human conscience has to find out the right course of action - not arbitrarily, but on the basis of sound values. He must probe into the truth. Investigation means a probe into for finding out the truth and crime investigation too means the same thing. Instead of an honest probe for finding out the truth, suppose, a police investigator, on the basis of a nexus understanding, harasses an individual, then people will not pardon him. In searching for truth, one may face several conflicts and the decision of an upright conscience is what is required in such situations. What are the scales which may help a police officer to arrive at a just, honest and true decision are ahead.

The third dimension of police conscience is the actual and concrete judgement which he makes pertaining to an issue at hand. After searching for truth, he takes a decision in specific issues. In nexus criminality, a police officer may be placed amidst many nexus temptations. He takes a decision and certainly, it is and it must be for not involving in nexus dealings. The dimensions of police conscience may be drawn as—

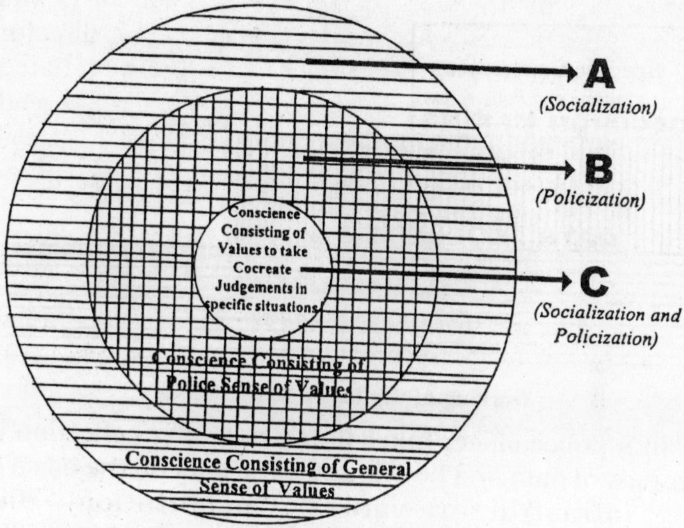

Police Coscience : Dimensions

In the above circle, 'A' represents the conscience formed by socialization. 'B' consists of values formed by policization. 'C' has the values formed from socialization and policization. The formation of conscience by inadequate policization may bring a defectively formed conscience–i.e., C - which will take decisions in concrete and specific situations. As pointed out earlier, the general conscience formed by adequate socialization will conflict with the police conscience formed by inadequate policization. The product, - i.e., the *specific conscience* ('C' in the above circle) will then take decisions which are unjust. In nexus criminals, it is seen that the specific conscience (C) is defective and that is the reason why he involves in nexus transactions without guilt feelings. The police conscience works in the following way.

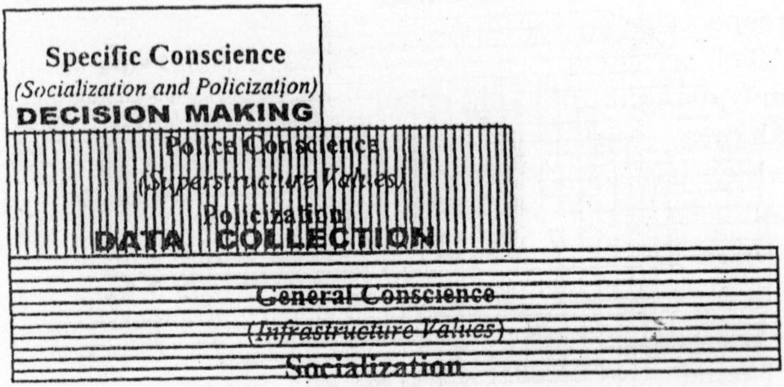

Working of the Police Conscience.

(i) A police officer takes a decision after collection of a variety of data and he evaluates the data on the basis of the infrastructure-values (socialization) and superstructure values (policization).

(ii) Values (socialization) and superstructure values (policization).

(iii) He applies his values and makes a decision in specific situations. "I follow my conscience"–a police officer says so. It means that his infrastructure is good and his decision is good. He has taken a decision after gathering sufficient data. The formation of his conscience is upright.

Socialization and policization are adequate. Following one's conscience does not mean that one can do as he likes. In nexus criminality, one notices violation of all values and therefore the violator must have conscience pricks.

Social Implications of Nexus Involvement

The social implications of nexus criminality are many as nexus crimes cause distrust on police sense of justice and damage to police image and reputation. Any person who involves in nexus transactions suffers from moral collapse and loses his status and postition which other respectable policemen enjoy in the department/society. All officers/men who have self esteem and respectability may ostracize him and will prefer to avoid his company. All these result from his nexus involvement/partnership which is prompted from his individual definitions and outlooks of the meaning of police duties and functions and sublimity of the profession. His act puts the entire department in ill-repute, humiliation and devaluation. If the nexus offender is in a high position of the hierarchy, he may be exhibiting a wrong role model. People criticize everyone in police department. When many people commit nexus crimes, then the result is the emergence of a disorganized department. Considering all ill-effects and consequences of nexus crimes, they doubtlessly become the most reprehensible of acts a policeman/officer can conceive of during his service in police department.

Every policeman/officer has certain legal and moral obligation to himself, to his department, to his society and committing nexus crimes implies feeling from the manifold legal and moral responsibilities. Any amount of justification to rationalize the act can not and does not mitigate the full vigour of the balme in the act.

Authority, Authoritarianism and Police Conscience

Police have authority and muscle power. They can be used - misused - abused. Authority is one thing and authoritarianism is quite another thing. Authority means *the power to judge, act or command* and authoritarianism means *favouring complete subjection to authority or domineering, autocratic* (The Random House College Dictionary). Policemen/officers take *authority* and *authoritarianism* to mean one and the same thing. Authoritarianism is using/misusing/abusing power to impose directives and to demand unquestioning obedience and observance of the directives so given. In nexus crimes, a policeman/officer is not exercising his authority, but is exercising his authoritarianism. This is the reason why he receives nexus benefits/advantages and he does so by giving a signal that he will misuse/abuse/use his power irrespective of its consequences. There is an element of threatening in every nexus crime.

Authority and the policeman's individual self meet in his conscience and that is specifically done during the period of policization. Police trainees have been seen taking an authoritarian attitude during their period of induction training itself. They get an idea of misinterpreted police authority and it influences their conscience formation. In nexus crimes, this may be seen.

Push-Pull Factors, Socialization, Policization, Conscience, Decision-making

The policeman/officer has push factors and they operate in them irrespective of their permission. They are present in man and activate people to do something. The pull factors exist outside the man and they work irrespective of man's permission. For example, a police officer will have emotions when he sees certain things. The police officer has no control over the emotions thus seen in him. Nevertheless, once emotions come into being, he can control them by applying the values which are in him through adequate socialization and policization. A man has no control over the push and pull factors. For example, unemployment, overcrowding, poverty in society, family collapse, etc, are pull factors and a man has no control over them. A policeman/officer too has no control over the pull factors seen in society.

A policeman has control over his conscience and the values in his conscience can control him. These are inculcated by adequate socialization and policization. Very often one sees a fight between the Push-Pull factors and police conscience (police conscience formed by socialization and policization). This may be represented as -

Push - Pull Factors

Police Conscience

(Socialization and Policization Values)

Decision - Making in Conflicts

How to make a decision during a conflict? For this, man is provided with a psychic filter. Before going further about psychic filters, it is important to know more about the policeman's mental approach to nexus crimes.

Men including policemen demonstrate in their own nature a pressure (Push Factors) towards the pull factors which in turn pull them further forward. A sort of double action is seen here. For example, the push factor may be an uncontrollable urge to become rich. The pull factor may be bootlegging by which one can make a lot of money. Here the role of the pull factors may be to help him to actualize his desires which work as the push factors. Thus there are two sets of forces pulling and pushing an individual to an end. It is like a push-pull train which goes in high speed because of the push and pull by two engines from back and front. The push factors are psychological and within the individual and the pull factors are sociological which are found operating *hic et nunc* on the individual. In nexus crimes, these two sets of forces push and pull an individual to an end. This is called the forces which can be put under a common heading: "What Are?"

Socialization and policization inculcate human values - conscience in a policeman - and the police conscience speaks about "What Ought To Be?" There starts the conflict between "What Are?" and "What Ought To be?"

"What are?"
"What Ought to be?"

The policeman/officer is necessitated to take a decision - "To be or not to be " - "to be a nexus offender?" The psychic filter comes to the aid of the police officer then.

Psychic Filters and Nexus Crimes

In nexus crimes, there is a wilful violation of norms, code of conduct, law and morality. There is a commission or omission to do what is and ought to be done by a police officer. The 'victimogenesis' - the factors which propel an individual policeman/officer towards becoming a victim (here an offender) of his own wilful action to become a nexus partner is of paramount importance. A police officer here must apply certain criteria to assess his own behaviour. A policeman who is identified as a nexus offender feels uncomfortable to confront people in police department and in society. It may be owing to a strong feeling of guilt in him. Why does he have such a feeling? Is it because he feels that he violate the norm/code/law? Nexus involvement is looked down upon by good many conscientious and civic minded people in our society/ culture. It means that the people are against this despicable and loathsome human act. As pointed out, for deciding the illegality/immorality of nexus crimes, one has to apply certain criteria and the first criteriaon towards this end is called 'Individualistic Scale'. The scales by the help of which one decides the legality/ illegality, the morality/immorality are in the 'psychic filter' of an individual.

Individualistic Scale

Every policeman/officer has his subjective concepts and highly individualistic values about human acts and the legality/morality of nexus involvement. Whereas one policeman/officer may say that nexus involvement is justified or justifiable, another may argue that it is not. Who is right and who is wrong here? Both individuals evaluate nexus involvement purely on the basis of highly personal standards and subjective values which may be objectionable to the dominant culture of the society. Apart from individual views about the legality of nexus crimes, what does the law of the land/dominant culture think about it?

Earlier we discussed the role of socialization and policization in the formation of human conscience. In fact, it is the socialization and policization which make the individualistic scale. The formation of individualistic scale may be adequate or inadequate. There are numerous examples to show that inadequate formation of the individualistic scale cause perversions in the interpretation of not only nexus involvements but also of many kinds of misuse of authority and abuse of power by police personnel. The experience of a person when he violates the law of his conscience is called "guilt feeling". How many policemen/officers experience guilt feeling when they accept corruption-money or when they manipulate records for nexus advantage etc? The inadequate socialization and policization exert influence to form perverted values in the life of a policeman/officer.

Nexus crimes are, it may be reiterated, crimes in every sense. Can the desirability of committing nexus crimes be evaluated on the basis of the individualistic scale alone? The answer to this question is an emphatic 'no', for each police misuse of authority/abuse of power has not only an individual dimension, but also has social, cultural, religious, legal and many more dimensions. As such, assessing the issue - or filtering the act - only from one angle - or through a single scale - i.e., the Individualistic Scale - can not and does not mean anything. It does not evaluate the issue in its totality. The Filtering is partial. The Individualistic Scale is not objective and the subjective content of the scale makes the judgement less reliable and realistic.

Scales of Assessment of Police Behaviour

In order to make a fair, just, objective, total and balanced judgement on a vital police behaviour - here the nexus involvement-, one may have to filter his behaviour from other means. One has to apply various scales like the: 'Ideal scale, Majority scale, Sociocultural Scale and finally Diagnostic Scale to arrive at a conclusion. They may be used in addition to or in lieu of the individualistic scale, either concurrently or consecutively. For, nexus criminality has multidimensional aspects.

Ideal Scale

Every policeman/officer has set forth certain 'ideals' for his job - or ought to do so. Police department has a motto. Anything done for the actualization of the motto will be quite acceptable and all right. The question here is: "Does the moto of any police department consider nexus criminality as desirable? - as justifiable/ - as acceptable?" No, the police department can not adopt an attitude in favour of anybody involved in the commission of nexus crimes.

The "Ideal Scale" is good enough to assess the legality/morality of nexus crimes? For, no sublime principle which the police department has will accept nexus involvement. In order to evaluate the legality/ morality of nexus crimes with sincerity, earnestness and objectivity, it is necessary to apply the departmental laws, norms, principles to nexus involvements. Police departments work and can work under principles which are accepted as just and fair and those principles come under the 'Ideal Scale'. When applying the lofty 'Ideal Scale' of the police department, it becomes evident that nexus crime can not be, on any account or stretch of imagination, regarded as legally/morally justifiable. The implications of people committing nexus crimes and the ill effects such illegal acts bring on them and the department are beyond human imagination and comprehension.

Every policeman/officer has to play certain roles for himself, for others, and for the department and the society at large. When young constables, sub-inspectors, assistant superintendents of police commit nexus crimes, they put an end to the long cherished aspirations of the society which recruited them to service. The picture is quite distressing when it comes to the level of superiors/ supervisors. The nexus involvement of the inspector general of police/director general of police means perverted role models and the absence of good leadership. Total chaos will be the outcome. The lower levels in such desperate situations do not get proper guidance and supervision. An unhappy department or lack of departmental solidarity and proper supervisory control are found to result in the development and ramification of the nexus epidemic. Considering the evil impact and irrevocable consequences of nexus crimes in society, any policeman/officer, irrespective of the fact that he is a constable or the director general of police, will admit that it is against all sorts of legality/morality to commit nexus crimes. It is illegal/immoral to commit nexus crimes, because the person who commits them does a great disservice to his obligations and responsibilities as such policeman/officer.

Majority Scale

While assessing the legality/morality of nexus criminality, it is but necessary to evaluate it on the basis of the frequency of occurrences of nexus crimes. Since nexus crimes and nexus consciousness are matters of serious concern for many people, both inside and outside the police, and many individuals constitute the police department and society and for whose benefits the laws exist, it is but essential that "majority scale" is applied to assess the legality/morality of nexus criminality. If the frequency of occurrences of nexus crimes is really significant, such a behaviour can not, as a rule, be regarded as immoral although it can be called illegal if there is a law against it. Therefore, if majority of people in Indian society/in different cultures think that nexus crimes are illegal/immoral, then they are, even if there is no law making nexus transactions as offences. No doubt, the people, press and media consider nexus crimes as real offences and precisely therefore they are. The "majority scale" is, probably, the best way to assess the legality/morality of nexus crimes.

Nexus crimes, their ramification and glorification in any society are likely to exert undue and undesirable influence on the weak-minded people. Casual studies conducted on nexus criminality reveal that the havoc caused by nexus offenders to social fabric is indeed alarming. Being influenced by the extent and intensity of nexus transactions in government services, people possessing weak ego strength and conscience become susceptible, suggestible or vulnerable to the oft-resorted foul practices of nexus involvements.

Sociocultural Scale

Police have certain unquestioned customs, traditions, cultural and subcultural norms, unwritten and written laws, rules, regulations and principles. It is in fact these codes of conduct which inspire the police to perform their duties. The totality of these written and unwritten code of conducts make the Sociocultural

Scale. 'Never commit a crime' - this is a social, cultural, moral and legal norm in so far as no law, by whatever name it is known, accepts nexus crimes as praiseworthy. Police cannot accept a value which is found unacceptable to the society. The police may have one thousand and one justifications to rationalize their nexus involvements. But, the sociocultural scale insists that everything must be justifiable before the law. Inadequate salary, political pressure, retributive approach to criminals, craving for status, position and authority, ego-vanities, relative deprivation, frustration in financial matters, desire for easy success, etc, cannot be brought as justifications to violate the sociocultural laws. The sociocultural laws form the non-material culture in society. The policeman's/officer's urge to become wealthier, authoritarian, etc, can not and must not clash with the non-material culture. Some of the explanations given by the policemen/officers would appear to be justifying individual involvement in nexus crimes. Every policeman/officer who indulges in nexus criminality knows fully well that he is violating the sociocultural scale. He also knows the consequence of his act.

Diagnostic Scale

In order to decide upon the legality/morality of nexus crimes, a policeman/officer may resort to the diagnostic scale which enables him to make a decision in an objective way. The diagnostic scale designed may be as under—

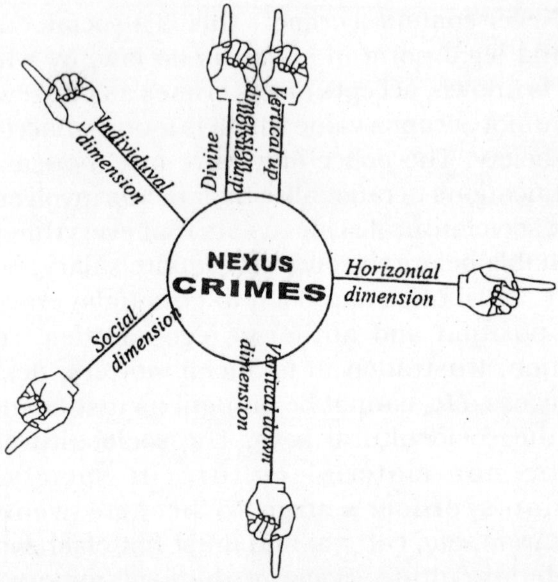

Every human act including nexus acts has an individual dimension - i.e., the act ensures individual happiness. Every policeman/officer has the power and capacity to choose right from wrong. If he chooses nexus involvement, it means that it ensures nexus benefits and advantages. Again, every nexus crime has horizontal, vertical up, vertical down dimensions. People around him, those who are above him, below him and equal to him are affected favourably or unfavourably by his nexus involvements. Some may be affected in a severe way while others may be in a slight manner as the case may be. A nexus offender puts many in difficulties. Hence, individual happiness which a nexus criminal gets does not ensure happiness for those who are around him. Further, every nexus crime has a social dimension. Nexus crimes do not guarantee social happiness and welfare. Precisely, therefore, the nexus crimes are social evils.

As believers in God and in His mercy and grace, some policemen/officers will see whether or not their act is pleasing to the Almighty. Usually, only those acts which are pleasing to individuals, to society and men will also be pleasing to God. Nexus crimes are not so.

Filtering, Push-Pull Factors and Human Conscience in Police

From the discussions above, it becomes evident that nexus crimes take place as under:—

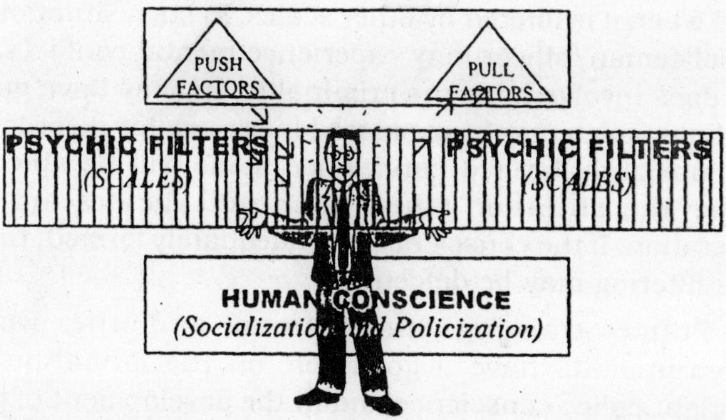

An individual has his push factors and pull factors. His conscience formed by socialization and policization fights against the push-pull factors. In order to do so, the human conscience filters the push-pull factors by the help of the psychic filters which are made of the scales. After filtering, if the conscience feels that the act is legal/ moral then it accepts it; otherwise rejects it. In the case of nexus crimes, the conscience can not but reject it. For example:—

In the case of bootlegging and nexus involvement, the push-pull factors may be very strong. The conscience filters it and accordingly, bootlegging is illegal/immoral as per:—

(1) Individualistc scale;

(2) Ideal scale;

(3) Majority scale;

(4) Sociocultural scale; and

(5) Diagnostic scale.

Hence an adequately formed upright conscience rejects the idea to involve in nexus criminality. There may be situations in which filtering through one scale may be good enough for him, but the same appears to be bad when it is filtered by other scales. In such situations, a policeman/officer may experience mental conflicts. If he does involve in nexus criminality, he may have guilt feelings which may be expressed in personality disorders. An uprightly formed conscience alone will be able to filter the situation when push-pull factors are in operation. If the conscience is inadequately formed, then the filtering may be defective.

Police training institutions and the work environments have a good role on the formation of upright police conscience and in the development of the police capacity to filter the act amidst the forceful operation of push-pull factors. Filtering will be OK if the police conscience is OK. Filtering will not be OK, if the police conscience is not OK.

Case Study: Applying the Different Push-Pull Factors

Once a police officer was suspended from service for his nexus involvement with blue film makers. On finding out the push-pull factors, the police conscience and filtering, the following facts were revealed. The police officer hailed from a lower middle class family. He had three brothers and four sisters. He lost his father when he was five years old and his mother had a tough time while raising her children.

Socialization : The police officers' mother had no time to socialize her children. She was busy in making money to feed her children. So the idea developed within him that money was everything in life. He studied in a local public school where he was not exposed to values in life. He lived amidst pupils who had many undesirable qualities. He had a poor religious training and his socialization was defective. He had an inadequate personality development and formation of conscience.

Policization: On probing more about his experiences and interactions in the police training center it was found that he had wrong role models. The instructor on the parade ground was a drunkard who used to borrow money from the trainees and never returned it. In the barrack, they discussed more about how to make money in official life and he came to learn many foul methods to make money under the cover of his uniform. Certainly, the policization was defective and the values inculcated in him were perverted. During his practical training in the field, he had many opportunities to see how his associates, superiors and subordinates made money through illicit means. He internalized a lot undesirable values from the field.

Application of Psychic Filters

Thus he had developed a contaminated conscience with perverted values. On probing further into his psychic filters, the following truths were brought out:

1. Individualistic Scale	"Without money, no status in society"
2. Ideal Scale	"It is the right of the poor man to adopt any methods to make money"
3. Sociocultural Scale	"Criminal is a label given by the society and culture to

	some human acts committed by people"
4. Majority Scale	"I find many in service making illegal income".
5. Diagnostic Scale	"Your pleasure is more important than the pleasure of the people around you.

He was found to be an agnostic in life.

Push-Pull Factors

He was found to have an uncontrollable urge to make as much money as possible and exploit the situation and become richer and richer in life. The push factors were very strong in him. Regarding the pull factors when he looked around, he found many temptations. They were pulling him and thus he saw a blue film maker and established nexus partnership with him to make money.

Necessarily, he became a nexus criminal. The push-pull factors were strong; the filtering scales were defective; the conscience was inadequately formed owing to defective socialization and policization. He became a nexus offender.

Many policemen/officers who had an upright conscience rightly formed were found to be honest people. People who had right socialization might become confused owing to inadequate policization. They could be found to suffer from mental conflicts and guilt feelings. Human conscience is *norma normata* and not *norma normans.* The guided principles are important and as such the conscience has to be guided or formed to take correct and just decisions. In police, this is very important as the policemen/officers often take decisions for others.

11

NEXUS CRIMES : EFFECTS, IMPACTS AND PREVENTION

Newspapers expose nexus crimes. Films and T.V. Serials show them to the public. People discuss them... and the nexus among bureaucrats - politicians and businessmen goes on. Dogs bark and the caravans continue to travel! In many nexuses in print or electronic media, the policemen/officers, somehow or other, come and certainly any nexus crime damages the police image; causes disruption in public trust on police. No nexus crime takes place or can take place in vacuum, in isolation or in darkness. For every nexus crime needs two or more people. Every nexus crime communicates many things to many people. The kind of relationship the police service develops with the people and vice versa depends upon what is being communicated - i.e., the communicative relationship the police have with the people and vice versa. What is expected of the police and what the police does to convince the people that the expected job is performed in the most satisfying way matters a lot.

How a Case Turned Argument in Favour?

Mohammed Ali was a deputy superintendent of police. The labourers working in a rubber estate declared a strike. The reason was that the management of the estate appointed some rubber tappers from a distant district. The rubber tappers in the locality objected to the appointment. The issue came for disposal before Mohammed Ali, the deputy superintendent of police who called the management and had a talk giving directions to appoint local rubber tappers. The DSP's argument was that they had the right to work in their locality and therefore the management was forcefully asked to see that the newly appointed tappers might be terminated. The representatives of the management got signals that they could get the goodwill of the deputy superintendent of police if they were able to establish a nexus with him. Accordingly he was humoured.

The deputy superintendent of police then called the representatives of the local rubber tappers and told them: "Look, I do not understand the logic of your arguments. If the rubber estate can appoint only local rubber tappers, then how can the people from here go for job in other distant places? - in other States? - in other countries? Any one can do job anywhere in the country". Saying so, he became violent in his tone of voice and spoke to them in a threatening manner that he would put them behind the bars if they refused to obey his orders. He took a decision in favour of the estate management.

The people in the locality said that the deputy superintendent of police was a corrupt man and the management told that they had an understanding with the deputy superintendent of police. During those days nobody spoke anything about nexus crimes, but now people know more about nexus crimes and therefore some of the corrupt practices are called nexus transactions. People identify easily the nexus police functionaries and they go down to any means and methods to reach a nexus understanding with police functionaries. The result is miscarriage of justice and unenviable image for the police service.

Nexus Transactions as the People see them

Nexus transactions may be visible or invisible. The policemen during the British rule were blamed by the people saying that they were executing the white man's orders for retaining their imperialistic regime in India. The policemen then had no option but to yield to the English man. People never said that the policemen established nexuses with the white men then. After India became independent, politicians in large numbers came into being. Somebody in a casual talk humourously said about democracy that "it is a system in which the fools elect scoundrels". Though the definition given by the humourist can not be accepted in totality, there is a lot of truth in what he says. A scoundrel, as the dictionary gives, is an unprincipled, dishonourable man and if that is so, it applies to many politicians from the village level to the national level. The people approach these politicians whenever they have a problem with the police. They do not approach just any politician, but only those who have some nexuses with the police. Some police officers want to establish such nexuses with politicians. To know people's opinions on police-politician nexuses, views of 318 people were taken. Some of the responses were:

* The 'police officer' here is the man of so and so politician. It is he who got the police officer posted here.
* Police cannot do anything now. Go to a police station through a politician of the ruling front, then one may get a decision in his favour. Police-politician relationship is very strong.
* The police officer was a party man before he joined the service. He will do only those things as directed by the political party in power.

* Before doing anything, the police officer gets in touch with so and so politician and gets instructions from him.
* So and so politician is his godfather, protector and guide.
* It is through political support that the police officer survives here. Nobody can touch him.
* He is a politician in uniform and his law is the politician's interest.
* He has no interest other than political interest. He collects money for political parties.
* During the last Government's rule, he was persecuted. Now he is activated by the politicians of the ruling government.

Thus the visibility of police nexuses with politician is very conspicuous and notoriously known to the people. Dramas, novels, films, T.V. serials bring the police-politician nexuses. They portray the development of police - politician nexuses after India became independent. Many films show vividly depicted police-politician nexuses. Many of the expressions found in the dialogue in films not only yield valuable information about unenviable police-politician nexuses, but also tell us the damages caused to people by such unholy relations. In a film, a head constable tells his sub-inspector: "Sir, though the cloth for the uniform is purchased by the uniform allowance given to us from the Government, we wear it not for the Government but for the politicians who are in the ruling front". Because of the popular appeal of the dialogues, they are spread very speedily among the public. One can not read a newspaper with some nexus stories - not necessarily the police - politician nexus. After enjoying a movie, viewing a T.V. serial or reading a newspaper, the people are inclined to think that: "there is definitely something wrong with the police".

Films, cartoons, novels, etc, picture the policemen having dirty dealings with the rich and the affluent. They make use of and misuse the policemen. They sit together - around a round table - drink foreign liquors - discuss things which please only them - take food causing a disliking to the people and so to say that the nexus thus shown on the screens create hatred to policemen among the people. The movie makers show an 'ideal policeman' who is beyond these temptations and such people are just handful. The nexus dealings of police and the rich are shown in theatres repeatedly in many places - making the image of the police unimaginably horrible.

What about the police nexuses with criminals and underworld criminals? - with unprincipled men? The theatres show it and the villains in many underworld activities are shown to the police officers in uniform - occupying high positions in the hierarchy. The characters who put on police uniform are stars who always play the role of villains in films. Nexus crimes as the people see them and nexus transactions as the people observe them are thus not necessarily from live situations, but from the screens, press, restaurants, train compartments etc. But, what they see there are not altogether baseless although some of them are exaggerated. Where is the sense of justice and dutifulness if the police involve in nexus transations? The most elementary quality expected from a man in uniform is his integrity in his service. He must not only possess such a quality - incorruptibility - but also must appear to possess it. If the people know that the policeman is a just man - not taking sides with nexus dealers - they will certainly respect the police functions and profession. As said elsewhere, the P in police must show to them the *Person* in the uniform, the *Power* of the Uniform, the *Purpose* of the uniform and the *Promise* of the uniform and in showing them, there is no scope for nexus dealings. Actually, the role of the police is prevention and control of nexus transactions seen among the bureaucrats, politicians and businessmen. If they can not do it, they must not transfer it to their subculture.

Nexus Crimes Communicate and Contaminate.....

Once a deputy inspector general of police was found using a scooter (a two wheeler) for his personal needs in a south Indian State when the officers occupying such positions could never imagine a DIG of police travelling on scooters. The people in that State have seen senior, middle level and junior police officers using and misusing police vehicles for their personal needs. The police know fully well that the police officers are not allowed to misuse departmental vehicles for their personal needs. They also know that many misuse police vehicles with a nexus understanding among them. A DIG of police-an officer occupying a higher rank in police hierarchy-using a scooter for his personal journeys communicated to the people that he was a man of different values. In fact, several of his colleagues who had resorted to the nexus misuse of police vehicles for personal needs were puzzled to see the DIG of police making use of his personal scooter for his personal needs. In their frame of reference, a scooter is associated with lower ranks in the service. It cannot be understood by many higher ranks in police and the affluent in society why a senior police official is seen using a lower-class vehicle like a scooter for his personal purpose. Necessarily, his behaviour loudly communicated to the people that he had some principles in life - at least a man who never misused departmental vehicles for personal purposes. A police officer who has a lower middle income, middle income or upper middle income background cannot afford to enjoy five star hotel facilities at home - cannot insist European/Chinese food always at noon - cannot smoke very costly cigarettes - cannot purchase readymade costly dresses every month - cannot make outings every Sunday to tourist spots - cannot always purchase articles that are imported or that have a European, American or Japanese look. If he indulges in such lifestyle, it communicates to the people very clearly that such officer's have income from other sources - and mostly from their nexus transactions!

The nexus police officers may not realize that they are indirectly communicating through their uppish lifestyles their self concept and group identity with nexus family. They clearly tell the people around: "You can also approach me with things that may please me. Let us have a nexus. Why not?" This is like an invitation to people and the businessmen, unprincipled people, underworld criminals to accept the invitation at the earliest and establish strong nexuses with such a nexus prone police officer. The nexus crimes contaminate the department with foul smell.

Finding out from 87 policemen/officers to write their preferences in police work revealed that their first preference (most of them) was to work in police stations/ police offices where they had direct contact with the public; next was to the crime investigation branch; next to the intelligence branch; next to the computer branch and the last was to the training centres. Reasons being:

1. They needed status, position, recognition, money and luxuries.
2. They loved interaction with people and could earn an income which was unaccounted.
3. They enjoyed the work which conferred on them authority, power and pseudo-authority.

4. They wanted a wide circle of acquaintances which could be used/misused for their personal advantages.
5. They valued more of personal freedom in their work.
6. They loved people-oriented jobs.
7. They welcomed varied experiences.

The responses indicated what was inside them for prefering a job in police stations/offices having direct contact with people. Necessarily, they will communicate their inner ideas when they work. Some of their inner ideas can be implemented only if they establish nexus contacts and it is they who contaminate the department with foul smells. One does not require to go to a nexus partner to become a member in the nexus family. The nexus people will approach a police officer if he has the inclination and attitude. Police officers who look upon their job as a source of economic security, prestige or financial reward become easily susceptible to nexus dealings. The personal values have a decisive say in the choice of becoming nexus partners. Such people manage and manipulate their job to confirm with their value patterns. Policemen/officers who are flexible, adaptive and receptive to nexus temptations achieve success in making nexus advantages. There is evidence showing marked changes in the attitudes of new entrants to service during their early years of police job - a change that is seen partly through their interaction with the norms of their superiors and partly through the influence of the culture that prevails in the working environment. The inclination to nexus involvement is more likely to rise when their superiors and the culture in their working environment express interest, support, tolerance, encouragement, etc., to nexus activities. They exert influence on the new entrants' values and presumably their nexus activities.

Growth of Nexus Psychology

One of the major problems which a conscientious police administration faces today is the extent and intensity of nexus crimes in law enforcement. Any one reading the reports in daily newspapers can not fail to discern that there is something very prominent about the different forms of unholy nexuses in all areas of administration. Whenever such reports come in print, immediately the politicians raise their voice not for administering justice, but in order to achieve political mileage from them eventually the matter may be entrusted to the vigilance and anti-corruption Bureau or to the CBI for investigation. It takes several years for the investigating team to say 'yes or no' in the matter. The nexus criminals know the weakness of the system and the new psychology prompts them to indulge in more and more nexus crimes. Undoubtedly some of the orders entrusting nexus criminality for investigation are no other than with a plan for a targetted closure of the cases in due course. Such issuing of orders for investigation of nexus crimes (Politician - Bureaucrat - Businessmen) have become a part of the administrative practices of nexus rulers in Indian democracy and the vested interests consciously press the investigation to have a natural burial. The police have not developed any special methods or scientific techniques for investigating nexus crimes. The investigations in certain nexus crimes are perceived as a calculated and a deliberate system response to wind up the entire matter with no evil consequences. The growth of nexus crime is alleged to be a well planned and neatly executed nexus decision at the top of political and administrative hierarchy.

A nexus psychology has thus emerged at various levels from the bottom to the top of administration. None are exempted. "How am I benefitted?" - this is what the nexus criminals ask. "What is it for me if the law is enforced in this way or that way?" - they ask further. "Time is limited and days are numbered when one can make nexus advantages. Exploit the situation" - that is how they think about their position, authority and power. All these perverted thoughts in law enforcement may be of recent origin. Many find nexus crimes and nexus involvement so thrilling and full of wonderful possibilities to make fortunes that they yield to nexus temptations whenever they get opportunities or they create opportunities. All people have some biologically based and psychologically seen inner nature which is natural. These push factors need actualization and they go after pull factors unless they are checked/controlled by an upright conscience rightly formed by socialization and policization. With an intention to inculcate human and moral values, both the police and the Government have now introduced a Code of Conduct for the police. The Code of Conduct prohibits nexus crimes of any description and it shows the need to check the growth of nexus criminality.

Community Policing, Decision Making and Nexus Criminality

These are the days of community policing. The emergence of nexus psychology makes community policing difficult. When nexus injustice is practised and perpetuated, the people develop a tendency to keep away from police. Decision making is a process that involves the application of an upright conscience rightly formed - involves the choice of some just course of action from many alternatives. If nexus plays a role in decision-making, then the decision will ensure only nexus advantages and not the desired result of law enforcement. Such decisions will help to create newer and greater problems and ultimately the people will lose their trust on police justness. The impact will be detrimental to the organization and to society as a whole. The nexus dealings which some policemen/officers had during the internal emergency period (1976) in India continues to be a topic of discussion among people who look at the police with contempt. A nexus policeman/ officer makes all decisions with a nexus understanding and he demands complete and instant compliance of his subordinates, associates and the people to all his decisions. Certainly, people suspect his designs and see them with resentment. 'Who gets what by police action' must not be the guiding principle in law enforcement - instead the object must be that the "people must get justice in a just way". Only one thought lingers on in a nexus criminal's mind and that is "What will I get?" The people easily sense this intention. Police in India is regarded as an organization for social control and just law enforcement. A nexus policeman/officer is a shame for the organization and for society of which he is a member.

Management by Objectives/Results

Management By Objectives/Results (MBO/R) system has emerged as a method of managing police organizations as well. A police officer from the sub-inspector to the director general of police determines the objectives and identifies the result he expects. If he is a nexus parter, he determines the nexus objectives and identifies the nexus results. A nexus police officer plans, organizes, motivates, leads and controls others with his objectives. In films, we may see such nexus operations in which crime syndicates make extensive plannings and they decide what the police officers must do for the success of their activities - in which the politicians make extensive plannings and decide what, where, when and how each police officer must function for the success of their activities. Raising fund for political activities, arranging vehicles for party conventions, etc., are just a few among the many nexus operations. People see such activities and talk about them. They see them not only on screens, but also in actual life.

What about the management by results? If a police officer is able to see that - no law and order problems are created in his jurisdiction—no headache is caused to the Government in power and for the police authorities, The politicians in the ruling front are kept happy and the organized criminals are not excessively harassed, then he is rated to be a successful officer in his jurisdiction. Is there any evaluation or performance appraisal on this account? The annual confidential report may be prepared in a ritualistic fashion and all is well that ends well! Human resources are the key to success of any organization and the way they are evaluated assumes a lot of importance. The allegation is that such an evaluation does not take place in a meaningful manner. That is said to be a cause for the nexus crimes to flourish in police organization. The nexus-support systems must be identified and done away with. What is seen today may be that the nexus support systems are allowed to survive which means that one does not interfere with the working of the system. It means that a passivity is seen. They may say that 'nexus involvement is OK'. They support the nexus involvement. Senior police officers, sometimes adopt a lenient and liberal attitude regarding subordinates who are notorious in their nexus dealings. Some of them say that they have no option but to take such an attitude. They themselves may be surviving in the department because these nexus subordinates are not against them. Once a policeman who was very active in his police association work disclosed that it was he who protected his deputy superintendent of police. He also said that his deputy superintendent of police was weak in many respects and corrupt in all ways and therefore he required the support to extend help for him so as to survive in the jurisdiction. True or false, the entire narration is unfortunate and tells the helplessness of the hierarchy in many areas.

In our newspapers and on TV, we are often confronted with unholy nexuses among bureaucrats, politicians and businessmen. Sometimes, the police too become a member of the nexus family. Of late, the situation appears to be desperate for many. Solutions appear to be difficult. Sometimes, it is tempting to yield to despair or to escape to numbness on reading of nexus involvement/ transactions in newspapers. Any nexus crime is a challenge to human sense of justice. Eradication of nexus crimes, therefore, becomes the foundation for positive administration of justice in a democratic society. To be faithful to a policeman's/officer's call to law enforcement may mean taking a stand against many of the presently practised strategies. When a policeman/officer accepts nexus criminality, it means that he accepts injustice. Nexus criminality has many faces - oppression of the weak and helpless, deprivation of basic human rights, corruption and corrupt practices, economic exploitation, neglect and abuse of power and authority, innumerable other acts of inhumanity. "If you wish justice, then defend justice"- this advice to policemen and officers has no scope to nexus involvement. *Just Justice To All*— should be the motto but nexus crimes do not and can not ensure this just justice to all. All policemen/officers hold that every person has the right to get the best justice possible, yet some of them involve in nexus activities, so much so, that they fail to execute what they preach to others.

Criminals of the Nexus World

It is amazing that in spite of the large proportions of nexus crimes these days, the criminals do not come to the notice of the police. This is so, because their activities fall outside the purview of the provisions of the Indian Penal Code - 1860, and other special and local laws which are currently enforced in India. How can the police know that the commissioner of excise has nexus transactions with bootleggers or the secretary, PWD has nexus dealings with contractors or the minister of education has clandestine understanding with school managers? The assumption that the police must have information on nexus dealings in society is absurd as there is no mechanism by which such transactions can be known to or by the police.

Persons occupying high, middle or low offices in government services may engage in many kinds of nexus crimes/activities and the police will have little or no information on such activities. Nexus crimes in many areas are invisible to the people outside the services. The field and scope of criminology is now extended to include nexus criminality as well. Criminologists are not very much concerned at present to study the causes of nexus crimes. A retired joint secretary to government once discloseed that he constructed his two storied residential building by utilizing the funds which he made through his nexus dealings with forest contractors. He was frank enough to confess that he was instrumental to see that some government orders got issued through his over-enthusiastic interest in favour of the forest contractors. The forest contractors made several millions of rupees through his mediation and he got Rupees eight lakhs for the service. The police did not know anything of the nexus involvement and there did not seem to be any scope for them to know anything too. If the police could know about nexus dealings, then many in government services would face serious problems - he added.

Thus we see that many nexus criminals in government services are not detected by police. They are not exposed to traditional criminals like thieves, burglars, pickpockets and so on; nevertheless, they involve themselves with nexus criminals who are generally affluent. When one person designs and devises a method to achieve nexus advantages, many others become aware of such methods to make nexus profits adopting either the same method or creating new methods. The nexuses that are seen in many departments are not conspicuously seen by people. But, the nexuses which the policemen/ officers with vested interests have are highly visible in many situations. And, therefore, there is a greater possibility of accusing police to be more nexus-prone than many functionaries in other government services. Many theories which explain traditional crimes are of no use or value to explain nexus criminality.

Information Availability of Nexus Crimes

Nexus crimes are illegal acts or series of illegal acts committed by two or more people after entering into a nexus understanding to obtain money, property, benefits, advantages, position, status and what not? It is just impossible to know the extent of nexus crimes because almost all of them go undetected - unreported - uncared. Police do not come to know of them and therefore the police records will not contain information on nexus crimes. At present, there is no column in police statistical records to show the extent of nexus criminality and therefore incorporating the data on nexus crimes is not possible. Yet, the fact remains that the people talk a lot about nexus crimes and unholy nexuses. Certainly, the impact of nexus crimes is very damaging. They are found to be harmful for the psychological and sociological well being of the people. The nexus crimes will not only damage the moral fibre of the society, but also will cause total chaos and confusion, unfairness and injustice, partiality and favouritism, etc, in government administration. Our study here excludes nexus crimes in departments other than police.

Nexus Crime and Personality Disorders

Since the conscience of the man is involved in the commission of nexus crimes, it is quite possible that some people committing nexus crimes experience personality disorders. Guilt feeling may be the underlying cause for such personality disorders. Anxiety reactions may be developed as a result of acute guilt feelings. One's feelings of self devaluation reveal themselves in his anxiety attacks. They start developing a feeling that they will somehow be punished for their nexus behaviour which is immoral. Those who have a strong and upright conscience are specially prone to experience severe guilt and self devaluation. A nexus criminal thinks that he is evaluated by others as a nexus partner. Symptoms of paranoid personality disorder may be expressed. He may show pervasive and unwanted suspiciousness and mistrust of people and may be hypersensitive and hypervigilant in his activities. He may also have difficulties in evaluating the whole situation in its totality. He questions the loyalty of others. Once a deputy superintendent of police was suspended from service for this nexus transactions with bootleggers. His associates later told that he was a man who always searched for hidden motives and special meanings in others' behaviour. He was argumentative and often found exaggerating/overexaggerating things. He was always tense and stubborn in his approaches. He was very defensive and could not accept criticisms against him.

Nexus criminals are noticed to exhibit generalized irritability. They dread the possibility that they may be caught some day for their nexus dealings. Their fears and general sensitivity keep them upset, uneasy and discouraged. If their conscience is rightly formed, then they worry excessively over unforeseen circumstances which may lead to misfortunes for them. They feel self-condemnation.

There is a case of an inspector general of police who developed an obsessive - compulsive behaviour out of his guilt feeling for having committed a nexus crime. When he was a superintendent of police, he caused a lot of harm to a subordinate due to a nexus understanding he had with the then director general of police who had hostility towards this subordinate who was subjected to harassment and victimization. The director general of police retired from service on superannuation while the superintendent of police continued in service. In due course, the then superintendent of police became an inspector general of police, but during his service he met with many vehicle accidents from which he escaped narrowly all the time. In the meantime, while he was the inspector general of police he developed the obsessive notion that his *nexus victimization* of the subordinate was the cause of his recurring vehicle accidents. The nexus victimization had been for a vehicle accident allegedly caused by his subordinate long back. Analysis of his disorder revealed that he was a self-centered man, but a highly sensitive and conscientious person. He had several MAs to his credit and a Ph.D. degree in English literature. He considered himself highly intelligent. On further analysis, it was learnt that his guilt feeling over the nexus injustice done to the subordinate haunted him very much and he had no opportunity to make an apology for the wrong he committed to his subordinate.

A nexus criminal who possesses a strong conscience may find it extremely difficult to tolerate self-devaluation resulting from his failure/inability to live up to his ethical convictions and high opinions of himself. Nexus criminals are found to be taking an opportunistic approach. Opportunism means the 'Policy or practice of exploiting opportunities without any regard to moral principles.' They stretch their conscience to any extent to please the nexus partners and stoop down to any level before the powerful superiors. They do not maintain integrity with their subordinates, associates, superiors or the people they come in contact with. They lose public trust and confidence. When this happens, these individuals face extreme difficulty to maintain their integrity.

Nexus Crimes and the Future of Police Service

People may forgive many things the police do - but never can they forgive nexus crimes in any form. Therefore it is upto the police to keep away from their nexus involvements. Nexus involvement means injustice. For preventing nexus crimes, the police themselves have to seek out and eradicate the underlying causes permitting and perpetuating nexus crimes. Moreover, they have to establish conditions which ensure fair justice administration.

A proper planning of the preventive strategies becomes necessary. Management by objectives and results (MBO/R) has emerged today as an effective method to control and prevent crimes too. There must be proper and intelligent planning, organizing, motivating and leading, controlling strategies adopted for the purpose. The activity must be result oriented.

Institutional Training : Policization

Formation of conscience in an upright way is of paramount importance to stop any kind of evils including nexus transactions. Police Training institutions have a positive role in this regard. They inculcate the finer values through policization. The policizing agencies, namely, the faculty of the police training institutions must have men of character. People who come to service after suspension, who are unwilling to work anywhere, who are unwanted elsewhere in the department, who are desperate and dejected, who feel relative deprivation, who lack morality and moral principles, who exhibit double or multiple personality, who suffer from character or personality disorders, who are addicts to liquors/drugs, who are misfits, and so on miserably fail to inculcate values in the trainees. Inadequate policization is a cause for inadequate personality development. Police trainees have been noticed planning strategies to work in a way calculated to ensure extra-income from service even when they undergo institutional training. They communicate the ideas among themselves and once they pass out of the training institutions, they may experiment them in the working environment. They get further information on various methods to make extra income from their association with the field staff in police service. Policization takes place not only during the institutional training, but also during their practical training in live situations outside the police training centres. Nexus transactions have been the foremost way of earning money through coocked means in police.

Proper vigilance and supervision by superiors who have the moral calibre and courage can put down nexus criminality. They only can do so. A nexus superior will multiply nexus transactions. Various constables have been heard talking about the nexus transactions of their superiors. Once a police driver loudly said: "If pilfering petrol is a midconduct, then misuse of the police vehicle for personal use too is a pilfering. All senior levels do pilfer petrol through nexus understanding but they take action against the poor constable drivers." Certainly, the constables see, listen to and experience nexus transactions of their superiors/supervisors. An unprincipled supervisor can have only negative influence to curb down nexus crimes.

There must be special laws enacted to detect nexus crimes and punish nexus criminals - not only in police service, but also in all other services. Prostitutes must not talk about chastity - this is an oft-quoted saying and likewise nexus offenders must not enforce law and justice. People living in glass castles must not throw stones and likewise, the nexus offenders are weak and fragile. Police Criminology is a developing branch and it deals with many crimes like enforcement crimes and nexus criminality.

Recruitment of Police

Psychological Evaluation of Candidate

Some people enter the executive wing of the government with wrong ideas about their work. Intelligence test, aptitude test, physical efficiency test - all these are good for recruiting policemen/officers although aptitude test is not conducted in many States in India for recruiting constables/officers. As nexus criminality, corruption, value deterioration, self-devaluation, inadequate socialization/policization etc. are seen in great measure, proper psychiatric evaluation and testing must be done at the time of recruitment. This evaluation will help to discover emotional disturbances, character defects or questionable motives of the candidates joining the police service. The psychological evaluation and testing during the selection process can help identify the nexus proneness among the candidates.

Polygraph Testing

Every candidate seeking employment in police must undergo a polygraph examination. Polygraph testing is expensive and the polygraph expert can bring out the crime proneness deviant nature, deceptive character, etc, of the candidates. There are countries where polygraph examination is made compulsory during the selection process. In India, owing to unemployment, many undesirable characters come to police service. This can be stopped if polygraph examination is done correctly.

Ascertaining the Background of the Candidate

A thorough background investigation is necessary for recruiting the right people to police service. The character of the constable upto the director general of police should be above reproach. It may be emphatically insisted that the police department should never accept a candidate until his background is comprehensively explored by honest people. The candidate's habits, prejudices, emotional stability, attitude to crime, aptitude to money-making, inclination to corruption and corrupt practices, etc, must be honestly inquired into. A policeman - the director general of police included - must perform his duties with credit to the uniform he wears. Anything less is unacceptable. Any investment in making an extensive background investigation pays well later.

Obtaining people's participation to fight against nexus crimes becomes necessary. There was a time when people used to make *Public Trial* of corrupt and nexus government servants in a south Indian State. The movement was suppressed as it was a way by which the general public played with law. Nevertheless, the fact remains that the *Public Trial* of nexus/corrupt government officials could deter them and stop the malady. Whatever that be, the public cooperation is a must to cure the disease. 'Community watches' have been seen in ancient India, modern India and in today's India. People, press and the political parties watch the police and they bring out many things including nexus involvement. Every nexus transaction/corrupt practice whether small or big, that the police involve in has some negative influence in some way on the world surrounding the police department. An account was taken of people, politicians and pressmen on the character analysis of the sub-inspectors, circle inspectors and the superintendents of police of two police stations, two circle offices, two district police offices. The assessment of majority was in the following order of priority-i.e., 1. corruption and corrupt practices including nexus dealing, 2. sense of responsibility and justness, 3. political affiliation and decision-making, 4. character vices including drinking, womanizing etc. etc. This showed that the nexus transactions of the police did have the first priority in assessing them. Police had to be impartial, fair and objective showing restraint, compassion and tolerance this was only possible if they were not involved in any nexus transaction whatsoever.

People's Role in Countering Nexus Criminality

Vigilance departments in some States (and Police departments too) used to release advertisements through television, radio, newspapers, etc, for obtaining public support to fight against corruption and corrupt practices. The output of such advertisements is not known, nevertheless, such attempts, if honestly done, must yield results. For the people know the fight against nexus dealings of their enforcement officers and their participation in fighting against nexus crimes is to be encouraged.

The people must be informed of nexus criminality and its evil effect upon administration of justice. Massive campaigning must be initiated with honesty. The contemporary campaigning is for creating an awareness among the people about the crimes people commit and not at all about nexus crimes committed by enforcement agencies. The people have a 'catching role' of nexus offenders. Police today deter the people and this deterrence is essentially for preventing crimes. The people too can deter the law enforcement agencies and the deterrence-strategies can certainly limit both opportunity and motive to engage in nexus crimes and corrupt practices. People's watch of police performance will frighten nexus prone officials and will create anxiety among them. The human rights activists and their organizations in some parts of the country today keep a constant vigil against the human rights violations by the police. A similar strategy by non-governmental organizations to watch law enforcement officers and their nexus activities may be a welcome step to stop the malady. The people and their civic organizations can place themselves in a positive and negative relationship to the law enforcement agencies depending on the methods they use to deal with nexus criminality and its prevention against corruption and corrupt practices.

The people have the role of enforcers of law against maladministration and miscarriage of justice. They have a proactive and reactive role. Proactive responses are those which are undertaken by the people in anticipation of or to prevent nexus crimes including corruption and corrupt practices. The reactive responses are those made after their detection of nexus crimes/enforcement crimes. People may observe the police taking a passive role-that is ignoring law violations (e.g., nexus bootlegging, corruption - money fixing, etc,) and avoiding of initiating any police action to deal with the situation. They should react against such strategies. The reason for police lethargy or inaction may be the nexus understanding, excessive political pressure, etc, on them. There may be situations in which the police will be activated to do many things against the principles of justice adminstration. In such cases too, the people must react so that deterrence is caused.

Media can be extensively used against the emerging and the emerged nexus criminality. A crime must be called by its proper name and there must be departmental vigil against nexus crimes. Deviations must be detected at the earliest and should be analysed. The underlying causes must be eradicated. There is no meaning in having a surface therapy. What is required is a source therapy. The nexus criminality may have a history of its own and therefore a deeper analysis of the multiple factors promoting nexus criminality ought to be researched and studied. Human resources are the key to the success of any organization and the way they are evaluated, controlled and directed assumes a lot of importance. It will ensure efficiency, effectiveness and productivity in the desired direction.

BIBLIOGRAPHY

Allen, Francis, A., *The Crimes of Politics,* Harvard University Press, Cambridge, Mass, 1974.

Asch, Sidney, H., *Police Authority and the Rights of the Individual,* Arco, New York, 1968.

Balau, Peter M., *The Dynamics of Bureaucracy,* (re.ed.), Chicago University Press, Chicago, 1963.

Baumhard, Raymond C., *How Ethical are Businessmen?* Harvard Business Review, XXXIX July - August, 1961.

Berkley, George, E., *The Democratic Policeman,* Beacon Press, Boston, 1969.

Black, Herbert, A., and Gilbert Geis, *Men, Crime and Society,* Random House, New York, 1962.

Bandura, Albert, *Principles of Behaviour Modification,* Holt, Rinehart and Winston, New York, 1969.

Bonger, William, A., *Criminality and Economic Conditions,* Little, Brown and Co., Boston, 1916.

Bordus, David J., (ed), *The Police: Six Sociological Essays,* Wiley, New York, 1967.

Bose, A.C., "What is wrong with our police force?" *Amrita Bazar Patrika,* 28, Jan. 1969.

Chambliss, William, "Vice, Corruption, Bureaucracy and Power", *Wiscosin E. Law Review* (No. 4), 1971.

—, *A Professional Thief's Journey,* Harper and Row, New York, 1972.

Chevigny, Paul, *Police Power: Police Abuses in New York City,* Vintage, New York, 1969.

Clift, Raymond, E., *A Guide to Modern Police Thinking,* W.H. Anderson, Cincinnati, 1956.

Clinard, Marshall B., *The Black Market: A Study of White Collar Crime,* Holt, Rinehart and Winston, New York, 1952.

—, *Sociology of Deviant Behaviour,* Holt, Rinehart and Winston, New York, 1963.

Clinard, M.B. and Daniel J., Abbolt, *Crime in Developing Countries,* Wiley, New York, 1973.

Cloward, R. and Ohlin, L., *Delinquency and Opportunity,* Free Press, New York, 1960.

Comming, E., "Policeman as Philosopher, Guide and Friend", *Social Problem,* Vol. 12, No. 2., 1965.

Curry, J.C., *The Indian Police,* Faber abd Faber, London, 1934.

Devlin, L., 'The Police in a Changing Society', *Police Journal,* February, 1966.

Dickson, Donald, T., 'Bureaucracy and morality: An Organizational Perspective on a Moral Crusade', *Social Problems* 16 (Fall), 1968.

Duster, Troy, *'The Legislation of Morality',* Free Press, New York, 1970.

Dwivedi, J.N., *Police Power and Duties,* Allahabad Law Agency, Allahabad, 1950.

Earayil Alphone L and James Vadackumchery, *Police and the Society,* Kairali, Trivandrum, 1985.

Geis, Gilbert (ed.), *White-Collar Criminal,* Atherton Press, New York, 1968.

Gibbons, Don C., *Changing the Lawbreaker,* Prentice - Hall, Englewood Clifts, N.J. 1965.

Glaster, Daniel, 'Criminality Theories and Behavioural Images, *American Journal of Sociology,* LXI (March), 1956.

—, *Crime in our Changing Society,* Holt, Rinehart and Winston, London, 1978.

Goddard, Henry, H., *Juvenile Delinquency,* Dodd, Mead and Co., New York, 1921.

Gouldsbury, C.E., *Life in the Indian Police,* Manu Publications, Delhi, 1977.

Govind Narain, 'A New Perspective for the Indian Police,' *National Police Academy Magazine,* November, 1953.

Hale, C.D., *Fundamentals of Police Administration,* Holbrook Press, Boston, 1977.

Hall, Jerome, *Theft, Law and Society',* Bobbs - Merril Co., Indianapolis, 1952.

—, 'Police and Law in a Democratic Socity', *Indian Law Journal,* Vol. 28, 1953.

Harijai Singh, 'A Look at Our Police,' *The Tribune,* Chandigarh, June 21, 22, 1977.

Hooton, Ernest A., *Crime and the Man,* Harvard University Press, Mass, 1939.

Iyer, Krishna, V.R., *Police in a Welfare State,* Asia Book Centre, New Delhi, 1958.

Kamte, N.M., 'Reforming the Police,' *Indian Express,* Dec. 7, 1976.

Kattakayam, J., and James Vadackumchery, *Crime and Society: Current Issues and Trends,* A.P.H. Publishing Corporation, Delhi, 1999.

Klein, Herbert T., *The Police: Damned if They Do - Damned if They Don't,* Little, Brown, Boston, 1968.

Klockars, Carl B., *The Professional Fence,* Free Press, New York, 1974.

Kooken, Don, L., *Ethics in Police Service,* Charles C. Thomas, Springfield, Illinois, 1957.

Korn, Richard R., and Lloyd W McCorkle, *Criminology and Penology,* Holt, Rinehart and Winston, New York, 1959.

Lafave, Wayne R., Arrest: *The Decision To Take a Suspect Into Custody,* Little, Brown, Boston, 1965.

Lemert, Edwin M., *Social Pathology,* McGraw-Hill, New York, 1951.

Letkemann, Peter, *Crimes as Work,* Prentice-Hall, Englewood cliffs, N.J., 1973.

Merton, Robert K., 'Social Structure and Anomie', *American Sociological Review,* 3 (October), 1938.

Merton, Robert, K., *Social Theory and Social Structure,* 3rd ed., Free Press, New York, 1968.

Mondale, Walter, *'The Accountability of Power,* McKay, New York, 1975.

Montagu, Ashley (ed.), *Man and Aggression,* Oxford University Press, New York, 1973.

Mukherji, U., 'Role of Police in a Democracy', *Indian Police Journal,* July - Sept., 1968.

Newman, Donald J., 'Public Attitudes Toward a Form of White Collar Crime, *Social Problems,* IV January, 1957.

Noorani, A.G., 'Police Excesses: Need for Institutional Safeguards, *Indian Express,* 9, March, 1976.

Packer, Herbert, L., *Policing the Police,* The New Republic, 4, December, 1965.

Radzinowicz, Leon, *Ideology and Crime,* Columbia University Press, New York, 1966.

Reid, Sue, Itus, *Crime and Criminology,* The Dryden Press, Hinsdale, 1976.

Remington, E.J., 'The Role of Police in a Democratic Society,' *Journal of Criminal Law, Criminology and Police Science,* Vol. 56, 1965.

Roebuck, Julian, *Criminal Typology,* Charles C. Thomas, Springfield, 1967.

Ruchelman, L., (ed.), *Who Rules the Police?,* New York University Press, New York, 1973.

Suksena, N.S., 'Police Unpopularity: Causes and Remedies,' *Indian Police Journal,* Oct-Dec., 1974.

Schafer, Stephen, *Theories in Criminology,* Random House, New York, 1969.

Sellin, Thorsten, *Culture Conflict and Crime,* Social Science Research Council, New York, 1938.

Shelon and Eleanor Glueck, *500 Criminal Careers,* Alfred A. Knopf, New York, 1930.

Sinha, S.K., 'The Police in India,' *USI Journal,* April-June, 1940.

Sutherland, E.H. and D.R. Cressey, *Criminology,* Lippincott, Philadelphia, 1974.

Tannenbaum, Frank, H., *Crime and the Community,* Ginn. Boston, 1938.

Tappan, Paul W., *Crime, Justice and Correction,* McGraw Hill, New York, 1960.

Trilok Nath, *The Indian Police: A case for a new image,* Sterling, New Delhi, 1978.

Vadackumchery James, *Police, Women and Gender Justice,* A.P.H. Publishing Corporation, Delhi, 1999.

—, *Third Millennium Police: Take Off Trends in India,* A.P.H. Publishing Corporation, Delhi, 2000.

—, *Police, Enforcement Crimes* and *Injustice,* Gyan, New Delhi,
2000.

—, *'Why I am not a Policeman?',* Kaveri, New Delhi, 2001.

Vold, George, B., *Theoretical Criminology,* Oxford University Press, New York, 1958.

Wallerstein, J.S., and Clement, J.W., Our Law-abiding Lawbreakers, *Probation* 35 (April), 1947.

Whisenand, P.M., *Police Supervision: Theory and Practice* (2nd ed.) Prentice Hall, Englewood Cliffs (NJ), 1976.

Wilson, James Q., *Thinking about Crimes,* Basic Books, New York, 1975.

Wise, David, *The Politics of Lying,* Random House, New York, 1973.

Wolfgang, M.E. and F. Ferracut, *The Subculture of Violence, Tavistock,* London, 1967.

Yablonsky, Lewis, *The Violent Gang,* MacMillan, New York, 1962.

—, 'The Violent Gang', *American Sociological Review,* XXVIII April, 1963.

Index